P54,66

Coming Up Roses

D0092118

Coming Up Roses

THE BROADWAY MUSICAL IN THE 1950S

ETHAN MORDDEN

OXFORD
UNIVERSITY PRESS

OXFORD
UNIVERSITY PRESS

Oxford   'New York
Athens   Auckland   Bangkok   Bogotá   Buenos Aires   Calcutta
Cape Town   Chennai   Dar es Salaam   Delhi   Florence   Hong Kong   Istanbul
Karachi   Kuala Lumpur   Madrid   Melbourne   Mexico City   Mumbai
Nairobi   Paris   São Paulo   Singapore   Taipei   Tokyo   Toronto   Warsaw

and associated companies in

Berlin   Ibadan

First published by Oxford University Press, Inc., 1998

198 Madison Avenue, New York, New York 10016

First issued as an Oxford University Press paperback, 2000

Oxford is a registered trademark of Oxford University Press

Library of Congress Cataloging-in-Publication Data
Mordden, Ethan
Coming up roses : The Broadway musical in the 1950s
/Ethan Mordden.
p. cm.
Includes index.
ISBN 13: 978-0-19-514058-3

1. Musicals—United States—History and criticism.
2. Broadway (New York, N.Y.)—History. 3. Popular music—United
States—1951–1960–History and criticism. I. Title.
ML1711.8.N3M77   1998
782.1'4'097471—dc21   97-42682

Printed in the United States of America

To Ken Mandelbaum,

because he was there.

Acknowledgments

Thank you to my intrepid agent, Joe Spieler, and, at Oxford, to Joellyn Ausanka and my classic editor, Sheldon Meyer.

Contents

Coming Up Roses

1

The Street, 1950

You hear it as soon as the overture starts: a fanfare of confidence, ingenuity, surprise. Once, musical comedy overtures were simply medleys of the choice tunes, one after another. Now, they're a touch symphonic, thematic, a kind of bragging: for in the 1950s the Broadway musical was beginning the fourth decade of its golden age.

The musical then was central to American culture. Its songs not only topped the Hit Parade but, unlike most pop music, often passed into classic status. Its stars were American icons; better, its ability to *create* stardom, at times "overnight," was awesome. Its earning power could be terrific. With production costs holding at about $150,000 to $300,000, a hit could start paying off inside of six months, with further profits from recordings, touring and foreign mountings, and Hollywood transformation, routine in a day when all Americans, it seemed, loved musicals.

This golden age, launched in the 1920s, when a new generation of composers teamed up with a new generation of librettists to rebuild the musical's style from the bottom up, counted some of these talents thirty years later. True, Jerome Kern, George Gershwin, Vincent Youmans, and Lorenz Hart were dead; Ira Gershwin and B. G. De Sylva had retired. (The latter died in 1950.) But Irving Berlin, Cole Porter, and Guy Bolton were still working, and Richard Rodgers, now partnering Oscar Hammerstein II, had given continuity to the age by reinvigorating the form with their highly influential "musical play" in the 1940s—*Oklahoma!*, *Carousel*, *Allegro*, and *South Pacific*. Then, too, the 1930s and 1940s had added to the mix such talents as Harold Arlen, E. Y. Harburg, Alan Jay Lerner, Kurt Weill, and Frederick Loewe. In all, the Broadway musical had never been more successful, sure of itself, and even prestigious. It claimed a noble tradition and, apparently, an endless future.

Of course, Broadway in general was enjoying this power. The ever-looming Eugene O'Neill typifies the decade's air of mingled conservatism and revolution, for though dead he was yet to present the theatre world with a few final productions, most notably *A Long Day's Journey Into Night*, arguably his masterpiece, in 1956. The once shocking O'Neill had long since been taken into Broadway's old guard, yet he was still shocking; this was good news. Furthermore, many long-established actors were still in trim—Katharine Cornell, Helen Hayes, Alfred Lunt and Lynn Fontanne, Judith Anderson, Eva Le Gallienne. Yet Broadway was only just absorbing the revelation, by Marlon Brando as Stanley Kowalski in Tennessee Williams' *A Streetcar Named Desire* (1947), of a new and stimulating naturalism, a style that shatters style (especially that of Cornell, Hayes, and company). As for playwrights, Williams, Arthur Miller, and William Inge were promising Broadway to be the Big Three, their each new title (not least when directed by Elia Kazan) fairly described as "eagerly awaited."

Broadway had some problems, widely assumed to be minor. The overexpansion of New York theatre realty in the boom years of the 1920s saw the second half of the overloaded 1927–28 season in real distress, with too many productions for an audience that had reached its maximum and could not expand further. A year later, the Stock Market Crash cut this audience back and tightened the flow of capital for new productions; simultaneously the development of the talking film lured away customers even more than the silent film had. The "road" shrank, from a gleeful network of anything and everything to a solemn touring of Broadway hits.

In all, this was regarded as regrettable but unavoidable. After all, what was lost was supposed to be a glut of lowly genre productions—the murder mysteries, domestic comedies, cheesy revues, and melodramas that no one really cared about, anyway. Oh—there was television, too. But in 1950 this was a laughable novelty, with its tiny black-and-white screen, its spotty scheduling on a mere four networks, its kiddie shows and *Amos 'n' Andy* and Milton Berle.

So the American theatre was on a roll, fielding some fifty-one productions in Broadway's 1949–50 season. (This is to ignore evenings of dance and Gilbert and Sullivan that occupied legitimate theatres that year.) Fifteen of these fifty-one shows were musicals, and perhaps a good place to start would be with Big Broadway, in a star vehicle produced by Leland Hayward for Ethel Merman with an Irving Berlin score, a Howard Lindsay–Russel Crouse book, direction by George Abbott, and choreography by Jerome Robbins: *Call Me Madam* (1950).

In fact, this is an ideal jumping-off place, for *Call Me Madam* is prototypal, a conventional piece in every respect. Technically an "original" (that is, not based on a prior source), it is little more than a three-hour novelty act—Merman as our ambassador to a tiny European country. Her character, Sally Adams, was modeled on Perle Mesta, a Washington, D.C., partygiver whose service to the Democrats was rewarded with just such a post, in Luxembourg. But the real fun in *Call Me Madam* lay in watching our anything-but-tactful Merman taking on the diplomatic set.

"The play is laid in two mythical countries," the program announced. "One is called Lichtenburg, the other the United States of America." There is a lot of topical fun—Merman on the phone with President Truman (whom she calls "Harry"), beltway jokes, contemporary D.C. compared with picturesque Lichtenburg, with its operetta costumes and its ocarina, something between a tin whistle and a recorder. Still, *Call Me Madam* has a story, an at times touching one: how naive American power comes up against crafty European politics . . . and both sides win. We make a friend, they get a power plant, and Merman charms an old-world conservative into loving America and marrying Merman.

The book is overlong and has dull patches, but Lindsay and Crouse gave Merman plenty of those raucous zingers that were her specialty. (Of her deluxe gown for a royal reception, she cries, "I don't mind a train, but did they have to give me the Super Chief?") There were a few choice jabs at America's political scene, as when Sally's vis-à-vis, Cosmo Constantine (Paul Lukas), complains about Lichtenburg's prime minister:

> COSMO: He has a mind like a steel trap. Unfortunately, it snapped shut twenty-five years ago and hasn't opened since.
> SALLY: He must be your Senator Taft.*

What's attractive about *Call Me Madam*'s book is how smoothly it integrates the more elaborate sets with the in-between scenes "in one" (downstage, in front of a traveler curtain, allowing the stagehands to prepare the next larger set). That was state of the art by 1950, a way to keep a story jumping from place to place while respecting fourth-wall "realism." The way the show organized its musical spots, too, is representative, with an assortment of functional songs, character songs, love songs, and atmosphere songs, every one of which is fairly evoked by the plot.

For instance, the first act begins in the office of Dean Acheson, the Secretary of State, the set created by a backdrop dominated by what looks like a Gilbert Stuart framed by partly drawn curtains. Typical Washingtonians, grouped at center stage, suddenly break their cluster—revealing Merman being sworn in by a Supreme Court justice as Acheson looks on. This is a real surprise appearance, as Merman normally made an Entrance, with a lot of buildup and furore. A relatively short book scene led up to another Merman zinger—"Hey, Dean, where the hell is Lichtenburg?"—and a blackout, as the curtains closed and the chorus bopped onstage for the first number, "Mrs. Sally Adams."

---

* Robert A. Taft, son of President William Howard Taft and senator from Ohio, who fanatically opposed the New Deal, led the isolationists in Congress during the 1930s, and three times nearly won the Republican presidential nomination.

The song establishes Sally's persona and sets up for the ensuing party scene, while choreographer Jerome Robbins planned it to play in one until the second, full-stage set was ready, when the traveler curtain parted and the chorus simply folded into the guests at Sally's big farewell bash. The new set presented a vaguely art nouveau living room with a double staircase upstage and three fancy sofas in front, leaving plenty of room for entrances and exits as Lindsay and Crouse banged out more exposition, mainly to introduce Sally's new secretary, Kenneth Gibson (Russell Nype), a young and idealistic foil to her older cynicism. It was Kenneth who cued in the first of what were to prove *Call Me Madam*'s host of standards, "The Hostess With the Mostes' on the Ball," a made-for-Merman number if ever there was one.*

By Broadway timing, one now expected some all-out, full-stage dancing, and Robbins obliged with "Washington Square Dance." This led to the next blackout, as ocarinas ushered in our first look at Lichtenburg—again, in one, as Cosmo addressed the audience on local politics while Lichtenburgers paraded past. Another number, "Lichtenburg," insured that the stagehands had readied the big U.S. embassy set and that the public had some understanding of the problems besetting the humble little nation that Sally hoped to help. So it went through the evening, small set to big set and back as the action remained fluid.

Note that Sally and Cosmo supplied one love plot and that Kenneth, with Lichtenburg's Princess Maria (Galina Talva), supplied the other. Musicals almost invariably counted two romantic couples, in a tradition that dates back to the eighteenth century. Typically, the main couple was grander, the other couple younger. *The King and I* fixes it for us, with Gertrude Lawrence and Yul Brynner sparring over who owns the show while dear little Doretta

---

* Has any other Broadway star generated so many personally stereotypical numbers? The torch song: "Down in the Depths (on the Ninetieth Floor)," "I'll Pay the Check," "Make It Another Old-Fashioned, Please," "He's a Right Guy," "I Got Lost in His Arms." The charm spot: "Let's Be Buddies," "Small World." The "hot" number: "Anything Goes," "Red, Hot and Blue," "When Love Beckoned," "Come On In," "The Leader of a Big-Time Band." The "I Own the World" rouser: "Rise 'n Shine," "Blow, Gabriel, Blow," "Ridin' High," "I Got the Sun in the Mornin'," "(Gee, but) It's Good To Be Here." A partial listing.

Morrow and Larry Douglas pine and die. As we'll see, however, the musical was ceaselessly protean in these years, usually conventional but always developing convention, twisting it, replacing it. Who's the first couple in *Guys and Dolls*? Nathan and Adelaide? Sky and Sarah? Aren't the pairs perfectly equal in importance? *Pipe Dream* has no second couple at all; *My Fair Lady* makes do with a sort-of triangle when Freddy tries to woo Eliza away from Higgins. *West Side Story* honors the tradition—Tony and Maria are romantic while Anita and Bernardo are sexy—or have we another triangle, the main love plot being that of Riff-loves-Tony-who-loves Maria? (More of this later.)

Note, too, that one absolute convention of popular musical theatre has lost grip—the curtain-up number. It was a mark of the musical's growing rationalization that this throwaway genre was starting to vanish. Why should every story start in the same way if every story isn't the same? Once deemed necessary though virtually pointless, the opening number, usually a chorus but sometimes a solo (as in *Mary* [1920], *Oklahoma!* [1943], or *Kismet* [1953]), was by 1950 likely but not requisite. *Call Me Madam* begins where the story begins, as Sally is sworn in on her new job. *Then* came the number, because that's where the number belongs in the story.

The overture, however, was a convention never questioned in the entire decade. As I've said, the fifties overture tended to begin imposingly, as if not auditioning but *proclaiming* its melodies. *Call Me Madam*'s overture takes off on a reveille in the brass: jazzy triplets over emphatic brass chords that move from an A Flat Major sixth chord to an a flat minor sixth, a bluesy effect that recalls Jerome Kern's famous reply to the question, "What is Irving Berlin's place in American music?": "Irving Berlin *is* American music." Something wonderfully basic occurs when Berlin is in form (as he is throughout this score), something that communicates instantly and effortlessly. Here, in 1950, forty years after his first published songs, Berlin still occupies the center of what middle-class Americans call music. Yet Berlin puts his personal spin on everything, as when he fills out each A quatrain in the AABA of the overture's first title, "Something To Dance About," with two bars of waltz at odds with the song's overall 4/4 time. It's as if

Berlin is trying to stuff his sound with dance. Indeed, the number itself, the second-act opener, puts the dancing ensemble through a cavalcade of styles—"Argentine Tango," Charleston, "Quasi Guy Lombardo Waltz Tempo," blues, rhumba (with a pride of needling brass), and fox trot.

Four of *Call Me Madam*'s thirteen songs are ensemble dance numbers, though all are strictly dance for dance's sake rather than narrative or psychological. The 1940s discovered the use of choreography to interpret or even advance the action (as in *Oklahoma!*'s dream ballet, "Laurey Makes Up Her Mind," or *On the Town*'s "Miss Turnstiles"). The 1950s exuberantly caught this ball and ran with it, most climactically in *West Side Story*. But many shows, like *Call Me Madam*, used dance strictly as decoration—even while employing *On the Town*'s and *West Side Story*'s choreographer, Jerome Robbins.

Berlin's songs themselves are tuneful and motivated. "It's a Lovely Day Today" became an overnight classic, along with "You're Just in Love," the latest in Berlin's long line of quodlibets, two separate melodies performed successively and then, to the ear's delight, simultaneously.* Yet *Call Me Madam* went out of town without "You're Just in Love"—without, truth to tell, a solid second act's worth of songs. One problem was the lazy, crazy "Mr. Monotony," a number Berlin was especially keen on but which had been dropped from several projects. It was so out of character for Sally Adams that even Merman couldn't make the audience like it. She also had a solo called "Free" (re-executed successfully for Rosemary Clooney in the film *White Christmas* as "Snow") that seemed preachy.

On the road, then, *Call Me Madam* was playing as a smash with a flop second act. So Berlin dropped "Mr. Monotony" and "Free" and put in "Something To Dance About." Now the second act

---

* Berlin's best-known prototype is "Play a Simple Melody" from *Watch Your Step* (1914), but he returned to it in *Stop! Look! Listen!* (1915), where a Berlin tune is sung in counterpoint to "America"; in the second and fourth *Music Box Revues* (1922, 1924); in the opening chorus of *Miss Liberty* (1949), "Extra! Extra!"; in *Mr. President* (1962); and in the new number for the 1966 Lincoln Center revival of *Annie Get Your Gun*, "An Old Fashioned Wedding." The quodlibet was virtually an Irving Berlin trademark.

opened with a spark. It continued well, too, with "They Like Ike,"
a bouncy salute to the man the Republicans were fingering as the
solution to twenty years of Democratic hegemony in the White
House. But the second act still needed an eleven o'clocker, a homer in the ninth inning. "Give me a song with the kid," Merman
suggested, in reference to Nype's crew-cutted, preppy charm.
That's when "You're Just in Love" went in. Then someone or other
had a brainstorm—as President Truman is continually mentioned
but never appears, why not finally bring him on stage . . . during
the curtain calls? An actor named Irving Fisher was a dead-ringer
for Truman, and, after Merman took her bow, he walked on to
lend her the presidential imprimatur.

Now *Call Me Madam* was *playing*. One thing remained—for
Berlin to rewrite the "dummy" (temporary) lyric to the verse to
"The Hostess With the Mostes'." Just before the New York open-
ing, Berlin triumphantly entered Merman's dressing room to pres-
ent her with the new couplets. Nothing doing: "Call me Miss
Birdseye of 1950," Merman barked. "This show is frozen!"

Eisenhower was in the audience for the premiere, for he was
then president of Columbia University. Ike liked the show, and
so did the critics. Brooks Atkinson of the *Times* called Merman
"an inspired pin-ball machine," which he meant as a compliment,
and he intelligently analyzed the show's strengths—an "ingratiating" if at times "dull" book, one of Berlin's "most enchanting
scores," Abbott's "jaunty" direction and Robbins' "festive" dances.
Atkinson even singled out the two ocarina players by name.

The nation fell into line with the *Times. Call Me Madam* ran a
year and a half and managed a yearlong post-Broadway tour (with
Elaine Stritch in Merman's part), a hit London production with
Billie Worth, and a successful movie version with Merman. It
never became a classic, but it was very profitable, and that was
all one asked of a show then, especially a musical comedy. The
few titles that had established themselves as perennials by 1950
were virtually all operettas or the like; anyway, the notion that
American culture might be building up a treasury of musical
shows, a legacy of national art, was considerably in the future.

The coming together of Merman, Berlin, Abbott, and Robbins
on a major success was not a lucky strike: it was what was sup-

posed to happen, for the writing and staging of musicals were by 1950 something of a science. An unsteady science, granted: with an ever-volatile chemistry and a well-nigh inscrutable physics. But the periodic table, the schedule, so to say, of elements, was secure: the star (or a team of promising youngsters) in an unusual story competently narrated and punctuated by captivating music and lyrics and unique ensemble dances, the whole organized by a veteran staging expert.

Compare that with the elements of a musical in about 1920: the star in a cliché story that was merely a framing device for generic musical numbers, hoary joke-book gags, and the usual specialty performers in a staging more often than not by a hack. Three crucial revolutions reinvented the musical, making it more complex and unusual but, paradoxically, all the more likely to enjoy a greater success than the typical twenties hit. That is, as the shows got unique they also became more popular, and they got unique because (first revolution) the storytelling became more imaginative, because (second revolution) the choreography became more imaginative, and because (third revolution) the subject matter became more imaginative. In other words: *Show Boat* (1927), *On Your Toes* (1936), *Lady in the Dark* (1941).

The three revolutions came together most spectacularly perhaps in *Oklahoma!* in 1943, but, as the 1940s wore on, the extraordinary power of the dances in *On the Town*, the haunting darkness of *Carousel*, the operatic intensity of *Street Scene*, the satiric vision of *Finian's Rainbow*, the experimental daring of the first "concept" shows, *Allegro* and *Love Life*, and the sheer expertise in balancing the elements in the essentially unambitious *Annie Get Your Gun* proved that virtually all the musical's most popular and prestigious talents were thoroughly imbued with the revolutions.

Interestingly, when these same people or their counterparts could in the 1920s suffer the most ghastly failures, by 1950 they were far more likely to succeed. For instance, around 1925, Jerome Kern, Vincent Youmans, Oscar Hammerstein, Sigmund Romberg, Cole Porter, and George Gershwin all saw at least one show fold out of town and watched other shows stagger through ignominiously short runs. In the 1950s, the elite tended to enjoy smash hits, the succès d'estime, or at least four-or five-month failures that still left behind a cast album and thereby the possibility of future resuscitation.

A case in point would be *Out of This World* (1950), elementally comparable to *Call Me Madam*: a star (Charlotte Greenwood), Cole Porter in one of *his* most enchanting scores, and a major choreographer (Hanya Holm) and director (Agnes de Mille, whose out-of-town firing brings us yet closer to *Madam* in her unbilled replacement, George Abbott). There was one major difference between the two shows: *Madam* succeeded, but *Out of This World* failed.

A retelling of the Amphitryon legend, the piece proposed Greenwood as Juno, chasing after Jupiter (George Jongeyans, later Gaynes), who lusts for the bride (Priscilla Gillette) of an American newspaperman (William Eythe), in Greece for a story on a gangster (comic David Burns). Add an impish Mercury (William Redfield) and some luscious local color (Barbara Ashley), and one has a fine follow-up to Porter's previous show, *Kiss Me, Kate*: antique subject but modern worldview, ribald atmosphere, lots of melody and dance, and elaborate decor.

Something went wrong, because after a hectic tryout period the show opened in New York to tepid reviews, and the gala score couldn't produce a single hit. (It had had one till Abbott threw out "From This Moment On" in Boston, apparently because William Eythe, a non-singer, was killing his half of the whirlwind love duet. Why didn't Abbott reassign the number to Redfield and Ashley, whose characters it would in fact have suited?)

I blame Dwight Taylor, for his original plan was misconceived and humorless. It's easy to mistrust a script whose author has so vague a grasp on his subject that he runs through a host of titles. Taylor fondled *Laughter in the Sky, Heaven on Earth, Day Dream, Stolen Fruit, Just Imagine, Summer Lightning*, and the one Cole Porteresque title (think *pun*), *Made in Heaven*.

Taylor, who had written the book for a Porter show almost twenty years earlier—*Gay Divorce*—had been working in Hollywood meanwhile and forgot anything he might have known about the structure of musical comedy, which would have been antediluvian by 1950 anyway. He had one odd idea: for the evening to start with a man in evening clothes to leap out of a box seat

onto the stage, to announce that he was Mercury, then to strip
down to godly tights and introduce the show. It's fresh, at least.
But Taylor's exposition was unbelievably lengthy, he did not include the comic gangster, and the Juno he wrote was little more
than a featurette. Reginald Lawrence was brought in for rewrites
even before rehearsals began, and when Abbott joined the show
in Philadelphia he enlisted F. Hugh Herbert for more rewriting.

By Boston, the script had been drastically improved, but it
wouldn't hold up. It was too silly, too given to masquerade and
unmotivated appearances, as twenties musicals had been. The
show got some publicity mileage out of Boston's pruning of certain erotic excesses,* and these were indeed many. (The all-time
gamiest Cole Porter double meaning occurs in this work, in
"Cherry Pies Ought To Be You," in a reference to "Erroll Flynn,
loose or tight," a jest on Flynn's bisexuality, unknown to the public
but a hot item in Porter's set.) But New York took these in stride
while regretting the book's shallow subterfuges. And this after *Kiss
Me, Kate*, too!

New York did greet Greenwood with affection. A longtime
Broadway veteran famed for her *Letty* series in the 1910s and early
1920s, she had been out of the musical for exactly as long as
Dwight Taylor had. But here was one of the great comebacks.
Wisely, Greenwood withheld her signature straight-leg high kicks
for her eleven o'clock number, "Nobody's Chasing Me," as the
house went mad. Everything else in the show was instant rubble,
unfortunately including the songs. Porter's most popular score, in
terms of sheer hit numbers, must be *Anything Goes*; his most
popular score *as a whole* must be *Kiss Me, Kate*; his own favorite
was *Nymph Errant*; and his best is *Jubilee*. Yet *Out of This World*
is his loveliest in its own odd way. All mature Porter scores have
their tender side and their sassy side; this score is the tenderest,
but also the sassiest. It's Porterissimo, so winsome and pure in
the American wife's ballads, "Use Your Imagination" and "I Am

---

* These include, to quote a letter from Mayor John B. Hynes's office, the
dropping of "All irreverant use of 'God,'" the dance "at end of Act One to be
greatly modified," the elimination of the gangster's "Blessing [i.e., crossing] himself after shooting Juno," and the rephrasing of a lyric that referred to "goosing."

Loved," and "No Lover (for me)," so impishly gold-digging in "Where, Oh Where," so randy in the gods' music. Just the fact that Juno and Jupiter never duet is notable—what, paste some makeweight over that black hole of a relationship? Porter keeps the two separate, Jupiter for the hot stuff and Juno for the comedy. His "I Jupiter, I Rex" is eruditely hot: the music goes all horny, but the lyric quotes "the croaking chorus from *The Frogs* of Aristophanes," as W. S. Gilbert put it. Mercury's "They Couldn't Compare To You," a salute to a bevy of showgirls, is plain hot, with a patter section on his many conquests (which range from Eve to Peggy Joyce, not excluding Pandora, who "let me open her box!").

When they build a highway, people buy cars. When they open a library, people borrow books. When they invent the long-playing record, people get to take show music home with them more or less as it was heard in the theatre, and this is a salient factor in our understanding of the American musical. Not counting a pair of piano-accompanied productions in the 1930s, there were no American "original-cast recordings" until the 1940s, at that only about two dozen, leaving some of the biggest hits unpreserved. Remember, only 50 percent of a given musical is what was actually written: the other 50 percent is how it was performed. Not till Columbia introduced the LP in 1948 did the recording industry have the flexibility and marketing power to capture some fifty minutes of a show's *original performance* for all time; and the relatively low cost of making the discs coupled with the popularity of show albums in fifties culture led Columbia, Victor, Capitol, and Decca (the inventor of the Big Broadway cast album, with *This Is the Army* in 1942) to vie for and ultimately secure literally every hit, every important score, and a good many *objets trouvés*. From the 1950s on, we not only know what was written, but how it sounded—and *Out of This World*, for all its book problems, sounded just fine. Consider this aspect of the cast recording: in the 1920s, even the biggest hit, once it finished its national tour, could be gone forever. Columbia's LP of *Out of This World* stayed in the catalogue for twenty years, and, rereleased on CD, it's still with us—along with a recording of the 1995 Encores concert per-

formance starring Andrea Martin that may well have been inspired
by Columbia's disc.

Merman's grand and Greenwood's vexed experiences in star vehicles remind us that no element in musical-comedy craftsmanship is invulnerable. One potential diva saw her career virtually
destroyed by poor craftsmanship. Nanette Fabray enjoyed a great
1940s. Still a teenager in her first ingenue roles, then a replacement lead in two huge hits, *By Jupiter* and *Bloomer Girl*, Fabray
made stardom in *High Button Shoes* and *Love Life* and seemed
poised to challenge the reigning queens, Ethel Merman and Mary
Martin. Fabray was cute, trim, and tomboyishly womanly, an ideal
musical comedy type: something special that hadn't already happened. Then, unfortunately, the Theatre Guild offered her *Arms
and the Girl* (1950) and she took it.

Actually, it must have seemed promising, a story rich in period
Americana and directed by Rouben Mamoulian, a recipe that, a
few years before, produced *Oklahoma!* and *Carousel*. However,
Arms and the Girl's authors were not Rodgers and Hammerstein
but Herbert and Dorothy Fields on book and Dorothy writing the
score with Morton Gould, whose *Billion Dollar Baby* music had
been so humdrum that only three songs were published, an
unheard-of economy for the day. Other less than encouraging
signs were Mamoulian's sharing libretto credit with the Fieldses—
what did Mamoulian know about writing a script?—and the participation, as sole backer, of the Consolidated Edison heir and
sometime producer Anthony Brady Farrell, whose taste was no-
toriously the worst on Broadway.

Still, the show offered Fabray a suitable role, as a Revolutionary
War heroine who runs around in uniform bearing a sabre, sniffing
for spies, and blowing up (the wrong) bridges. Her colleagues included Georges Guétary as a Hessian mercenary who defects to
our side in admiration of democracy, and Pearl Bailey as a runaway slave who takes the name of whatever state she happens to
be in. (Originally Virginia, she was recently Pennsylvania and is
now Connecticut.) In the event, Gould and Fields came up with
a tuneful score with two solid comic numbers in the loafing but
gritty Bailey style, "Nothin' For Nothin'" and "There Must Be

Somethin' Better Than Love." The choreographer was the excellent Michael Kidd, Horace Armistead designed sets reminiscent of the simplicity and harmony of Grandma Moses, and Farrell did not, to Fabray's relief, demand that she revive her by then abandoned signature trick of whistling through her teeth.

The show was lively and bright. Once again, there was no opening number: the curtain rose on a hayloft during a battle. Soldier Guétary ran in to take shelter and there met Bailey, also in hiding:

> GUÉTARY: Slaves . . . I read about you in Europe.
> BAILEY: They know about me in Europe already? I only run away last Sunday!

Now it was Fabray's turn, in a novel entrance, dashing in with sabre waving to shout, "Draw your sword, Hessian swine!"

So Fabray and Guétary meet cute. They court cute, too, because *Arms and the Girl*'s source was a forgotten play called *The Pursuit of Happiness*, which featured a "bundling" scene, recalling the colonial custom of setting a young man and woman in bed together with a board between them, supposedly to insure warmth on winter nights. No authority whom I have consulted can or is willing to explain whether or not the kids were supposed to have sex, but *The Pursuit of Happiness*'s bundling scene was considered highly titillating, and *Arms and the Girl* gave one not only to Fabray and Guétary but also to Fabray and John Conte, as an American general Fabray suspects of espionage. Thickening the plot, Connecticut names him as her owner, yet, in a scene of comic suspense, he fails to recognize her. *Ha*, an *imposter!*

So Guétary wanders around disguising his natural French accent in Pennsylvania Dutch ("Well, for dying I am too young yet . . ."), as if reserving a part in *Plain and Fancy* later in the decade, and Fabray finally gets into women's clothes in a gala Dressing Number, "He Will Tonight," during which the chorus girls build her a frilly outfit by retooling napkins, ribbons, Martha Washington caps, and so on. By the time General Washington strode onstage as deus ex machina to order Fabray to "stay the hell out of the Revolution!," it was clear that *Arms and the Girl* was no *Oklahoma!*. First of all, 1950 was late for the costume

Americana that had flourished during the war years, and in any case a show that was merely competent needed something special if it was to run—a couple of hit tunes, something astonishing in design or choreography . . . or a theatre-filling personality who can exalt ordinary material. Fabray was to do exactly that a decade later in Irving Berlin's bomb *Mr. President*—but not, unfortunately, in *Arms and the Girl*.

Even more damaging to Fabray's career was *Make a Wish* (1951), the first time her name headlined alone above the title. This was an adaptation of Ferenc Molnár's *The Good Fairy*, first seen on Broadway in 1931. A triangle involving a French adventuress with both a protégeur and a protégé, it was sweetened and chastened for a delightful Hollywood version with Margaret Sullavan and further tamed in a remake for Deanna Durbin as *I'll Be Yours*. Preston Sturges, who had written the first film script, was hired to repeat himself for *Make a Wish*, but he knew nothing of how a musical is put together. Moreover, personal problems and an obsessive interest in his California theatre company led him to abandon the show in Philadelphia, where Abe Burrows (very hot because of the flash success of his book for *Guys and Dolls*) attempted to doctor a mirthless, heavy-handed script.

But then the show itself was heavy. At $340,000, it ended up as one of the most costly shows in Broadway history to that time, with elaborate sets and costumes by Raoul Pène du Bois that strove to fill the Winter Garden Theatre with the Parisian feeling that the show badly needed. Choreographer Gower Champion helped, with two ballets, "The Students' Ball" in Act One and "The Sale" (a spoof of department-store turmoil) in Act Two.

The designs and the dancing were the show's strong points. Hugh Martin's score was amiable but conventional, with the cliché opening number that doesn't really matter (so why do it?), the heroine's cliché character introduction number, "I Want To Be Good 'N' Bad," the cliché salute to Paris, "(Meet the lady known as) Paris, France," and the cliché late-in-the-second-act novelty, "Take Me Back To Texas With You," that finds two French girls suddenly conversant with cowboy folklore. The rewritten book still lacked humor, for Burrows, so clever at finding the ironies in Runyonland or the Corporation (in the later *How*

To Succeed in Business Without Really Trying), had nothing to work with in Sturges's version of Molnár.*

In all, *Make a Wish* had no reason for being, outside of its profit potential. The play and movies had succeeded—why not a musical in this very age of musicals? Maybe a drastic reworking would have discovered something in it; its authors certainly didn't: Fabray is an orphan waif who is befriended by rich Melville Cooper so she can befriend penniless lawyer Stephen Douglass. The non-singing Cooper blandly steers clear of the music while Fabray and Douglass go through the outline of a romance and dancers Harold Lang and Helen Gallagher provide the comic subplot of an American dating a Parisian—though a Parisian Helen Gallagher (as Poupette) was quite a contradiction in terms. "For some reason or other," Brooks Atkinson thought, "there does seem to be more scenery than show."

The reason was that *Make a Wish* had no personality, no outlook, no real story in the story. Everything that so captivated in Molnár had by now been adapted out of him, so there was nothing left but new stuff—the scenery and dancing, which, ironically, almost put the piece over. The critics were so impressed by these two factors that one reads a tone of grudging respect in notices that would otherwise have been damning. (George Jean Nathan, who really panned it, considered the $340,000 and estimated that five cents of it was spent on humor.) Fabray's personal notices ran short of the all-but-necessary wow! mark, and *Make a Wish*'s three-month failure all but finished Fabray on Broadway.

Call Me Madam, Out of This World, Arms and the Girl, and *Make a Wish* are all examples of musical comedy, by 1950 the dominant form of Broadway musical: as opposed to revue (which was in steep decline), operetta (which almost invariably flopped), the musical play (which was becoming increasingly popular), and, oddly enough, opera. There had been four operas on Broadway

---

* Burrows did at least seek out Molnár, a Hitler refugee living in New York, and was thus able to revitalize some of the wit of the original Hungarian play. Oddly, neither Sturges nor anyone else connected with the writing and rehearsing of *Make a Wish* had thought to consult with its original creator.

between 1948 and 1950: Benjamin Britten's *The Rape of Lucretia* (1948); Marc Blitzstein's adaptation of *The Little Foxes* as *Regina* (1949); Britten's *The Little Sweep*, presented as *Let's Make an Opera* (1949) because the audience takes part in the show; and Gian Carlo Menotti's *The Consul* (1950). Only the last succeeded, in part because it is one of the few Menotti works rich in melody and also because its look at an Eastern European family trying desperately to emigrate to the free West was very timely.

The revue, once a Broadway staple in everything from lavish annuals such as the *Ziegfeld Follies* and *George White's Scandals* through themed evenings such as *At Home Abroad* down to little more than vaudeville with a title, had degenerated so badly that the fifties revue produced some of the most forgotten shows of the entire postwar era. Forgotten? Who heard of them then? *Alive and Kicking* (1950) at least boasted Jack Cole choreography (and Cole's lead dancer then, Gwen Verdon, in her Broadway debut), and Paul and Grace Hartman somehow found enough to do in *Tickets Please* (1950) to sustain business for seven months. But *Pardon Our French* (1950) brought back the eagerly unawaited Ole Olsen and Chic Johnson, who had perpetrated the *Tobacco Road* of musicals, *Hellzapoppin*, back in 1938, following it with sequels, of which this was the fourth and last. Then there was *Michael Todd's Peep Show* (1950), a genuinely slapdash affair of decent acts mixed with throw-it-in-anyway horrors. Todd did nothing for the dignity of revue by featuring in the score a song called "Blue Night" that was composed by Bhumibol Adulyadej—"His Majesty the King of Thailand," as the sheet music proudly proclaimed.

Operetta's big problem was that the musical play had stolen all its best qualities—passion, musicality, idealism—and left it with hoary jokes, pointlessly exotic decor, and Irra Petina. Actually, Petina was about all that operetta had going for it by 1950: a marvelous singer with a comedienne's delivery who was far too good for the *Gypsy Ladys* and *Hit the Trails* that she kept ending up in. What Petina really could have used was not operetta but one of those musical plays. Like, say, Rodgers and Hammerstein's *The King and I* (1951).

Here's the science revealed at its surest, in fact by the two men who had recatalogued the table of elements. *The King and I*, amusingly, was in effect a commission, by Gertrude Lawrence, who wanted the boys to turn the Twentieth Century-Fox film *Anna and the King of Siam** into her starring vehicle. The finished work, however, was the opposite of *Make a Wish*: not a routine product of the serial transformation of material from, say, novel to play to movie to musical to movie musical (as with Patrick Dennis's novel *Auntie Mame*, more or less the same event in all its forms), but something so transformed by its adaptation that it becomes a thing in itself. Certainly, none of *The King and I*'s tragic rhapsody can be found in the movie; and the novel doesn't even have a plot.

Coincidentally, we meet up with another King of Thailand, for such is the modern name of the nineteenth-century Siam in which *The King and I* takes place. Now, watch how artfully Hammerstein lays out his exposition. After the overture, a glowering march† in the brass under brightly trembling strings and woodwind runs warn us that this is a musical play, a drama rather than a romp. Flute and strings then sound an Asian-or-so tune in canon as the curtain rises on Captain Orton's ship and young Louis runs on. A few lines between him and the Captain establish that they are approaching Bangkok, their port of call, Gertrude Lawrence calls to her son from offstage, and Louis's bit of repetitive fill as Lawrence enters is drowned in the audience's traditional Greeting of the Star. Fifteen seconds later, the Captain takes the opportunity to state the evening's central conceit: "I wonder if you know what you're facing, Ma'am—an Englishwoman here in the East."

But now the royal barge approaches, bearing the Kralahome (ORTON: "The King's right-hand man, you might say"), and the conceit is developed:

---

* *The King and I*'s official source credit cites only Margaret Landon's novel *Anna and the King of Siam*. But the musical is much closer to the movie in theme, story, and characters. Perhaps legal considerations pertaining to Landon's copyright made it impossible for *The King and I* to state fairly where its inspiration lay.

† This is in fact "Song of the King," his second-act solo: as if he were surveying Anna's arrival, not only all powerful but omniscient.

ORTON: That man has power, and he can use it *for* you or
against you.

ANNA: (*laughing*) Oh.

Her laughter tells us how used Anna is to the amenities of Western
Civilization and how unaware she is that she is about to lose them.
Then, as the barge closes in, comes the first number, prompted by
the situation—danger may threaten, but we're not afraid, are we?
In fact, we're so nonchalant that we're whistling. "I Whistle a Happy Tune" establishes the mother-son relationship but also under-
lines Anna's ignorant boldness. She thinks she can't ever be in trouble because everyone in England is reasonable. She realizes that
she's not in England any more during a scene with the Kralahome's
interpreter, these two interjecting a little color into the show by
miming their Siamese to piquant orchestral accompaniment.

The interpreter's questions become personal; Hammerstein shows
us Anna's courage but also her inflexibility while warning us just
how unWestern Siam is and giving the scene a surprise twist:

ANNA: (*stiffening*) Tell your master his business with me is in
my capacity of schoolteacher to the royal children. He has
no right to pry into my personal affairs. (*Orton tries to signal a warning, but she turns to him impatiently.*) Well, he
hasn't, Captain Orton!

(*The Interpreter gives the Kralahome her message. The Kralahome gives the Interpreter a kick on the shoulder which
sends him sprawling out of the way.*)

LOUIS: I don't like that man!

KRALAHOME: (*Herewith revealing that he in fact speaks English*) In foreign country is best you like everyone—until
you leave.

Anna and the Kralahome continue in English, wrangling over a
contractual point that, it appears, the King may not honor:

ANNA: I shall take nothing less than what I have been promised.

KRALAHOME: You will tell King this?

ANNA: I will tell King this.

(*The faint suggestion of a smile curls the corner of the Kralahome's mouth.*)

KRALAHOME: It will be very interesting meeting.

Thus Hammerstein introduces the King—unreliable, difficult—
even before we've seen him, and though Anna and Louis exit whistling their happy tune, the air of wonderment set up at the scene's
first moments has become one of anxiety.

Compare *The King and I*'s exposition with *Call Me Madam*'s: a
quick look at Ethel Merman taking her ambassador's oath, a silly
chorus number, then an endless party scene that does little more
than introduce Merman to Russell Nype. *Call Me Madam*'s
through-line—an American woman in postwar Europe—is no
more than a hook, an angle. *The King and I*'s through-line—an
Englishwoman in the East—pits two monumental characters in a
war literally to the death (his) in a clash of cultures as well as
personalities.

This West meets East is no hook but the very substance of the
show, impelling the book and dominating the score in many small
and large ways—in one procession of Buddhist priests while
Anna's Siamese students pass singing "Home Sweet Home" in
counterpoint; Louis and the Siamese prince reprising the King's
first-act solo, "A Puzzlement," emphasizing in their racial diversity
the song's sociopolitical ambivalence; the second-act opening,
"Western People Funny," as the King's head wife, Lady Thiang,
gives an ironic view of Western dress; a Siamese staging in Eastern theatre style of *Uncle Tom's Cabin*, "The Small House of Uncle Thomas"; Anna teaching the King to polka; and, even as the
King dies, his son directing the court to bow and curtsey in the
Western manner instead of making the customary kowtow, the
scene played to the strains of Lady Thiang's "Something Wonderful," as if stating that the democratizing of Siam was in fact
set into motion by the King.

We should compare also *The King and I*'s score with *Call Me
Madam*'s, not to take advantage of the latter, but simply to show
how integrated the best fifties scores were. *Call Me Madam* runs
its plot, for the most part, between the numbers, which are not
strongly characterized in any case. (Yes, "The Hostess With the
Mostes' " is flavorful, but much of the rest is enjoyably generic.)
However, navigating through "My Lord and Master," "Hello,
Young Lovers," "A Puzzlement," "Getting to Know You," "We Kiss
in a Shadow," "Shall I Tell You What I Think of You," "Something

Wonderful," and "Shall We Dance?"—that is, hearing the songs alone—one can actually tell what the show is about. Even "I Have Dreamed" would be just another love song were it not for the fact that its singers risk death simply to utter those words. But then, Rodgers and Hammerstein's scores are unusual not because they were looking for out-of-the-ordinary topics but because they wrote about out-of-the ordinary characters.

For instance, consider the secondary couple: not frisky and young but senior and contemplative. Not only do they never duet—they share but one brief book scene. And they love not each other but the King: Lady Thiang and the Kralahome. This unqualified worship of their monarch enriches his persona, gives us an alternate context in which to view him, because we naturally assume Anna's view at first. She sees him as selfish and tyrannical. They see him as devoted to his people and struggling to break with his totalitarian traditions, Siam's first democrat.

The more orthodox supplementary couple is of course Tuptim and Lun Tha, young, pretty, and doomed. However, unlike the typical second pair, these two bear heavily on the story. Most of their counterparts maintain the most tenuous connection to the show; their main contribution lies in keeping the audience amused during scene changes. One thinks of *Annie Get Your Gun*'s Tommy and Winnie, featured players with two numbers of their own but of such little value to the story that, for the 1966 Lincoln Center revival, they were entirely written out of the show, songs and all.

One could not stage *The King and I* without Tuptim and Lun Tha. She in particular is essential on a thematic level, as a slave who most vividly presents the horror of living as another person's property. Here is another side of the King revealed to us, for to Tuptim he is vindictive, destructive. Not surprisingly, she is the author of "The Small House of Uncle Thomas," arguably the greatest of all set-piece dances in this age obsessed with Big Ballet. Tuptim's attraction to Harriet Beecher Stowe's novel is, obviously, its denunciation of slavery (and, in a touch of feminism avant la lettre, simple pride in a woman's having written a novel). But our interest in the ballet lies in how Jerome Robbins utilizes the pageantry of the East to give a familiar story a new glow. And, because Little Eva must enter heaven as a sacrifice at the ballet's end, so must Tuptim serve as a sacrifice, her tragedy bringing in a new King of Siam, one who will govern, under Anna's tutelage, even more democratically than his father.

This brings us to the central couple, Anna and the King. Which is the protagonist, the character bearing the moral weight, the cultural superiority? The play's title (from her viewpoint) and its stated source (the King barely appears in the novel) suggest Anna as the ultimate principal, and of course Lawrence was billed alone above the title during the show's first run. Yet, from the very faithful movie version on, Yul Brynner began to crowd the Annas, and, in two major revivals, it was he who got solo headline billing.

In fact, the parts are equally weighted, though Anna pits a sympathetic democracy against the King's sometimes rash totalism, and though she has five major numbers to his one big number, one small number, and his minor share in "Shall We Dance?" No matter: each musical play in the Rodgers and Hammerstein style rebalances the elements, which is one reason why they prove so successful in revival: they lack the conventions that date a work, "type" it. It's difficult to imagine any other writing team tackling such unusual material in 1951, but if one had made the attempt, *The King and I* would surely have come out an operetta with a baritone King, not unlike *The Desert Song*'s Red Shadow in pyjamas.

To my mind, Anna and the King are the two greatest roles in all Rodgers and Hammerstein, because they contend not for each other's souls but for the fate of a people. The King wants to accommodate, gradually, some form of enlightened monarchy; Anna wants to turn him into F.D.R., and not later than next Thursday.

It is an incendiary relationship, not only because of their political differences but because cultural taboos forbid them from consummating any physical desire they may feel. Certainly, the King, to refer to Brynner's performance in the film, harbors an overt interest in Anna, implicit until "Shall We Dance?" Not that this harmless polka is erotically metaphorical. But at one point Brynner takes Deborah Kerr in a firm grip as if annexing a disputed province; it's war, and it's love.

The entire Anna–King relationship is war and love, which gives it its unique richness. There is only one way to play Nellie and Emile in *South Pacific* and perhaps two or three ways to play *Carousel's* Julie and Billy. But Anna can be bossy or gently guiding, reckless or prudent, shrewish or eager; the King can be Brynner, Farley Granger, Darren McGavin, Rudolf Nuryeyev, or Lou Diamond Phillips, each of whom found something valid yet different to play. Granger was a charmer, only showing power when goaded. McGavin thundered and worried. Nuryeyev was heedlessly childish, as the dancer himself was. Phillips was warily boyish, not altogether sure of his power even as he exercised it.

It is the scene just after "Shall We Dance?" that defines each Anna and King. Rodgers and Hammerstein set it up with brutal irony, for the dainty polka tune and the shy lyrics emphasize all the unspoken substance of their bond. Anna sings of saying good night and meaning goodbye, but the number's subtext is is Shall we ever be able to be truly honest with each other? For their gala whirl around the room as the orchestra blasts out the melody—a great memory for theatregoers of this era and wonderfully preserved in the movie—brings them into an impossible moment: they finally agree on something. On the achievement of having brought off a diplomatic tour de force in eighteen hours, on how well each brings out the other's best qualities, on the refreshing vitality of the dance. At its end, they are closer than ever, laughing and carefree. The King demands an encore. This is excellent showmanship—but ingenious playmaking, too, for even the most alert member of the audience, disarmed by the warmth of the moment, has forgotten that Tuptim and Lun Tha are attempting to escape together to Burma. The encore lasts but seconds, for now comes the brutal part. A gong crashes, the music halts, and the Kralahome rushes in: "We have found Tuptim."

Instantly, the temperature on stage changes. Anna is terrified, the King cold and hard—"Miles away from Anna," as Hammerstein's stage directions tell us, and perhaps more apart from her than ever before. So intimate one moment and so opposed the next: that has been the pattern of their relationship almost from the beginning.

This night they really will mean goodbye, for the King prepares to whip Tuptim as Anna entreats him to forgive:

> ANNA: She's only a child. She was running away because she
> was unhappy. Can't you understand that? Your Majesty, I
> beg of you—don't throw away everything you've done. This
> girl hurt your vanity. She didn't hurt your heart.

The King appearing obdurate, she abandons her plea—*too soon!*—
and starts hacking away at him in frustration. In fury, it may be,
at being denied control. Suddenly she is less concerned with Tuptim's fate than with the king's refusal to submit to her guidance.
Watch how she changes tack in the line that directly follows the
above:

> ANNA: You haven't got a heart. You've never loved anyone.
> You never will.

Again, let's read Hammerstein's stage directions: "The King, stung
by Anna's words, seeks a way to hurt her in return." That way is
to whip Tuptim, who is by now no more than a pawn in Anna
and the King's war for power.

In the event, the King cannot bring himself to beat Tuptim
under Anna's fiercely challenging gaze. She has so transformed
him that he now gauges his self-esteem on her rating system. His
instincts demand Tuptim be punished, but his reason knows she
shouldn't be. Trapped between the safe place of his authority as
monarch and the dangerous place of Anna's authority as keeper
of his self-respect, he panics and runs. Anna has finally made the
King feel something he never felt before: shame.*

It's trivia to note that *The King and I* was the fifth consecutive
Rodgers and Hammerstein show in which someone dies (three of
the six principals), but it does help reveal the adult nature of their
subjects. If the 1950s was the decade that promised a continua-
tion of the musical's crucial place in the culture, it was at least
partly because the Rodgers and Hammerstein revolution in the

---

* The moment is obviously the climax of the role; Brynner was supreme in it.
Farley Granger was too shallow an actor to bring it off, but Darren McGavin,
even with nothing but Risë Stevens to goad him, strongly tasted of the King's
humiliation. Rudolf Nureyev was embarrassing, with his ballerino's exit flying,
and Lou Diamond Phillips curiously chose to play it for a stuttering slow-motion
exit, as if he had been admonished rather than destroyed. His replacement, Kevin
Gray, made far more of the moment.

1940s urged the musical to seek beyond typical fare for stories based on realistic character development: to become drama. Thus, the 1940s introduced the notion and the 1950s exploited it.

So this is the first decade filled with shows that are revived not just for their music (like *The Student Prince* or *Anything Goes* or *Song of Norway*) but for articulate, searching storytelling. I'm not going to list such titles here—this book is full of them—but I will offer *The King and I* as a show-and-tell exhibition for its wealth of psychological detail, not least in Hammerstein's ruthless dissection of his heroine's flaws.

This was the key to the musical's confidence, the security of its science: once, the great shows were the best of a particular kind. Now the great shows are unique.

2

Guys and Dolls

Michael Herr's novel *Walter Winchell* finds writer Ernest Hemingway asking writer Damon Runyon, "How come you never use the past tense in your stories?" Runyon answers, "I dunno . . . saves time, I reckon."

This snippet of Runyon's story "The Idyll of Miss Sarah Brown" shows what Hemingway was referring to:

> One Sunday evening The Sky is walking along Broadway, and at the corner of Forty-ninth Street he comes upon a little bunch of mission workers who are holding a religious meeting, such as mission workers love to do of a Sunday evening, the idea being that they may round up a few sinners here and there, although . . . at such an hour the sinners are still in bed resting up from their sinning of the night before, so they will be in good shape for more sinning a little later on.

Runyon, a sportswriter, all-around journalist, and short-fiction retailer of the gamblers, girlfriends, crooks, freaks, and other denizens of the Broadway Tenderloin, became one of the leading mouthpieces of hot-town New York from the 1920s to the 1940s.

Nothing fades faster than old newspapers, of course—what now remains of Runyon's colleague and, in the last days of Runyon's life, friend Walter Winchell, once thought to be the most powerful man in America?

Nevertheless, Runyon's stories, all underworld comedies narrated in the first person with, usually, an O. Henry twist ending, are American classics. They were even popular in England, though Runyon's argot (money: "sugar, "scratch," cook: "swing a mean skillet," theatre tickets: "ducats," man: "guy," woman: "doll" and his characters (such as Gigolo Georgie, Sam the Gonoph, Dream Street Rose, and Johnny One-Eye), and the immortally relentless use of the present tense conjure up a culture out of language itself, one difficult for foreigners to grasp.

Hollywood heard it, when the early talkie crime melodramas began to give way to comic or pathetic crime dramas, and there were rather a number of adaptations of Runyon's tales. Yet they were all B-budget programmers, as if the movies didn't get Runyon's uniqueness and mistook him for a conventional yarn-spinner. Warner Brothers produced *A Very Honorable Guy* (1934) and *Midnight Alibi* (1934), Universal *Million Dollar Ransom* (1934), *Princess O'Hara* (1935), *Butch Minds the Baby* (1942), MGM *The Three Wise Guys* (1936), RKO *Racing Lady* (1937), Fox *Little Miss Marker* (1934), with Shirley Temple. There were a few others, but all are forgotten today, though Temple's film was remade twice. Warner Brothers' *A Slight Case of Murder* (1938), from a play by Runyon and Howard Lindsay, does boast a noted comic turn by Edward G. Robinson, and Runyon himself was in charge of *The Big Street* (1942), in which busboy Henry Fonda loves selfish, crippled showgirl Lucille Ball. In fact, for all his classic status, Runyon's fables never provisioned a major film until Frank Capra's *A Pocketful of Miracles* (1961).

However, in the late 1940s, Broadway producers Cy Feuer and Ernest Martin, looking for a successor to their first and very successful effort, Frank Loesser's *Where's Charley?* (1948), chose "The Idyll of Miss Sarah Brown," planning it not as a funny show but as a dark romance. Something, maybe, like Rodgers and Hammerstein, only with the dirt and deals of Winchell's and Runyon's Broadway, though gentling down the murderous violence that

Runyon took for granted. Feuer and Martin hired Jo Swerling to write the book and Loesser again to write the songs. But while Swerling gave his employers what they asked for, Loesser went off on a tear into the real Runyon, whimsical and absurd yet, on his characters' hard-bitten terms, entirely logical.

By the time Swerling and Loesser had finished Act One, Feuer and Martin realized that they had the script for one show and the score for another. Swerling had done his work well—but he had the dark Runyon and Loesser had the light. Losing Swerling, the producers brought in radio writer (of *Duffy's Tavern*, comparable to Runyon in tone) Abe Burrows to rewrite Swerling around Loesser's songs. Burrows and Loesser would then collaborate on Act Two—and now the piece was in trim. To Runyon's story of how gambler Sky Masterson ("because he goes so high"—this is Runyon—"when it comes to betting on any proposition whatever") woos Salvation Army lass Sarah Brown ("She puts the blast on sin very good, and boosts religion quite some"), *Guys and Dolls* added a new second couple, Nathan Detroit and Miss Adelaide.* He's the guy who organizes the crap games, and she's the doll he has been engaged to for fourteen years. (Adelaide refers to herself at one point as "the well-known fiancée.") Both Sky and Nathan have an aversion to bourgeois mating procedures, which Loesser set out early on in a duet, "Travellin' Light."

The number was cut out of town because the Nathan, Sam Levene (who had been in *The Big Street*), couldn't carry the tricky tune. Otherwise, however, Levene was excellent; the entire production team saw him as the key player of the four leads. Actually, they were all fine: Robert Alda (father of Alan) a masterful Sky, absolutely in control; Vivian Blaine a wonderful Adelaide, so nagging yet so thwarted; and Isabel Bigley's Sarah fielding an ingenuous little soprano to counter Blaine's nasal belt.

Better, all four were perfectly in balance. Here is one musical

---

* It has been suggested that Hot House Herbie and Miss Cutie Singleton, in Runyon's "Pick the Winner," are the source of this second couple. But, other than a long engagement, the pair have nothing in common with Nathan and Adelaide.

with not a main and supplementary couple but two exactly matched couples, their two stories ingeniously intertwined. Nathan and Sky are old friends and cross paths early in the action, while the two women don't meet up till the show is almost over. But drop even a single scene of *Guys and Dolls* and the entire structure would collapse. It's that well made.

It's interesting, too, that while most fifties musical comedies treat the decade as a source of sardonic commentary (for instance, in jokes on Truman, wheat thins, Tennessee Williams' decadence, automobile tailfins, Hollywoodiana, and so on), *Guys and Dolls* holds to the boundaries of its timeless Runyonland. Only when the two heroines, in "Marry the Man Today," strive to imagine a bourgeois life *out* of their natural habitat does the text permit the citing of epochal placenames—*The Reader's Digest*, bandleader Guy Lombardo, the conservative men's clothier Rogers Peet.

Thus, while Runyon's Broadway itself is long vanished, *Guys and Dolls* remains extremely revivable. "Not only a young masterpiece," Kenneth Tynan called it, "but the Beggar's Opera of Broadway." *Guys and Dolls* opened in New York in 1950, the same year as *Call Me Madam*. But where that show's here-and-now attitude rooted it in an era, *Guys and Dolls* is wonderfully rootless: universal. It's not about postwar attitudes. It's about a technically illegal subculture operating within the main culture.

Choreographer Michael Kidd established this in the pantomimed opening number, set at something like Broadway and Forty-sixth Street: Texan tourists, a cop, a sidewalk vendor, a training prizefighter, a pickpocket, two bobbysoxers, a celebrity, and the passing crowd, all seen and reseen in the whirling pace of midtown. A sidewalk photographer snaps the Texans, takes their order and money for pictures, and tosses their order away when they leave. The bobbysoxers beg for an autograph from an elegant couple till his shirtfront lights up to promote Pessimo ("the worst") Cigars. The street vendor, selling dancing paper dolls, converts his "counter" into a baby buggy when the cop appears. The pickpocket points to the sky and the Texan looks up, losing his watch and chain. A streetwalker steals the loot from the pickpocket, the Texan gives chase, the cop chases the Texan, and the stage erupts in riot, everyone at last dashing off to reveal three touts doping out their racing forms as the characteristic racetrack bugle call peals out of the orchestra.

That's the cue for "Fugue for Tinhorns," a trio in canon and the first sign in the fifties musical that the form was still youthfully vital: because it was still capable of renewal. Irving Berlin, a month before *Guys and Dolls*, and Cole Porter, a month after, proved in *Call Me Madam* and *Out of This World* that both were yet at full power. But that was old news. The new tidings gave us Frank Loesser's sudden development from *Where's Charley?*'s popmeister into a wizard—and this is not to mention the dazzle of Kidd's opening, actually called "Runyonland" and, even this late in the musical's history, one of the few curtain-raising numbers that is neither sung nor danced. Indeed, Kidd—with de Mille, Robbins, and Fosse—would make this *the* decade of the choreographer, a venerable collaboration in the musical suddenly liberated to twist each show into something with its own style, look, tempo.

New book writers, too, were essential now that the musical expected substance in its narrative. Newcomer Burrows' confidence was almost embarrassing. The Runyon atmosphere is there:

> HARRY THE HORSE: Is [Nathan] got a place for his crap game? I'm loaded for action. I just acquired five thousand potatoes.
> NICELY-NICELY JOHNSON: Where did you acquire it?
> HARRY: I collected the reward on my father.

The Runyon characters are there:

> NATHAN: I'm having terrible trouble. Everybody's scared on account of that lousy [Detective] Brannigan—
> BRANNIGAN: (*suddenly making an appearance*) Something wrong, Mr. Detroit?
> NATHAN: I hope you don't think I was talking about you. There are other lousy Brannigans.

Or:

ADELAIDE: (*To* SKY, *after* NATHAN *has let her down again*) Will you see Nathan before you go?

SKY: Maybe.

ADELAIDE: Tell him I never want to talk to him again and have him call me here.

Guys and Dolls' book is nothing but narrative and atmosphere. Burrows establishes his premise in the very first book scene: Nathan needs one thousand dollars to rent a garage for the crap game. From then on, character is destiny. To get the thousand, Nathan bets Sky he can't date Sarah, the mission doll. Sky does, and the two fall in love, but are sundered when the mission is raided because Nathan held the game there. Meanwhile, Adelaide has been pressuring Nathan to give up gambling or lose her. Fat chance, either way, but so it continues, the plot ever logically twisting until the authors come up with the ultimate twist—well, two twists, really. The guys all lose Sky's wager on their souls and attend a mission rally that in fact saves the mission; and the two dolls meet up near Times Square while singing quodlibet reprises of Sarah's "I've Never Been in Love Before" and "Adelaide's Lament." They then figure out the happy ending in "Marry the Man Today": you don't wait for the guy to reform *before* marriage. Marriage—and this is so Runyon—is *itself* reformation.

With its sneaky structure of one bar of vamp before each bar of song, its echoing voice lines, its emphasis on the minor key, its baaing mordent on the first syllable of "laughter" so that the two in effect "sing" a laugh, and its two-octave violin glissando at the close, "Marry the Man Today" is yet another of the show's numbers announcing a special talent. Consider the dueling duet of a love song, "I'll Know," in which Sky and Sarah match romantic icons—she's got Him all cast and he wants Her to be a surprise. (They're both right in their descriptions; and though they've just met, they are but hours from the wedding bell.) Consider Sarah's "If I Were a Bell," a metaphorical list song that charts the progress of the romance by repeating their "Chemistry?" "Yeah, *chemistry*" exchange from the first number but taking the controlling reply from *him* and giving it to *her*.

Consider "Sit Down, You're Rocking the Boat," which manages

to spoof revivalist hymns while serving as a perfectly legitimate revivalist hymn. Consider the repeated-note recitative of the title song's verse, each new statement reaching up to a higher repeated note like newspaper headlines increasing in size till the banner at last clicks us into the show's moral: guys were born to love dolls and dolls were born to tame guys.

Or consider how well Loesser worked the comedy songs into the fresco, as just another color, not as intrusive blots. For that's what the musical's comedy songs so often were. Think of *Brigadoon*'s "The Love of My Life" and "My Mother's Wedding Day" or *Kiss Me, Kate*'s "Brush Up Your Shakespeare." In *Guys and Dolls*, "The Oldest Established," "Adelaide's Lament," and the title song are respectively, plot, character, and thematic numbers; and "Take Back Your Mink," ostensibly a nightclub floor number, really opens up to us Adelaide's deeply conservative moral code under the showgirl facade (though the song was written some years before, for Loesser to perform at parties).

"Take Back Your Mink" is the second-act opener,* and this brings us to another of *Guys and Dolls'* premiums: a brilliant second act. Most musical comedies ran out of plot in Act Two because—as in the classic Feydeauvien farce layout of exposition, mad scramble, and dénouement—that final act was little more than the third X in tic-tac-toe. The strong character development of the musical play gave its last act something to work with, but musical comedies, turning more on plot than character, would exploit the exposition and mad scramble in their first act and thus had little more to do in the second than close up the plot and say good night.

But *Guys and Dolls* continues the mad scramble, ever gaining energy as it reaches the "Luck Be a Lady" sequence, first "The Crapshooters' Dance" (in the infrastructure under Forty-eighth

---

* A musical number directly after the intermission and entr'acte was all but inevitable in this time. Even shows that began Act One with a book scene wouldn't think of attempting to launch Act Two without song and dance in some helping or other. Of all early fifties shows, *Paint Your Wagon* gets in the most dialogue between the end of the overture and the first number—one full scene right up to the blackout. But what's doing when the curtain goes up on Act Two? The utterly extraneous frolic "Hand Me Down That Can of Beans."

Street) and then Sky's own prayer to Lady Luck, perhaps the most characteristic number in the score because it is so unlike numbers in other shows in subject, melody, and even harmony—the vamp shifts back and forth between D Flat Major and the extremely foreign D Major, building to a climax as Sky finally throws. "Ha!" the gamblers shout, straining forward to read the dice. Blackout.

Of course, he won the toss, effectively reconciling him with Sarah; and the infinite engagement of Nathan and Adelaide having reached critical mass, they too hit the church, or wherever Runyonkind get married. Feuer and Martin not only had their hit successor to *Where's Charley?*—they had a Classic. *Where's Charley?* ran two years and made it to London and Hollywood; now it's gone. *Guys and Dolls* has never left. Samuel Goldwyn, a sucker for Broadway prestige, paid one million dollars plus 10 percent of the gross for the film rights, reminding us how bottom-line profitable the musical was then. Literally longer than the stage show, Goldwyn's film (1955) retained an overflowing Vivian Blaine, three of the gamblers, and Michael Kidd from Broadway, dropped five and added three numbers, and castrated the role of Nathan Detroit for a strangely spineless Frank Sinatra while discovering in Marlon Brando and Jean Simmons two non-singers who nevertheless found the microphone empowering and left unchallengeable performances.

An all-black version, directed by Billy Wilson under Burrows' supervision, played Broadway in 1976, England's National Theatre staged a superb revival (with Ian Charleson, Julie Covington, Bob Hoskins, and Julia McKenzie) in 1982, and a second Broadway revival in 1992 with Nathan Lane, Faith Prince, Peter Gallagher, and Josie de Guzman was the hit of its season and the longest-running musical revival in Broadway history. Please note that I have been inconsistent in laying out these casts, starting now with Nathan–Adelaide, now with Sky–Sarah. But, of course, it's never clear exactly who the leads are, as I've said. The original billing, in 1950, featured, below the title, Sky, Adelaide, and Nathan, leaving Isabel Bigley in smaller type on the next line with Pat Rooney, Sr., who played her grandfather, the mission chief.

I emphasize this wonderful character structure of the four absolutely equal principals because this makes *Guys and Dolls* unique. Yes, its setting is unique and its patois is unique and its score is unique. But what's *uniquely* unique here is the way the show concentrates on this quartet and its two very separate networks, of life on the street (gamblers and cops) and life in the Lord (the mission folk). This is a young show but a wise one, something that shouldn't be possible. And it was Big Business but subversive. After all: gangsters for heroes?

It embarrasses me no small amount to say so, but it is now a more cockeyed time of an era than formerly, and it is all bets off exactly how this came about. But I would as soon take a quiet sneak away from Brick McCloskey while he is in a mood for some talk of the social life, such as who is killing who lately, as I would fail to regard how it is once again those Rodgers and Hammerstein fellas that deal this particular hand. You would think their interest in the opera kind of story, in which, what with this and that, everyone is coming off very passionate and a few characters are even getting sanded, does not work for musical comedy.

But I am saying that these certain parties known as Rodgers and Hammerstein are making it tough on every kind of diversion of a Broadway nature. Because it now seems that what these two are doing in their own private musicals is what the public wants to get in every musical of whatever kind.

And that, while I should not make a big fat legal case of it, is what is coming on these days.

3

A Tree Grows in Brooklyn

As we investigate the American musical in this age when it was hailed as America's contribution to theatre history, we should remember that one of its strengths was its relative youthfulness in comparison to the popular music theatre of other cultures. After all, by the end of the nineteenth century, French opéra bouffe and opéra comique (in the lighter style favored by Audran and Adam) were in their prime, English "comic opera" had produced Gilbert and Sullivan, German Singspiel doted on a history so venerable that it ran back to before Mozart, and Spanish zarzuela was in its *second* flowering.

By contrast, the American musical was in its infancy at this time, even after exposure to Offenbach and Johann Strauss. Story shows tended to behave like revues, and the musicality was primitive. I think of this period as the musical's First Age (circa 1850–1899). The Second Age (1900–1919), dominated by the lavishly musical Victor Herbert and the highly theatrical George M. Cohan, is a time of absorption of European styles even as the musical eventually subsumes these styles in a wholly American format.

Think of *Lady, Be Good!, Good News!, Show Boat,* and *Whoopee,* all in the 1920s. That decade launches the Third Age (1920–1969), only thirty years old in 1950 and thus still fresh, crisp, novel. It's a kid, arrogant and wiseass and discovering itself. Those European forms were by 1950 in dotage. Broadway's musical was randy.

Yet some of its essential elements were ancient. The star comic and les girls had been around from the start. The star heroine, personified by Lillian Russell, came into prominence in the Second Age. The composer and lyricist and, less notably, the librettist took power in the 1920s, and the artistic choreographer (as opposed to the master of the hoofing chorus' cliché "combinations") was introduced during the 1930s, picked up major prestige in the 1940s, and will assume near-total power as these very pages turn.

Yet the definitive honcho of the current era, the High Maestro Director who collaborates with the writers, "conceives" the staging, and takes full responsibility for its success or failure, came into being only with the rise of the "concept" production in the 1970s, though of course every musical that ever lived had a director of some kind. No one knew or cared who they were in the First Age, and though the Second Age hosted two very gifted directors, Edward Royce and Julian Mitchell, they were not celebrated. By the start of the Third Age, George M. Cohan, in reality the first of the High Maestro Directors, was the only staging talent in general notice—and that because he was mainly famous as a producer, writer, and actor. Then, in the mid-1930s, came George Abbott.

A former actor and still a playwright, Abbott virtually steered musical comedy (he seldom worked on operettas or musical plays) through the 1940s and 1950s, when he was the director of everyone's first choice. Here was a formidable character: tall, trim, energetic, reasonable but impatient with fools, resistant to fads, and an absolute authority on how a musical must unfold—what kind of number goes here, when to cue in the dream ballet, where the story stands when the first-act curtain falls, how to cut when a scene is sagging. Abbott had little contact with the adventurous musical; he was a journeyman, not a visionary. But he knew Broadway. He knew talent. He knew the public. And he had a remarkable record of successes because he could apply this knowledge creatively. That is, he was not a hack. Nor was he a genius. He was very, very good at what he knew how to do and, like all conservatives, never attempted to do anything else.

Many found him intimidating. He often worked with youngsters, who instinctively fell into the tradition of calling him "Mister Abbott" (though Joel Higgins, on *Music Is* [1976], found this affected and, unreproached, called him "George"). Abbott disdained the subtle psychological preparations that became popular in this age haunted by the Method, and when an actor, stumped on a scene, asked what his motivation was, Abbott replied, "Your paycheck."

Abbott himself denied that story, though it is true that he discouraged such discussions. He preferred to give line readings—say it like *this*—and get on with the blocking. In one sense, Abbott was an engineer, keeping the complex machinery of a big musical humming. Let me give you three anecdotes to fix for us Abbott as man and thespian, and then I'll explain why I think Abbott was in the long run a destructive figure in the musical's history.

Anecdote Number One gives us Abbott the keeper of order in the often pointlessly explosive backstage world. On *Call Me Madam*, Abbott has edited down one of Lindsay and Crouse's more garrulous scenes and, at a general rehearsal, the ridiculously touchy Lindsay notices the changes and huffs out, "Well, I hope at least we still have the same title!"

Abbott immediately calls for a break, and takes Lindsay and Crouse out to the lobby for a Talk. There is no more carping at Abbott's editing.

The second anecdote gives us Abbott as Broadway's God. Late in the second act of *Damn Yankees* (1955), a blackout is covered by a sports announcer's voice-over, putting the audience into great suspense about the any-second-now outcome of the game deciding whether the Washington Senators will finally take the pennant from the Yankees. The pitch is thrown—and the auditorium was suddenly plunged into the blinding illumination of night lights as the stadium came into view, a great theatrical stroke. Supposedly, at one performance, a startled spectator cried out, "That's a mistake!" Then, thinking it over, he said, "No, George Abbott would never have okayed a mistake like that."

The third anecdote gives us Abbott the sage. In 1956, Edith Adams was simultaneously offered leads in two big fall shows, *Li'l Abner* and *Candide*. Having learned a good deal from Abbott on *Wonderful Town* three years earlier, Adams asked Abbott whether to play Daisy Mae or Cunegonde. *Candide*, Abbott reckoned, would be wonderful but a failure, and anyway Cunegonde would be another ingenue part: "You need a sexy role in a commercial hit." Adams took *Li'l Abner*, the smartest move of her career.

He knew his forks, Abbott. But his recipe for sound musical comedy structure was: get from A to B as directly as possible, from B to C even more directly, and so on. Psychology, atmosphere, realistic details, and, yes, motivation would not slow him. So character was established in broad strokes, as in a comic strip. The stage picture was about movement, never about meaning. The scores were integrated with the action, but if the second act needed a lift, someone—anyone—would entertain at a party or something.

This was the kind of dramaturgy acceptable before Rodgers and Hammerstein. The musical had been rationalized now, but Abbott saw it as more efficient than rational. His participation in *A Tree Grows in Brooklyn* (1951), then, as producer, co-author, and director, is problematical, much as his history in the musical is problematical. He streamlined and clarified, yes. But he ignored character development. He disliked ambitious musicality. He said Your motivation is your paycheck. Don't ask why. Just wrap it up by 11:00.

Like *Guys and Dolls*, *A Tree Grows in Brooklyn* was based on fiction, as more and more musicals were in the 1950s. Previously, musicals were adapted from plays or were built around a hot new topic such as ballet-versus-hoofing or psychoanalysis. But after Rodgers and Hammerstein proved that anything could be a musical if the material was treated properly, all sorts of unlikely subjects underwent transformation in the late 1940s and early 1950s—Jules Verne; a novel about the black subculture in old St. Louis; Alan Paton's tragic *Cry, the Beloved Country*, on South African race relations; Anita Loos' Lorelei Lee spoof; the Damon Runyon stories, as we know; and now Betty Smith's nostalgic look at growing up poor yet hopeful in turn-of-the-century Brooklyn.*

It is not a readily adaptable novel, episodic and almost epic as it follows three generations of an Irish family in Williamsburg. A film version in 1945 showed how to trim down the view to center on Katie and Johnny Nolan, their two children, Francie and Neely (though the boy was dropped from the musical), and Katie's gala "character" of a sister, Cissy. With a deliberately unglamorous Dorothy McGuire as Katie and the naturally unglamorous James Dunn as Johnny (though he won an Oscar), Joan Blondell made the most of Cissy, too sensual and fun-loving for the moral code of her day but, in the end, the encompassing energy that holds a troubled family together. Johnny, latest in a line of ne'er-do-wells, drinks and fails and dies, leaving his survivors to find the power to go on from deep in themselves, in their culture, in their hope for the future.

A very American saga, it has a taste of *Carousel*, perhaps. It was typical of the age that musical comedy people—Abbott, composer Arthur Schwartz, and lyricist Dorothy Fields—were folding themselves into the Rodgers and Hammerstein form of musical play. So far, so good. But the musical play's salient feature was its emphasis on character development within the social background of a particular time and place, something Abbott had no patience for. A great Abbott show was, say, *On the Town* (1944), a piece so mercurial that it covers a very crowded twenty-four hours yet seems to rush by in about fifteen minutes. There is no character development, no social background—no time for it. This is one moment in six people's lives that will change those lives forever. However, the *Tree Grows in Brooklyn* book, which Abbott wrote

---

* Ironically, it was not until late in their partnership that Rodgers and Hammerstein themselves adapted a novel. *Oklahoma!* and *Carousel* derive from plays, *Allegro* is original, *South Pacific* was, really, suggested by a few pages in a short-story collection, and *The King and I* was based on a movie script. Still, all these shows were special, and that's what led the fifties musical to strengthen its story content by raiding the library. Special became a genre: labor relations in a pajama factory; baseball; the mañana culture of Montery, California; a Tibetan Brigadoon; a satiric picaresque through eighteenth-century Europe; a cockroach and a cat; Tom Sawyer; Harlem life; backstage Broadway; San Francisco's Chinatown; Jane Austen; a stripper's memoirs . . . all fifties musicals, all from books.

with novelist Smith herself, covers some thirteen years in the life of a family, as seen within the milieu of the Irish-American working class. I'm worried.

One must state up front that Schwartz and Fields wrote one of the decade's finest scores, romantic, comic, and streetwise to mirror the story's unusual blend of doomed love (Katie and Johnny), domestic farce (Cissy and her current "husband," Oscar), and local color. For instance, the opening chorus, "Payday," is no mere curtain-raiser but a kind of rhapsodic laborers' anthem as they are all set free to enjoy a weekend, the scene teeming with the kinds and the types, and the set (by Jo Mielziner) is a dazzling street scene under the arch of the Brooklyn Bridge.* A few minutes later comes another number, "Mine Till Monday," led by Johnny, taking in his three cronies and eventually the chorus as everyone marches into the pawn shop for the weekly redemption of a treasure: china, a cutaway suit, a trumpet, a lamp, Johnny's watch.

The second-act opener, "That's How It Goes," sees an old-clothes man's call erupting in a full-scale ensemble jig to some front-stoop philosophy that views all existence as inevitable but meaningless. It's full of joys and sorrows, but in the long run it's just a cycle, like the seasons, or a year of washdays—"Laugh in 'em, cry in 'em, live in 'em, die in 'em." That's how it goes. This is sharp thinking, slipping what is virtually the show's motto into the inevitable second-act opening number.

Still, Schwartz and Fields did their most lasting work in the ballads, Katie and Johnny's "Make the Man Love Me," his overconfident "I'm Like a New Broom" (because he ain't), his even tragically bragging "I'll Buy You a Star," which tells us why Katie loses her faith in but not her love for Johnny: he's got the gift, the beauty, the love. He just doesn't have the strength. Katie does, as the libretto makes clear. In fact, the Nolan family scenes in the second act show us why musical comedy wanted to behave like the musical play—because there lay the drama, the depth, the almost spooky new power that the musical had discovered in

---

* Mielziner designed a similar perspective for Maxwell Anderson's play *Winterset* in 1935. But that Brooklyn was sour, political, cowering under its bridge. This new Brooklyn was all light and festival.

itself. No wonder the overtures were like symphonies of triumph: the musical had gone to bed as pop and awakened as art.

A Tree Grows in Brooklyn is above all a touching story, even a very touching one—something that *Guys and Dolls* is never going to be. It's those Nolans. Late in the evening, Johnny, reduced to playing piano in a bordello, wins the piano in the house raffle but is bullied out of claiming it, and faces his family with, for once, a dreadful honesty:

> JOHNNY: Francie, you've got to finish school. That's your mama's big ambition. That's why she works so hard. Look at me. See me for what I am.
> KATIE: (*anguished*) Johnny!
> JOHNNY: (*holding up the raffle ticket*) I hold in my hand the whole meaning of my life—a winning ticket on a second-hand piano that I can't even claim. (*He throws it from him.*) I always meant to do better. I thought I had time. I thought I'd be young forever and it ends like this. . . . Don't ever throw away your bright young years, darlin'. Don't be a failure like me.
> FRANCIE: You're not, Papa! You're not!

This follows a dream ballet—actually a nightmare ballet, on Halloween, in which a drunken Johnny is stalked and shamed by demons—very much in the Rodgers and Hammerstein mode. And the two act finales are beautifully judged, each freezing a characterological moment for us. In the first, Johnny sings "I'll Buy You a Star" on a Brooklyn roof in the carefree summertime while Katie, employed as the building's janitor, stoically scrubs away with pail and brush, consigned to her private heaven-hell. In the second, at Francie's junior high school graduation party, everyone is waltzing and some young beau asks Francie for her first dance. As they glide into it, we look at Katie. Johnny's dead and Katie's alone, but she swells with pride in her daughter. And just when Katie seems almost happy, the lights of Brooklyn Bridge flip on. And the curtain falls.

All this is superb musical-play thinking. But the tone is not consistently upheld throughout the show. A scene in which Cissy pretends to give birth (to an adopted baby) is terrifically funny, but plays almost as a self-contained revue sketch. Furthermore, when the stubborn Oscar demands that the child be named after him, boy or girl (Oscarina, in the latter case), Cissie says, "That ain't a name. That's something you play on—like a sweet potato." This unmistakable reference to "The Ocarina," from *Call Me Madam* the year before, is anachronistic in the way only a saucy, unreal musical comedy can dare to be. Imagine *The King and I* pulling such a stunt.

Even worse is the way Abbott establishes a powerful allegiance among Johnny and his three friends. We sense genuine fraternity. Later, in the second-act raffle and nightmare episode, Abbott needs villains, and the three friends will do. They treat Johnny with a brutality as false as it is startling.

Studying the show today, one can see exactly the moment in which *A Tree Grows in Brooklyn* went wrong. It comes midway through the first act, in the furniture store where Johnny and Katie have just bought the bridal bed. Elated, Katie breaks into "Look Who's Dancing," which naturally leads into a general dance. But then Cissy sings a chorus—and this isn't Cissy's song. It isn't her emotion. It isn't her scene. Trouble is, when you've got a great Cissy, you don't want to waste her.

Cissy was Shirley Booth, one of the most unusual actresses in American theatre history. She came in so long ago that the Lunts had only just teamed up. Charm and elegance were the fashion then—Ethel Barrymore, Jane Cowl, Jeanne Eagels, Marilyn Miller, Pauline Lord, Eva Le Gallienne, and Ina Claire were Broadway's reigning ladies. Booth was more like something out of vaudeville, with her baby voice and eccentric mannerisms, which might best be described as "wistfully coarse." She found her *Fach* in wisecrack comedy in the prewar years, with *Three Men on a Horse, The Philadelphia Story* (as one of the reporters), and *My Sister Eileen*, then suddenly revealed a singing voice in *Hollywood Pinafore* (1945), a Gilbert and Sullivan send-up of the movie business. Another revelation came with William Inge's *Come Back, Little Sheba*, in 1950, Booth now dazzling Broadway in a serious part as the slatternly wife of a recovering alcoholic. Doting on young people, flirting with delivery boys, and obsessing in an oddly now and again way about a runaway dog, Booth suddenly seemed to be the most versatile of stars.

The second half of Booth's career should have found her at the top of the profession, but instead she played in minor works and maintained a long run in the repellently vacuous TV sitcom *Hazel*. But her Aunt Cissy remains one of the grand memories; an oft-revived photograph of her slouching in a chair at a kitchen table, left hand on hip, right ring finger in mouth, dressed in a ruffled-bust lace slip under an open Japanese kimono and black stockings with elaborately sewn insets summons up not only this portrayal but the entire career. Booth was what the musical loved: a delightful freak. She was a clown, but an actress of uncommon depth, out of this world yet utterly believable. No beauty, she nonetheless possessed infinite appeal, and, like all great musical stars, she had a unique singing style, an infantile timbre pitched largely in the belt range, with startlingly potent high notes. She even danced—and, unlike Ethel Merman and Mary Martin, she looked natural in period costumes, as that famous photograph attests.

Then, too, Booth lucked into the lyrics of Dorothy Fields, so right for how Booth was going to play Cissy that Fields might have invented both of them. As lyricist and librettist, Fields had proved an essentially urban, lowdown talent, though she also worked in antique Americana (*Annie Get Your Gun* and *Arms and the Girl*) and even an operetta (*Up in Central Park*). Fields was a stayer, too: having started in *Blackbirds of 1928*, she was still at it forty-five years later in *Seesaw*. Yet hers was an ever-youthful talent, smartass but sensitive and wondering.

Fields's humor could be forced, but it wasn't here. Cissy's monologue "He Had Refinement" is that rarity, a truly funny comedy song, the kind only Cole Porter and Stephen Sondheim write at will. Cissy's more dramatic number, "Is That My Prince?," Is sad-funny, depicting the meeting, after fifteen years, with her first "husband," a deaf wreck whose refinement nows seems prissy affectation. (Swanswine is the guy's name, an agglutination of what he was with what he is.)

Fields and Schwartz were smart enough to celebrate Booth's instrument with an uptempo number as well, "Love Is the Reason," a catalogue of the fads and peeves of romance. It's cutely structured, ABABC with no rhymes except three in the first B and one in the second B, to match "Love is the reason for it all." And the song has a tick, a four-syllable throwaway word that kicks in the second A—"personally," "obviously," "generally," and so on, the kind of thing that only Booth could pull off as absolutely colloquial and absolutely bizarre at once. And just to hear one of Fields' second B lines—"If you shut your big mouth when his relatives call"—is to realize how well she caught character, social class, and period in the show.

Unfortunately, this valentine for Booth tells us how wrong a piece like *Brooklyn* can go. You can't do a star vehicle and a musical play at the same time. A musical play can have stars, yes— *The King and I*, for instance. But its star is not set free to entertain. Its star is set within the entertainment. Shirley Booth, in *A Tree Grows in Brooklyn*, was set free as great comics should be. It threw the show off.

The rest of the cast was of no great éclat: Johnny Johnston as Johnny (a sharp agent, or something, got him top billing with Booth), Marcia Van Dyke as Katie, musical comedy regular Nathaniel Frey as Oscar, and Nomi Mitty as Francie, with a fine veteran of the past, Harland Dixon, a dancing comic prominent in the 1920s, as the old-clothes man of "That's How it Goes."

Mostly good reviews (and a critics' ovation for Booth) did not fail to point out that *Brooklyn* was two shows: one, the story and, two, Shirley Booth. Still, the piece ran eight months, enjoyed some Hit Parade play without quite producing a standard, and vanished; and I blame Abbott. Somewhere in what he okayed for the Broadway premiere was one of the best of the musical plays not by Rodgers and Hammerstein, but it got lost in that darned "let's get there" efficiency-without-sensitivity that Abbott favored— and this at a time when audiences were looking for intelligence, substance, consistency. Crazy, silly diversion that it is, *Guys and Dolls* has them, and this is why it will age along with Offenbach, Lehár, and *Show Boat*. *A Tree Grows in Brooklyn* became, in the end, another of those canonical cast albums, a slate of songs rather than an in-the-theatre experience. For years, there were rumors that Sammy Davis Jr. would play Johnny in an updating set in Bedford-Stuyvesant, which would have piled Ossa upon Pelion. There's one star too many in the script as it is.

The playwright and director Moss Hart once told Alan Jay Lerner, "Every show makes you feel like an amateur": because, unless you did the same show every time, you were bound to be puzzled and challenged no matter how expert you were. Maybe that was George Abbott's problem—he never felt like an amateur because he kept doing the same show.

No matter how different the shows were getting.

4

The Street, 1952

It is the coming together of Irving Berlin and Frank Loesser, Ethel Merman and Vivian Blaine, Moss Hart and Michael Kidd, slam-bang musical comedy and the stimulating musical play—the old guard and the newborns—that tells us how vigorous the musical was. Here is a community of old and young talent egging each other on, everyone a student and teacher at once.

Cole Porter was probably as old time as one could have been, counting a Broadway debut in 1916. Yet his *Can-Can* (1953) was somewhat new wave, an old-fashioned show bursting with relative newcomers—producers Feuer and Martin, book writer Abe Burrows, choreographer Michael Kidd, and, in a featured part, the biggest musical comedy star to arrive since Mary Martin sang "My Heart Belongs to Daddy" in another Porter show fifteen years before.

So here is more Big Broadway, the kind of project whose first full-page advertisement in the Sunday *New York Times* would address a wide and eager public. And, of course, with "I Love Paris," "It's All Right With Me," "C'est Magnifique," and "Allez-Vous-En," it's a classic show—or is it just a classic score? It has been revived, but without success, even in revision. Yet its tale of a dance-hall hostess defying the judge who wants to close her place because he doesn't approve of it should be timely in any age.

Can-Can was, like Call Me Madam, a typical piece of work. Let Guys and Dolls popularize a new vocabulary, even sing in it; let A Tree Grows in Brooklyn wrestle with generical problems as it balances tragedy with comedy. Can-Can was all for fun. It had a look and a style, vaguely suggestive of Paris in 1893. But what it mainly had were the Cole Porter things—sex, speed, great songs, and a lot of personality in the cast. Quick, what's the opposite of Guys and Dolls?: period sets and costumes; so much dancing that it intrudes on the thin storyline, but so much the better; a clear hierarchy of star, co-star, featured and lesser players; bait-the-censors bawdry; and a brass section that gave poor Sandy Wilson, visiting from London to discuss the New York production of The Boy Friend, the shakes.

Can-Can showed its strength as early as 8:35 of an evening, as the orchestra struck up the overture and the Shubert Theatre's house velvet rose on the "show curtain" (as they called it then), an amazingly detailed "Plan de Paris." This was the inspiration of the show's designer, and the greatest Broadway designer of the middle third of the twentieth century, Paris-born Jo Mielziner.* As I've said, there were no real innovations made in stage design in the 1950s, but that was because Mielziner had anticipated all of them in the 1930s and 1940s. He was not only an artist but a brilliant technician. What more to say than that every producer always called Mielziner first?

With Can-Can's overture ended, the action began as the lights came up behind the show curtain, turning it transparent and thus revealing the stage as the show curtain lifted. Can-Can began in court, real fast, as our hero, Aristide Forestier (Peter Cookson),

---

* The show curtain was de rigueur for musical comedy, disdained by the musical play and operetta. Basically just something for the public to look at while listening to the overture, the show curtain created atmosphere—in Seventeen's small-town trees and fences, in "Wish You Were Here"'s collection of souvenirs (the summer camp's brochure, a timetable, a map, and, at center, a postcard bearing the title clause), in Mr. Wonderful's impression of Newark's after-dark neon, in The Music Man's collection of band instruments.

was introduced and les girls—charged with lewd dancing—were hustled in, screaming, grabbing the gendarmes' hats, and generally carrying on. The accused were then called by name, apparently assumed ones:

> BAILIFF: Duchess of Clichy.
> GIRL: Here.
> BAILIFF: Catherine de Medici.
> GIRL: Here.
> BAILIFF: Josephine Bonaparte.
> GIRL: Here.
> BAILIFF: Marie Antoinette.
> GIRL: Here.
> BAILIFF: Martha Washington.
> GIRL: Here.

Forestier notes that "The only one that seems to be missing is Joan of Arc."

> GWEN VERDON: Here.

That was the moment when a semi-featured ensemble dancer took hold of her green card in stardom. Yet Verdon, who was for the next few scenes bound into the ensemble, was not Can-Can's star. Verdon was the heroine of the subplot. The nominal star was Lilo, as La Môme Pistache, who ambled into the piece about five minutes later in her Bal du Paradis to reprove her dancing girls for their habit of supporting their boy friends in "Never Give Anything Away." A robust blond doll with a solid belt and great comic delivery, Lilo set one foot on a chair with her girls ringing her in a semicircle and put the number over with the self-confidence of a duchess, the erotic *oui* of a Bardot, and the curious tendency to stick an "m" onto the ends of words ending in a vowel (as in "Try to remember, ma belle-em").

Can-Can's action really gets going when Judge Forestier appears to see this place of sin for himself. He asks for mineral water but the waiter can't serve him: "The sink is broken." Meanwhile, Burrows nudges the subplot along: Verdon's Bulgarian sculptor boy friend (Hans Conried) wants Verdon to "be nice" to an influential critic (Erik Rhodes). Trouble begins when Rhodes presents Verdon with a wardrobe and Conried bristles:

VERDON: But you never buy me any good clothes.
CONRIED: You don't make enough money.

Can-Can is a show with everything that the form can afford. If Mielziner (and costumer Motley) provided the look, choreographer Michael Kidd provided the style, in highly physical dances that brought the apache to Broadway, not to mention a lengthy ballet on how sin came to Eden, with Verdon as Eve. The look and style came together in one moment that serves to showcase the pace and timing of fifties musical comedy. This occurs just after Lilo and her judge have touched base. She has been whining, excusing, throwing her breasts in his face, changing her clothes as he stands there; and she has had an effect. After he more or less staggers out, she raptly cries, "My first judge!," and, as the audience roars, the orchestra immediately breaks into an Offenbachian gallop, the lights black out, and Mielziner's technology demands only seconds before they come up again on a new set for Michael Kidd's "Quadrille," a mad dash of a ballet more or less devoted to the eroticism latent in dance-hall etiquette. Thus, Can-Can has taken us fluidly from plot scene to atmosphere scene, from comedy to dance, from dialogue to music, all without a break, simply using the public's laughter as a transition.

Burrows was Can-Can's weak link. By the second act, the sharp and funny book has degenerated into nonsense. The supposed through-line about democrats fighting censorship is forgot. There's something about Conried getting into a duel and the Judge and Lilo opening a dance hall. What? All right, Can-Can is a leggs-and-laffs show, but an altogether too loopy one for its era. The critics didn't know what to make of it. "It is generally agreed," wrote Theodore Hoffman in Theatre Arts, "that Can-Can has first-rate dancing, second-rate music (for Cole Porter, that is) and an also-ran book." Hoffman thought Lilo "a frenetic, wiggling, yapping device designed to cut men to pieces." Actually, Lilo afforded New Yorkers a rare chance to enjoy the type of sportive droll that the French call a "fantaisiste" (as opposed to the more dramatic "réaliste," like Edith Piaf), and gave *Can-Can* a well-needed shot of authenticity. Whom did Hoffman envision singing "I Love Paris" in Lilo's place? Gwen Verdon?

Verdon was the critics' darling; the show was not. Yet it ran a bit over two years, lasted nearly a year in London, and underwent major Hollywood translation, in one of those sleazy (in tone) yet chaste (in plot) jobs that pass tricky subject matter off as family entertainment and make a bundle. True, Soviet Premier Nikita Krushchof, visiting the set on an American tour, found the climactic title dance shocking, but you can't please everyone. The movie suggests that the show was worse than it was, losing Michael Kidd for the inferior Hermes Pan, lacing what was left of the score with tired Porter standards, and actually expanding that worthless storyline. Worst of all is the lack of Parisian flavor, emphasized in the casting of Shirley MacLaine and Frank Sinatra. Somehow or other, the French Louis Jourdan and Maurice Chevalier got into this thing, Jourdan as the judge and Chevalier as his uncle. This was the same relationship that they had had in the as it happens infinitely more evocatively Parisian *Gigi*.

Interestingly, after the movie, *Can-Can* started bombing—on Broadway in 1980 with Jeanmaire and in 1988 in London with the score again eviscerated and amplified. A new book favored the Hollywood storyline, with uncle Milo O'Shea, nephew Bernard Alane, and a vastly miscast Donna McKechnie, who at least was no less French than Shirley MacLaine and does not claim to be reincarnated.

Clearly, what saved *Can-Can* at first was the score and the production; at length, its dippy book destroyed it. To paraphrase Mussolini's famous remark about governing the Italian people, it is not impossible to revive *Can-Can*, it is simply unnecessary. For *Can-Can* never really had a story to tell; it had a collection of entertainments to present. These are very different things. Rodgers and Hammerstein were worshipped as the authors without a formula, but they did have a sort of very loose formula: Start with a good story. No wonder *Can-Can* baffled the critics. By the early 1950s, even the bad shows had stories.

Or, let's say, even the shows that didn't go over. Take, for instance, *Three Wishes for Jamie* (1952). Charles O'Neal's 1949

Christopher Award–winning novel, *The Three Wishes of Jamie McRuin,** told of an Irish lad who "had taken to dreaming as other Irishmen took to drink, and at times grew almost as drunk upon dreams as they upon poteen." Jamie claims that the fairy queen Una has granted him three wishes for his having returned her stolen gold. The wishes promise travel, true love, and a son who speaks "the ancient tongue." Matchmaker Tavish, however, has arranged a marriage for Jamie with Tirsa Shanahan, and when an altercation with Tirsa's brothers ends in Jamie and Tavish's appearing to have been swept away in a torrent, Jamie allows everyone to think them dead and takes Tavish to America. That's travel; and Jamie meets Maeve, and she's true love. But their marriage is barren. Then the couple adopt an unwanted boy, a mute named Kevin whom Tavish befriends in a curious symbiosis that finds Kevin able to speak only in dreams—and only in Gaelic. When Tavish dies, leaving Kevin a legacy, the boy's father suddenly demands legal rights to the terrified child. Unable to recognize him, the father will know him by his inability to talk. But Tavish, from beyond the grave, has one last thing to say to Kevin—or, rather, through him. "Cuevin moc Ruin is ainm dom," the boy cries, "agus se seo mo baile": Kevin McRuin is my name, and this is my home. The third wish has come true.

I have recounted this story in detail because one cannot comprehend the musical in the 1950s without understanding that, ten years earlier, this novel would have all but unthinkable as a source. All that auld sod Irish lore, the whimsey, the fantasy! A beloved character dies, a cute little boy is mute, and the heroine is barren! Charles O'Neal, like Betty Smith with George Abbott, collaborated on the script, with *Can-Can*'s Abe Burrows, and they hewed remarkably close to the original. The show opened with the wake of Jamie (John Raitt) and Tavish (old-time baby-faced comic Bert Wheeler), so we could be theatrically surprised—and relieved—when they turned up among the spectators, albeit outside, unseen by the others. The unwanted bride, Tirsa, who gets

---

* The Christopher Award singled out works promoting "Christian principles and the welfare of all men." Charles O'Neal was the father of movie actor Ryan O'Neal.

two or three pages in the novel, was built into a featured comic
(Charlotte Rae) who comes chasing after Jamie with her father
(operetta veteran Robert Halliday, the original Red Shadow in *The
Desert Song*) but ends up paired off with Me-Dennis O'Ryan, the
name from his mother's constantly addressing and referring to
him as "me Dennis." As with much of O'Neal's heavy Irish coloring, this was gentled down in the show to plain Dennis (Peter
Conlow).

Otherwise, *Three Wishes for Jamie* was in every respect a faithful retelling, even including Maeve's genetic inability to bear children and letting a spurned suitor angrily invade the first-act finale,
her wedding, to pass the information on to a stunned Jamie, and
later letting Anne Jeffreys express Maeve's regret in one of those
introspective monologue song scenes that Rodgers and Hammerstein had introduced into the musical's vocabulary.

The critics were very mixed, and the show failed, despite an
engaging score (by Ralph Blane) and wonderful performers, especially Rae, who made the most of her trick contralto-with-
Lakmé-extension in her wooing of Dennis, "I'll Sing You a Song."
Maybe the show's ethnicity was too heavily explored. Maybe the
"barren" thing was too dark even for a musical play—a number
of the reviewers expressed reservations about it.

If Rodgers and Hammerstein made certain shows possible, they
also re-empowered certain writers by inspiring them to develop
their talents. Surely Lerner and Loewe, after one musical comedy
flop, were thinking Rodgers and Hammerstein for *The Day Before
Spring* (1945), a succès d'estime, and particularly *Brigadoon*
(1947), the show that made them. Cole Porter openly noted that
his *Kiss Me, Kate* (1948) score, teeming with character and situation, was a response to the Rodgers and Hammerstein challenge.

Most encouraged of all was Harold Rome, famed in the late
1930s for *Pins and Needles*, a long-running amateur revue with a
distinctly working-class voice. Except for one book musical called
The Little Dog Laughed (1940) that closed out of town, Rome was
strictly a composer of variety shows. But revues were getting thin
on the ground in the story-conscious 1950s. So, while retaining
his natural inflection, Rome moved into the story show, abandoning the revue forever.

"*Wish You Were Here*" (1952) was the reconstituting title. Arthur Kober and Joshua Logan wrote the script, from Kober's 1937 comedy "*Having Wonderful Time*" about a long-vanished institution: the upstate summer camp for Jewish singles from New York City, where the women hoped to snag a husband and the men tried to settle for a date. Though no historian ever says so, "*Having Wonderful Time*" is part of the twenties-thirties folk play movement, in which a work incorporated a subculture in its very language and lore. Here's a sample of Kober:

> MR. G.: (*To* SAM) I'm just now telling a story is something funny heppening this munning. So like I say, I'm looking on Pinkie's puttch—Pinkie is here in camp a fella. And I see this girl, and she's coming fomm the bungalow, and right away quick she's jumping in lake.
> SCHMUTZ: Dijja see her face?
> MR. G.: A question! Of cuss I see the face!

Just as two more famous folk plays, *Porgy* (1927) and *Green Grow the Lilacs* (1931), on southern black and farmer-cowboy cultures, respectively, sired *Porgy and Bess* and *Oklahoma!* while keeping the originals' dialect and worldview intact, so did "*Having Wonderful Time*" endow "*Wish You Were Here*".

Rome was the ideal songwriter for this milieu; he had virtually grown up with the characters—heroine Teddy Stern (Patricia Marand) and her boy-mad sidekick Fay Fromkin (Sheila Bond), the drab older businessman whom Teddy's mother wants her to marry, Herman Fabricant (Harry Clark), the young hero she falls for, Chick Miller (Jack Cassidy), Itchy Flexner (Sidney Armus), the ambitious yet frustrated camp social director, and sly Pinky Harris (Paul Valentine), Teddy's would-be seducer. (As the quotation of Kober's 1937 script suggests, he is unsuccessful.)

The "*Wish You Were Here*" book, by Kober and Joshua Logan (who also co-produced and directed), provides the many details to develop these stereotypes into people, as when we note that Fabricant instinctively calls Teddy by her given name of Tessie, as if reproving her independent spirit. But it is Rome's score that really paints campers and staff—in Fay's boogie-woogie flirtation number, "Shopping Around," certainly, but also in her utterly colloquial gossip song, "Certain Individuals"; in Itchy's numbers, "Ballad of a Social Director" and the mock-tango "Don Jose of Far Rockaway," which manage to be frantic, wistful, intelligent, and nutty all at once; in the chorus's exploration of courtship rituals, "Tripping the Light Fantastic."

Better yet, Rodgers and Hammerstein's opening up of the standard score into a program with bite and point liberated Rome. His Chick is vocally extraordinary, a tenorino who has to field musical comedy's equivalent of "Stouthearted Men" and "Ah, Sweet Mystery of Life." For surely Chick's are "power" numbers: "Mix and Mingle" is a camp waiter's somewhat bitter review of his status as a law student paying tuition as a laborer by day and an escort at night. "Where Did the Night Go?," lyrically soaring, exalts these unsophisticated people by revealing their hunger for romance. "They Won't Know Me" is one of those so useful character-undergoing-personality-development numbers, and "Wish You Were Here" is a rapturous torch song to a rhumba beat. With his tense delivery and dramatic high notes, Jack Cassidy got as much out of Chick's music as any Ravenal or Billy Bigelow got out of his; it's strange to learn that Cassidy had spent much of the preceding decade on Broadway in choruses.

Perhaps *"Wish You Were Here"*'s best quality is its ingenuousness. For these naive people, Rome somehow contrived a canny yet artless-seeming score. There's technique—Teddy's first number, "Goodbye, Love," consists of verse, chorus, and middle section, after which the other girls sing the middle section while Teddy repeats the chorus; and "Relax!," Pinky's attempted seduction of Teddy, is a conversation in music. Still, above all, there's naturalism: a score made of the way this culture speaks and thinks.

Maybe that's why Joshua Logan, when Rome and Kober offered him the project, wanted to stage it around a swimming pool: *show* the camp, the fun, the flirting. The pool, built right into the Imperial Theatre, prohibited the show's traveling out-of-town, so Logan scheduled three weeks of previews in New York, common now but unheard of then. The reviews were a shock—almost entirely negative, as if *"Wish You Were Here"* were truly grisly, like *Happy as Larry* (1950) or *Great To Be Alive* (1950), to name two deservedly excoriated shows. "Joyless," said Atkinson, of Logan's baby. "Amateur Night," said Vernon Rice of the *Post*. The premiere occurred on an especially humid June evening; was that the problem?

Any musical that gets *"Wish You Were Here"*'s reviews closes promptly; co-producer Leland Hayward shrugged and sailed off to Greece with Alexander Korda. But Logan—with two weeks of good ticket sales ahead and very little after—decided that the critics were wrong and plunged into a heavy rewrite job. It had suddenly dawned on him that the piece did have one flaw, a small mistake that, ironically, threw the entire evening off. Opening with Teddy blithely casting off her awful fiancé, Logan had unwittingly made *him* sympathetic and her seem hard. Now Logan went back to Kober's original plan, in which the fiancé is a cross that Teddy bears almost to the end of the story. Out went Teddy's revelling "Goodbye, Love" (replaced by "Nothing Nicer Than People," not as snappy but sweeter) along with virtually a quarter of the script. Jerome Robbins jumped in to restage Logan's deliberately clunky choreography (again, striving for naturalism; it had worked for *South Pacific*), and Eddie Fisher's hit recording of the title tune was a staple of summer radio listening, amusingly repeating the show's name ten times per chorus. With all the tinkering, Harold Clurman called *"Wish You Were Here"* "the last experimental theatre in New York."

All this redeemed the show. After a couple of half-empty weeks, word of mouth pushed the box-office above breakeven through profitable to sellout, one of the very few instances in which a musical ignored a bashing and ran. *Theatre Arts* dubbed it "the season's most successful flop," and when it closed it had lasted a year and a half and also took London, where the English tradition of "holiday camps" broke the ice for this intensely ethnic exercise. Summer theatres favored it throughout the 1950s, pool and all, and Equity Library Theatre gave it an airing (without the pool) in the 1980s. Now it is all but gone—not dated, just no longer performed. Like many fifties musical comedy hits, it played its role in American civilization not by joining the canon but simply by keeping a theatre warm and a cast and crew employed and a huge audience entertained. The cast album survives on CD.

Of all those influenced by Rodgers and Hammerstein, Lerner and Loewe are virtually acolytes, for *Paint Your Wagon* (1951) could be seen as *Oklahoma!* by a different route. Like the earlier show, *Paint Your Wagon* is a period western (set during the California gold rush) with little plot but a lot of Agnes de Mille and background color. Both works deal with murder, intolerance (farmers versus cowboys; whites versus Mexicans), and the sometimes homemade lawfulness of a frontier community. And there are the Rodgers and Hammerstein this-time-only touches: the protagonist, founder of a mining town, charms rather than sings his way through three numbers, including one of the score's major ballads; the male chorus ("miners" in the program) are mainly singers and the female chorus ("fandangos" = saloon girls) are exclusively dancers; and a Mormon with two wives provisions an arresting episode when the womanless town persuades him to auction off one of his spouses.

Like so many of the shows we'll be considering in these pages, *Paint Your Wagon* raises its curtain on a tootle from the pit and a book scene—a funeral, it develops, led by our non-singing charmer, Ben Rumson (James Barton, the original Hickey in *The Iceman Cometh*). During the eulogy, Ben's daughter (Olga San Juan) becomes distracted by something shiny in the dirt. It's *gold!* As the kneeling mourners catch on and prepare to "call" ownership of the land as soon as Ben pauses, he wraps up his speech with "So, anyhow, here's Jim, Lord. I hope You'll make him happy up there [suddenly planting his foot on the soil] and for-ever-and-ever-I-stake-this-claim-Amen!" He lets out a roar of laughter. A blackout follows, as the orchestra stokes it bigtime, and the lights come up on the first number, a musical scene in rondo form—spoken vignettes each capped by a refrain, showing all the different men heading west for Rumson Creek, a little melting pot that even yields one chorus sung in Chinese. "Got a dream, boy?" the men lustily carol. "Got a song?" The scene's title is "I'm On My Way," but it includes the phrase "Paint your wagon" and is in feeling a kind of title song, especially when it reappears to round off the evening. In the ensuing decades, shows enclosed at either end by essentializing anthems became almost ordinary. Think of *Cabaret, A Little Night Music, Into the Woods, Grand Hotel.* Rodgers and Hammerstein surrounded *South Pacific* with "Dites-moi," but this little throwaway tune is not thematically central.

Was anything in *Paint Your Wagon not* Rodgers and Hammerstein in style? Even the love plot, between the daughter and a Mexican (Tony Bavaar), was somewhat anticipated in *South Pacific's* Cable and Liat. At least de Mille's dances jumped in at unexpected moments on unlooked-for subjects—but then, isn't that Rodgers and Hammerstein all the way? One wonders what the two men thought of de Mille's work here. The first dance number, "Lonely Men," rises out of a book scene of miners discussing their past and speculating about their future. An alto saxophone sounds a slow, keening minor-key tune, the tenor sax echoes it, and the tempo picks up as other instruments enter to create an Irish jig that soon moves into the major key as the men triumphantly career about the stage. Then, as they cool down, one remarks that it was his wife's idea that he come west. " 'What do you want to do, work in a factory all your life?' I says, 'No.' She says, 'Then put your fat carcass on the wagon and go out there and dig.' That's how she is. Always thinkin' of me.' " Another man starts picking at his banjo, and the first man encourages him: "Let's hear somethin' besides the wind blowin' through them damn hills," the cue for the banjo player's big solo, with the men's chorus ganging up, *fortissimo*, behind him: "They Call the Wind Maria."

That male chorus gave *Paint Your Wagon* its *tinta*, its unique sound. "There's a Coach Comin' In," relating the miners' eagerness to get acquainted with the town's first influx of women, is one of the biggest choruses (in sheer breadth of vocal power) of the postwar era, the kind of thing one thought had died with operetta. Then, capped by an F Major chord that took the tenors to a high A, came the coach itself and the entrance of the fandangos, which de Mille staged as a kind of tease-off, as they sauntered appetizingly among the lonely men and finally broke into a mad dance with them.

Choruses and ballets, that was *Paint Your Wagon*, along with a semi-hit tune, "I Talk To the Trees," and while all that was on the show was in trim. But it really did lack story; Barton, though the protagonist, served mainly as a kind of emcee. Lerner even-

tually reckoned that, while the show was strongly realistic as a
composition, the staging counted on unrealistic sets and abstract
choreography, creating a performance at war with itself. It was a
bold show, to be fair—husky and romantic where musicals are
usually racy and contemporary. But then, the musical play so
changed the rules that no one knew what the rules were any more.
Maybe the science was more an alchemy, magical rather than
procedural.

Let's compare two musical comedies (as opposed to the many
musical plays of the time) to show how right and how wrong a
work could go—and, to illustrate how rich and unpredictable musical production was in the early 1950s, let's use a pair of wholly
un-alike shows, *Seventeen* and *Flahooley*. They have three things
in common—their year of production (1951), their playing venue
(the Broadhurst), and their geographical setting (Indiana).

Seventeen is a period domestic comedy from Booth Tarkington's
1915 novel about a coquettish summer visitor to Indianapolis in
1907 who drives all the boys crazy. (As so often in Tarkington,
the aim is to get down the flavor of American life, not to show
who gets what in the end. These aren't quest novels: they're social
studies.) Nobody famous had anything to do with the production,
except Milton Berle, who co-produced it—and of course he was
famous only as a comedian. *Seventeen* was a little show, a sleeper.

Flahooley brings us to some big names in a contemporary satire
on an original story set in a toy factory. *Paint Your Wagon's* producer, Cheryl Crawford, was in charge, though the real muscle
behind the production was its lyricist and co-librettist, E. Y. Harburg. There was a star, sort of: Yma Sumac, a kind of Inca goddess
who sang in a reported four-octave range ("I'll give her at least
seven," said the stunned Vernon Rice) that ran from bird calls
that only dogs would receive to the suggestion of Eldorado sub-
siding in an earthquake.

Seventeen first. This was the ultimate in unassuming storytelling. Miss Lola Pratt comes to town with her baby talk, her flattery,
and her insufferable lap dog, Flopit, accepts the helpless homage
of smitten Willie Baxter, and finally departs, leaving the boy be-
reft. There was no opportunity for spectacle or production numbers. There was not even a chorus as such, their duties being

assigned to the fourteen boys and girls who played the friends of Willie and of May Parcher, Lola's hostess. There were as well Willie's father, mother, and sister, Jane, and Mr. and Mrs. Parcher, plus a collegiate visitor, George Crooper, who throws alarm into Willie by making a play for Lola, and the Baxters' black servant, Genesis, and Genesis' father. Other than the Mr. Baxter, Frank Albertson, known to movie buffs as Katharine Hepburn's impedient brother in RKO's *Alice Adams* sixteen years earlier, the cast was all unknowns. There were some promising young newcomers such as Dick Kallman, Richard France, Ellen McCown, Ann Crowley, and especially the Willie, Kenneth Nelson, later to originate The Boy in *The Fantasticks* and Michael in *The Boys in the Band*, both off-Broadway in the 1960s.

With so little plot, scriptwriter Sally Benson concentrated on character relationships, as indeed she did in the *New Yorker* stories that were the source of MGM's *Meet Me in St. Louis*, like *Seventeen* a piece of smalltown, period Americana. So librettist and novelist should get along. Once a canonical figure in American literature and now never mentioned, Tarkington specialized in what we might call the de-stereotyping of middle America. What could be more conventional than puppy love with a visiting flirt during an idyllic middle-class summer? But the novel *Seventeen* is anything but conventional in its characters. Willie is self-important, precocious, and so desperate to win Lola that he courts her in his father's tails suit and perfects an imitation of Flopit's barking that has Mr. Parcher ready to kill him. Lola is so over-the-top in her self-presentation ("Fwopit an' me think nice-cums" is a typical statement) that she approaches science-fiction. Mrs. Baxter is a lovely creation, holding her at times vexing family together through intelligence, tact, and a sense of humor.

Tarkington's masterpiece, however, is little Jane, so absurd yet so true, showing up at the tenderest times with her dress half off, her hands holding bread and butter doused in applesauce and powdered sugar, and her voice shrill and demanding. She sees and, worse, *tells* all, relentless as an Old Testament prophet. Reading the novel, one is impressed by how constantly Tarkington surprises one with his everyday honesty.

Sadly, Benson left out a lot of this. She re-stereotyped Tarkington—and the score, by Kim Gannon and Walter Kent, is a tuneful collection of songs that reinforces the stereotype. The senior Baxters were completely betrayed by "A Headache and a Heartache," a limp generation-war piece, and George Crooper got to sing "Ooo-ooo-ooo What You Do To Me" on the most transparent pretext since Rose-Marie asked Jim if he'd like to learn an Indian love call. "Say—how's it happen you got this [record] out here?" Crooper says, as the gramophone is wound up at a party. "Why, I saw a fellow do that at the opening night of the *Ziegfeld Follies* on the New York Roof. It went like this . . ." and he goes, like that, into the number.

Critics singled out the trio "I Could Get Married Today," which Willie sings with Genesis and his father, who, it turns out, got married for his first time when he was seventeen, like Willie. The number had Tarkington's charm. But the authors' failure to delve into their material is encapsulated in the finale. Remember, this is a story that has no real ending. Lola Pratt leaves town; Willie's wrecked; curtain. But Tarkington found an amusing way to round off his book, by telling us that Willie, last seen shouting furiously at Jane's mischievous little confederate, Mary Randolph Kirsted, will most certainly fall in love and marry one day. The future is always in tune with the present, Tarkington states, and "the bright air of that June evening, almost eleven years in the so-called future, was indeed already trembling to 'Lohengrin.'" If only Willie—or any of us—had the sensitivity to see more than the moment, now, today. It's the *Our Town* thing, the epic of plain life. Willie doesn't get it. He just goes on shouting, and the little girl runs off, and Tarkington springs his surprise in the very last line: Mary Randolph Kirsted is Willie's future bride.

That's so Tarkington, so life-is-lovely-if-we-only-stopped-to-look-around. How beautifully a musical might have fixed that aperçu for us. But this musical opted for a trick ending that has nothing to do with Tarkington. Willie misses seeing Lola off, and enters the railroad station set inconsolable, his hands covering his face. Genesis tries to cheer him up, visualizing his wedding. As offstage voices carol the show's main ballad, "After All, It's Spring," the lights come up behind the station scrim, revealing Willie's wedding party—Willie and Lola united, surrounded by friends and family with that ghastly Flopit in Willie's arms (for, of course, the Willie in the train station was a double). It's cute, but it misses Tarkington's wonder and rightness.

Now, *Flahooley*. The word itself is Irish for "flighty," "whimsical." (Charles O'Neal uses it in *The Three Wishes of Jamie Mc-Ruin*.) Those two words surely describe E. Y. Harburg's conception. Where *Seventeen* is methodical, *Flahooley* is volatile. *Seventeen* is sweet; *Flahooley* spits. *Seventeen* is daily life; *Flahooley* is fantasy, complete with Aladdin's lamp and a genie. Finally, *Seventeen* is about American culture; *Flahooley* is about America. It's a big, wild thing, an omnium-gatherum that took in not only the Machu Picchuan Sumac but the Bil and Cora Baird marionettes, not only a host of references to high art and low art but to McCarthyism and American business, not only the—can I say irrespressible?—Irwin Corey* but the very young Barbara Cook. Now you know that we're dealing with a cult flop.

Flahooley was a bomb, in fact, and commentators have been trying to figure out why ever since. That it has an excellent score is beyond rebuttal: Harburg, teamed with the sometimes on-and-off but here gushingly melodious Sammy Fain, was at his best; Cook and her vis-à-vis, toymaker Jerome Courtland, essentialized dynamic youth in the ballads and charm songs; and Sumac went off like a volcano in her chant-of-the-untamed-fire-deity-in-headdress-and-sandals specialty material (by her husband, Moises Vivanco).

But a good score can't save a terrible script (by Harburg and his habitual collaborator, Fred Saidy). *Seventeen* has a very light story, which is already dangerous for a musical. *Flahooley* has *no story whatsoever*. Instead, it has a premise: in a land of Betsy-Wetsys and crying dolls, a doll that laughs—she's called Flahooley—would be a sensation. But then what happens? Well, the doll's inventor wants to marry his girl friend. Okay: the love plot. And Sumac wants her broken lamp fixed. Okay: the subplot.

* Corey's career as a comic was based on his ability to spiel gobbledygook that sounded authoritative even as it produced logorrheic nonsense, a likeness of the academic poseur that once was exaggeration and now, in the age of "semiotics," is descriptive. Oldtime Johnny Carson viewers might recall Corey, always announced as the "Professor."

But then there's Harburg's eagerness to take on capitalist economics, a Harburg trait since he wrote the anthem of the Depression, "Brother, Can You Spare a Dime?" (with composer Jay Gorney). Harburg's *Finian's Rainbow* (1947) was almost obsessive in its jokes on the interior contradictions of American money culture; now Harburg wants *Flahooley* to fight McCarthy as well. Okay: topical satire, endemic in the musical since the nineteenth century.

However, while stacking romance and magic and satire and Yma Sumac on top of each other, Harburg never developed his premise. Some forty minutes into Act One, nobody in the audience had the vaguest idea what was happening. A rival doll is underselling Flahooley . . . The genie comes out of the lamp and produces too many Flahooleys, precipitating an economic crisis . . . A sort of McCarthyist riot breaks out, as people hold Flahooley-burning rallies . . . The toy executive turns up in Arab dress, mainly for no reason . . . The genie disappears, reappears, dies, and is reborn . . . Puppets sing cheer-up songs and dance around, as alive as Pinocchio . . . It's chaos without a throughline. As Atkinson wrote, "More plot crosses the stage than Macy's Thanksgiving Day Parade. But it seems to this columnist to be a colossal *non sequitur*."

One thing we have to credit Harburg with: he was absolutely fearless of McCarthyism. *Flahooley*'s witch-hunting spoof includes, one, the toy executive (Ernest Truex, the original title-role player in Jerome Kern's *Very Good Eddie* in 1915) protectively saying "God Bless America" when he answers the telephone; two, the worried cry, at a strange noise, "A concealed dictaphone!"; three, the voice-over PA system announcing a meeting with "Bring birth certificates, citizenship papers, list of magazine subscriptions, library cards, and receipted gas bills."

Unfortunately, *Flahooley*'s dialogue veers too often from the clever:

> GENIE: What is science, after all, but magic with an Oxford accent?

to the puerile:

SYLVESTER: I don't know how to make wishes any more.
GENIE: Nonsense! You've read the *Arabian Nights*! You've
seen *Finian's Rainbow*!

to the clever again:

GENIE: (*as he expires*) I am dying, Egypt, dying.*

Some may marvel at Harburg's open defiance of McCarthy.
However, the witch hunt for Communists, former Communists,
fellow travelers, mere liberals, utter innocents, and even guys who
had simply joined leftist groups to meet girls only took hold in
radio, television, and movies. There, corporation thinking dominated, and of course the corporation is profit driven and thus
willing to accommodate market pressures amorally. In the theatre,
everyone was freelance and most were liberal in the first place
and defiant of the blacklist that terrorized other media. In fact,
Harburg wrote *Flahooley* specifically to use Broadway to retaliate
against Hollywood's surrender to the Red Scare: a cartoon feature
based on *Finian's Rainbow* was scuttled in mid-production when
Harburg's name was Mentioned to a Committee.

On the other hand, Harburg's timing could not have been
worse. The Korean War had started in June 1950, grimly inform-
ing Americans that, having barely finished fighting Fascism, they
were now going to have to fight Communism. Worse yet, the war
was going badly. On April 10, 1951, General MacArthur was recalled, an almost universally depressing event stateside, and the
Communists launched another successful offensive on April 20.
On May 14, *Flahooley* opened; this was simply not the time to
lampoon—in effect, to criticize—American society. While prais-
ing the show's handsome production, most of the reviewers hit
hard at the intricately errant narrative, and John Chapman of the
Daily News called the show "the most elaborately coated propa-
ganda pill ever to be put on a stage."

Then, too, *Kiss Me, Kate, South Pacific, Gentlemen Prefer
Blondes, Call Me Madam, Guys and Dolls, The King and I*, and *A
Tree Grows in Brooklyn* were all playing at the time, stiff com-

---

* From Shakespeare's *Antony and Cleopatra*, so elevated from *Flahooley*'s wild-
ride spoof that its evocation is, in effect, a stroke of wit.

petition indeed. *Seventeen* failed at a disappointing if not shameful 182 performances, but *Flahooley* was an embarrassing dud at 40. There have been attempts to revise it, most notably on the West Coast as *Jollyanna*, with Bobby Clark and Mitzi Gaynor. But for all the lovely music, delightful puppets, and gorgeous scenery, *Flahooley* was an act of revenge, a show without content.

Seventeen and *Flahooley* illustrate two different facets of musical comedy as it was *before* Rodgers and Hammerstein. If operetta is passion and the musical play is drama, musical comedy is lively fun, sometimes sweet and sometimes satiric. *Seventeen* as a novel was something of a sweet satire, but *Seventeen* the musical is entirely sweet, all for youth and nostalgia. Its only wish is to charm. *Flahooley* emphasises the satire side—imagination, tempo, mockery. Its wish is to excite. One form is a valentine, the other a cartoon. *Seventeen* virtually capped a fifty-year-old tradition—of the fondly eccentric, small-cast, even smalltown show—whose high point may well have been the Princess Theatre musicals of Jerome Kern, Guy Bolton, and P. G. Wodehouse in the late 1910s. By the 1950s, that tradition was over. *Flahooley*'s tradition is even older, yet it was still vital at this time.

Consider *Top Banana* (1951). This salute to the comics of burlesque (featuring some of them in its cast) made a cartoon of Milton Berle, who besides being one of *Seventeen*'s co-producers was one of the nation's biggest celebrities because of his Tuesday night television variety show. Berle's Texaco Star Theatre was so popular that many people bought their first TV set simply to see Berle. Seizing this new piece of American mores, *Top Banana* took a look at the world of egomaniacal TV star Jerry Biffle.

Like Berle, and like Phil Silvers, who played the role, Biffle has come up the long way, learning his trade as comic till he is its ranking expert—and does he know it! Entering, Biffle cries, "The king is here! Kneel, you swine!" Actually, *Top Banana* did not make all that much of Biffle's self-importance; nor was it very interested in the triangle love plot involving Biffle, his girl friend (Judy Lynn), and a singer on Biffle's show (Lindy Doherty) or even in the fact that Biffle ends up with the girl friend's roommate (Rose Marie). The main thing in this show was comedy, the lower the better. "Burlesque with antennas" is how Biffle describes television, because in its infancy it had not yet developed its own comic style and simply inherited styles from vaudeville, radio, and especially the burlesque of zanies and show girls. Much of this was pure corn:

> MAN 1: Where are you going, Elmer?
> MAN 2: How'd you know my name was Elmer?
> MAN 1: I guessed it.
> MAN 2: Then guess where I'm going!

or:

> MAN 2: (*remarking on* MAN 1's *heavy outfit of bandages and cane*) What happened?
> MAN 1: Everything was lovely. I was living the life of Riley . . .
> MAN 2: Well?
> MAN 1: Riley came home!

More humor came out of Silvers' unique character: that of the tense, fast-moving wise guy who thinks he's the only one on the planet with smarts. He's suspicious:

> JERRY: (*When someone starts to help him retrieve his dropped money*) Just stand there. (*Clapping*) Do this. I want to know where you are all the time.

He's sarcastic:

> JERRY: They don't use actors in Italian pictures—they use people.*

He's the star, and don't you forget it, as when he shouts at a noisy animal in a Dog Number, "Not on my lines! Just wag your tail!" And he's a kind of mad control freak, as he coaches his girl friend for her big debut as Miss Blendo (after the soap company that sponsors Biffle's show):

---

* This is a reference to the habit of neorealist directors such as Rossellini and De Sica of using non-actors to perfect their films' realism. Think of the father and son in De Sica's *Ladri di Biciclette* (Bicycle Thieves), utterly convincing in their naturalism and in fact naturals: not actors, people.

SALLY: I'm standing on my Blendo soap—
JERRY: Who's standing? *I'm* standing. This is your big moment
in the show and you've got to make it mean something. *I'm*
standing. Say it with conviction. You're as good as anybody
else. (*Stamps his foot*) Sock it across.
SALLY: (*Stamps her foot*) *I'm* standing on my—
JERRY: No. Remember, soap is a romantic article. . . . Flirt
with the audience . . . be a girl. Okay!
SALLY: (*Wiggling her hips*) I'm standing on my Blendo soap
box—
JERRY: Honey, we don't want to be investigated. (*To* BETTY)
Better warm up another girl. (*Back to* SALLY) Go ahead, do
the lines.
SALLY: You won't let me.
JERRY: (*as if shocked*) I hardly know you.

This goes on till Biffle loses it in a long monologue, a paranoid
harangue taking in Freud and Spinoza and as much a performance
as it is a release of tension. Finally, we get to the number, the
first-act finale, "Meet Miss Blendo," and just before the chorus
hits its last line with high notes and upraised arms—the works—
Jerry calls out, "If this scheme doesn't work, you bastards are out
of a job!"

Top Banana is a very funny show, the kind you forgive for slipping into a number on almost any pretext. Rose Marie meets one
of Biffle's staffers (Bob Scheerer) and asks what he does in the
show:

SCHEERER: I'm the leading dancer.
ROSE MARIE: So dance.

Scheerer swings into "My Home Is In My Shoes" and the ensemble sneaks on to turn up the heat for a dance number with no
purpose but to supply one of the essential ingredients of the fifties
musical, as I've probably made clear by now: the choreography.
Top Banana even had a dream ballet, late in Act Two, after Biffle's
show has been canceled and he looks back on his career.

Top Banana's choreographer, Ron Fletcher, made no major his-
tory, and the score, by Johnny Mercer, is one notch above terrible.
As lyricist, Mercer was without question one of the best of the
Third-Age names who never quite made it into everybody-knows-

him fame. Let me run some of his titles by you, to demonstrate his vernacular poetry: "Ac-Cent-Tchu-Ate the Positive," "Blues in the Night," "Any Place I Hang My Hat Is Home," "My New Celebrity Is You" (a Porter list song with Mercerian spin), "This Time the Dream's On Me," "Sleep Peaceful, Mr. Used-To-Be" (a murderous lullaby), Moon River," lovely stuff. Unfortunately, Mercer also composed—seldom, and *Top Banana*'s music shows why. What lifeless ballads and bossy choruses! *Top Banana* ran a year but failed to pay off, and this time a flop musical had not book problems but score problems.

The same trouble haunted the revue. After 1950's *Alive and Kicking*, *Michael Todd's Peep Show*, *Pardon Our French*, and *Tickets Please*, the variety format desperately needed an infusion of class talent. It got that in the star revues *Two on the Aisle* (1951) and *Two's Company* (1952), the first with Bert Lahr and Dolores Gray and the second with Bette Davis.

Jule Styne and Betty Comden and Adolph Green wrote *Two on the Aisle*'s score around the fact that Lahr and Gray sang but that featured comic Elliot Reid and featured dancer Colette Marchand did not. It's music for two. Kathryne Mylroie and Fred Bryan contributed a ballad called "Everlasting" and the chorus spelled the stars now and again, but this was a Lahr and Gray evening. In matching checked suit and dress they closed Act One as vaudevillians taking over the Metropolitan Opera (an allusion to new impresario Rudolf Bing's "theatricalizing" the house with movie directors, English translations, and a sell-out *Die Fledermaus*) in "Catch Our Act at the Met": "I'll be Lucia," sang Gray, to Lahr's "And I'll be Sextet." They also acted in a sketch on adultery played first in burlesque style, then as written by T. S. Eliot, and last as in a Cole Porter show.

The two stars worked better alone, however, possibly because Gray was infuriated that Lahr had top billing (and in larger print). But, after all, he had been a top banana since the late 1920s; all she had in her kit was a sensation as Irving Berlin's Annie in London. Lahr could be difficult, an anxious performer (though never unprofessional), and Gray had her turbulent side: the ensuing feud was the second biggest in the fifties musical. (The first was that of Ethel Merman and Fernando Lamas in *Happy Hunt-*

ing; in good time.) So Lahr no doubt rejoiced to bound onstage alone in 6/8 meter, carolling in his characteristic gloomy hysteria, "A clown! A clown! A clown! They call me a clown!" Thank God, a spot without Dolores.

Gray was one of the musical's great singers. Hers was a suave belt, a smooth, *smooth* contralto with absolute pitch and phrasing that placed a song on the first hearing. Her most noticeable number was "If," which began with a torchy verse and led up to "I hope I don't miss you," whereupon Gray revealed a gun and shot the dude. But her triumph was "There Never Was a Baby Like My Baby," a slow one that rises to the line, "There never was a doll or guy baby who looked exactly like my valentine"—so sturdily vaulted, yet caressed, that one feels that no one else should dare sing the song.

Two on the Aisle did not succeed; *Two's Company* did even less well. Again, top names furnished the score—composer Vernon Duke with lyricists Ogden Nash and Sammy Cahn—and they did mostly good work. Certainly, as an opening number, "Theatre Is a Lady" outshines *Two on the Aisle*'s dumpy "Show Train," in which the chorus sings stupid digest versions of current hit shows.

Then came what the French call the *sortie*, as Bette Davis made her entrance in the second spot to sing "(Just) Turn Me Loose on Broadway" and . . . let George Jean Nathan tell us: "She can't sing; she can't dance; she has no knack for comedy." *Two's Company* wasn't as star-centered as *Two on the Aisle*, so Ellen Hanley and Peter Kelley could make the most of some lavish ballads, and two supporting comics, David Burns and Hiram Sherman, were busy all night. Still, Davis was why the show was put on, Davis in all her versatility—in a *Sadie Thompson* takeoff, in a Hatfields-McCoys spoof, in a painfully unfunny eleven o'clocker, "Just Like a Man." "She is attracting trade," said Nathan, "not by an expectation of talent but whimsically to delight in the courageous demonstration of a lack of it."

As it happened, the outstanding revue of the day lacked both stars and famous bylines: *New Faces of 1952*. In fact, this was probably the last first-rate revue ever—revue, that is, as an agglutinative vaudeville, as opposed to the songwriter's anthology so popular today. Leonard Sillman had been producing *New Faces* revues since 1934, with the eponymously stated intention of presenting fresh talent. Alumni included Imogene Coca, Henry Fonda, Van Johnson, Irwin Corey, and Alice Pearce, but the 1952 edition was stuffed with gifted debutants, such as Ronny Graham, Eartha Kitt, Paul Lynde, Robert Clary, Alice Ghostley, and Carol Lawrence (though the last was given no opportunity and wasn't noticed till *West Side Story* five years later).

More important, this edition harked back to the revue's prime in the 1920s and 1930s as a showcase for wonderful new *writers*: the time of George Gershwin and B. G. De Sylva; Noël Coward; De Sylva, Brown, and Henderson; and Arthur Schwartz and Howard Dietz. Unlike *Two on the Aisle* and *Two's Company*, *New Faces of 1952* had no set writing team but rather a crowd of contributors (mainly Graham, Arthur Siegel and Sillman's sister, June Carroll, and Sheldon Harnick as both composer and lyricist). Somehow or other, they wrote what may have been the most consistently entertaining vaudeville in history. There were rather a lot of spoofs, of Tennessee Williams, Laurence Olivier and Vivien Leigh, canasta, Johnnie Ray, Restoration comedy, and Gian Carlo Menotti's opera *The Medium*. Here was one show that required a smart audience. Still, much of the piece simply offered the one-of-a-kind, self-contained scenes that integrated musical comedy couldn't use.

So there was Alice Ghostley in a motheaten sweater alone in one to deliver Harnick's "Boston Beguine," the lament of a wallflower who knew one night of passion in the most exotic city on earth. There was "Love Is a Simple Thing," a harmless ballad suddenly handed over to creepy June Carroll to extoll Charles Addams's idea of romance (". . . soft as a mummy's hand"). There was Paul Lynde, in Safari attire and a mile of bandages, recounting the thrill of an African vacation (". . . and so, my late wife and I would like to thank you . . ."). There was "Nanty Puts Her Hair Up," a Scots thing, indescribable, though the word "twee" comes to mind. There was the Siegel-Carroll "Monotonous," Eartha Kitt's long-remembered solo on the boredom of international celebrity. There was a sad, even cruel nostalgia piece, as a woman of means looks back on her Lower East Side youth in "Penny Candy." There was June Carroll singing "Guess Who I Saw Today?," a wife's monologue to her her husband, unseen behind his newspaper, on her shock at seeing an adulterous couple in town that afternoon. "Guess who I saw today," she concludes—"I saw you." And the newspaper slowly begins to lower as the lights fade. Through it all, there was the dishy Virginia de Luce, as the emcee, ever trying to steal the show with "He Takes Me off His Income Tax," and ever being silenced by an offstage voice.

The revue had nowhere to go from here. Narrative was now the musical's absolute, and television was loaded with revues, with star talent, for free, Besides, the best writers disdained revue. Even specialists—Harold Rome, for instance—were abandoning it.

Another form on shaky ground was the revival, for old shows disappointed a public now used to sharper storytelling. Such classics as the Kern-Hammerstein *Music in the Air* (1932) and the Gershwins' *Of Thee I Sing* (1931) returned to Broadway in 1951 and 1952, and both failed. A rewritten *Shuffle Along* (1921), with co-author Flournoy Miller, composer Eubie Blake, and lyricist Noble Sissle in the cast, collapsed within a week.

True, a new mounting of *Porgy and Bess* with Leontyne Price achieved the biggest success for this title since the original had failed in 1935. But this was in fact a larger-than-Broadway project, an international tour that lasted four years, taking in a sellout booking at La Scala and a Russian visit. Anyway, *Porgy* is an opera, and operas live not in original runs but in revival. The sole profitable revival of a musical in this time was that of *Pal Joey* (1940), so successful in 1952 that a legend grew up telling us the first staging had failed. No; but the second ran longer, almost certainly because of the immense popularity of an LP that Columbia had published, with Vivienne Segal and Harold Lang, in 1950. The revival even used Segal and Lang from the disc: as if making a show out of a recording. (Segal, of course, had starred onstage in *Pal Joey* in 1940 as well.) It is also worth noting that a revival of another Rodgers and Hart show, *On Your Toes* (1936), in 1954, bombed. "Dated," the critics said.

This flurry of revivals in the early 1950s—there were few in the 1940s and none in the late 1950s, except off-Broadway and in the City Center's annual spring season of classic shows in authentic stagings—suggests a feeling that the musical now had an honorable history to look back on: an ontology in American culture. And it is interesting that this occurred right in the middle of the Rodgers and Hammerstein era, because that was when the musical realized that it had an opulent future, that it was still in development. So it is amusing to drop on the pair at this time, because this is when they decided to abandon the musical play for a snazzy here-and-now piece, a musical comedy: *Me and Juliet* (1953).

A backstager exposing the personal lives of the cast and crew of a six-month-old musical, *Me and Juliet* was the most taken-for-granted hit of the decade, a very enjoyable yet somehow not quite distinguished piece that was never sold to the movies and never managed to endear its score to the public in the way any classic title must do. In fact, the cast album sold sluggishly, went out of print early on, enjoyed a brief reissue, and did not appear again until the CD era.

What went wrong? Nothing—with the writing of the show. There was something very wrong in its staging, and I'll get to that in a moment. First, let's consider what Rodgers and Hammerstein didn't want to write.

They didn't want any of that phoney geschrei that Hollywood's backstagers had invented—the youngster taking over for the star, the backer threatening to pull out at the last minute, the producer's talentless girl friend, the hit tune that turns a flop into a smash, the failing director who, this time, *must* have a hit.

What they wanted to write was what it's like to be in a show— the bare stage with the lone work light, auditioning for replacements, rehearsing numbers that have grown untidy, the personal attachments (and alienations) within the company. Even the audience* was on view, in "Intermission Talk," set in the theatre's downstairs lounge, where buffs chat about the first act, Broadway in general, and whatever else is on their minds. ("I don't think it's

---

* There's an odd playwrighting error in this scene, for a member of the audience does little reprises from the score, confusing one song with another. Fine—but one of the snatches that she sings is from "It's Me"—a character song in the real-life plot, not an onstage number, and thus a melody that she couldn't possibly have heard.

right to be sulky all night," one woman tells her husband, "over one little bill from Saks!").

Also unlike virtually every Hollywood backstager, *Me and Juliet* does not range all over town. It is set almost entirely in the theatre in which its play-within-the-play is running, venturing only as far as the alley outside the stage door and the bar across the street. Rodgers and Hammerstein intended a valentine to their profession, full of naturalistic detail that only veteran insiders could share. It's a dramatic piece as well, centering on a triangle involving a soft guy, a bully, and the woman they both want. She wants the soft guy, which leads the bully, one of the show's electricians, to drop a sandbag inches away from her *during* a performance and then to come after the soft guy with the intention of killing him.

Another of Hammerstein's many villain figures that seem to enjoy humiliating and hurting people, the electrician, Bob, is *Me and Juliet*'s most arresting character. Unlike the somewhat conventional bullies who proliferated in twenties operetta, Bob has an emotional motivation, an undernourished sense of self-esteem that leads him to strike out at anyone who thwarts his will out of sheer ego-defense. That sounds like Jud Fry, *Oklahoma!*'s villain, but Jud is so low he seems beyond human; Bob is almost reachable. He has a sweet side—as long as he's in control—and a sense of humor. Moreover, the author-producers assigned the part to Mark Dawson, a giant hunk with a boyish face and a charming lyric baritone, exactly the contradiction that Bob presents to those he works with: appealing but dangerous. At one point, he actually picks up his girl friend and carries her offstage like a caveman.

The show gives Bob a great first act, revealing his sadistic side within the first fifteen minutes, then, pulling a characteristic Rodgers and Hammerstein switch, giving him *Me and Juliet*'s main charm song, "Keep It Gay." This would be too ingratiating a piece if it were Bob's character song; rather, he sings it on the lighting bridge over the stage, again during a performance. "Sh!" his partner whispers. But Bob sings it anyway, aggressively selfish yet, because of the way the number shows off his voice, attractive.

Bob's soliloquy, "It Feels Good," his second-act number in the bar after the sandbag incident, develops this contradiction of a man capable of rationalizing his own irrational behavior. A wonderful touch: Hammerstein has Bob refer to his inferiors as "weasels" full of "lousy weasel talk." It's a Nietzschean conception. Ultimately, Bob is defeated by a banding together of his co-workers: Hammerstein believes in community.

Flanking Dawson in the love triangle were Bill Hayes and Isabel Bigley (of *Guys and Dolls*), like Dawson wonderful singers, better than the average for musical comedy. The stars of the play-within-the-play were either singers (Arthur Maxwell and Helena Scott) or dancers (Bob Fortier and Svetlana McLee, who is then "replaced" in her part by Joan McCracken). Two other roles are speaking parts—the magisterial stage manager (Ray Walston), who has been dating McCracken but coldly breaks it off when she joins the show because of a personal rule against intramural romance, and the haughty conductor (George S. Irving), whose fond habit it is to drown out Maxwell on his more soaring phrases, carefully holding the orchestra to pianissimo for Scott. All told, it was a highly personable cast; it had to be, for the story as such was ordinary after the exotic coloring of Indian Territory, old New England, the south Pacific in wartime, and Yul Brynner's Siam.

The authors made an extremely crucial decision about the play-within-the-play, also called *Me and Juliet*. In order not to detract from the complex proceedings of the real-life people, the onstage scenes could bear neither plot nor character relationships. Instead, the audience would encounter iconic types that it could easily place—the hero, Me; his heroine, Juliet; Don Juan; and Carmen. Then, too, their surroundings must have a look all their own, airy and pixilated, to contrast with the real life going on behind the scenes.

That's brilliant. Then the authors made a second extremely crucial decision, one that guaranteed that *Me and Juliet* would last no longer than its first season and disappear thereafter: they hired George Abbott to direct and Robert Alton to choreograph.

True, this was the first Rodgers and Hammerstein title to call itself a musical comedy, and Abbott and Alton were musical comedy honchos. But Abbott was mystified by the play-within-the-play, and Alton was all danced out. What *Me and Juliet* should have had, as both director and choreographer, was Jerome Robbins, who would have exploited the bizarrerie of the onstage numbers as he did "The Small House of Uncle Thomas" and made something marvelous of them. Unfortunately, the age of the director-choreographer had not quite kicked in, though Robbins would do double duty on a show one year after *Me and Juliet.**

I'd like to say that, with Robbins, *Me and Juliet* would have entered the golden book of classics, but the score isn't good enough. It's tuneful, no question. But with half the songs devoted to the—remember, characterless—onstage doings, the authors had little room in which to create those "Stonecutters Cut It on Stone" or "Twin Soliloquies" numbers in which something superb hurls the very center of the show into the ear. There are enjoyable titles—"No Other Love (have I)," adapted from Rodgers' symphonic accompaniment to TV's *Victory at Sea*, "Marriage Type Love," "I'm Your Girl," "We Deserve Each Other." Some of them even swing, as befits Rodgers' return to his roots in musical comedy. But not a one of these songs, deleted from the show, would hurt it. Even "No Other Love," the show's basic love song, is from the play-within-the-play, not from the real-life romance (though at one point it is used subtextually, as the soft guy rehearses his girl friend in it). Worse, any one of these songs could have been smuggled into any other musical and sounded fine. That can't be Rodgers and Hammerstein at their best.

At his best in this show was the set and lighting designer, Jo Mielziner. I have said that stage technology did not appreciably advance during the 1950s, but Mielziner did pull off some nifty stunts for the first time, tricks with time and place that gave *Me and Juliet* the fluidity of cinema. Mielziner's greatest feat was the "moving" of the very stage of the theatre ten feet to the right, as if a camera had panned ten feet to the left, to catch up on what's happening in the wings. We see the soft guy kissing the girl—but

---

* Very late in tryouts, Rodgers and Hammerstein realized their error and asked Robbins to take over the show. He said no, apparently seeing how much he could do with the numbers and knowing that this would destroy Alton. As it was, Alton did one more show and retired.

so does the hard guy, because he suddenly swings a light on them from overhead. As the girl makes her "entrance" into the onstage number, a crowded nightclub scene, that light stalks her from on high like the wrath of God, while the dancers, heading for the first-act finale of both *Me and Juliet* and *Me and Juliet*, stare upward in terror, the aforementioned sandbag crashes down, and the curtain falls.

Mielziner got the reviews, "No Other Love" hangs on as a standard, and that's the all of *Me and Juliet*. It's tempting to blame Rodgers and Hammerstein for setting into motion a revolution that overwhelmed even them, that left them unable to write musical comedy on the level on which they wrote musical plays. But that's not what happened. *Me and Juliet* is a fine but not great show from authors of greatness. That makes for a bad press. What's key here is that the American musical had room not only for classics like *Guys and Dolls* or ephemeral smash hits like *Call Me Madam* but for a *second* level of ephemeral smash hits that utterly fade from view. *Call Me Madam* wasn't half the show that *Me and Juliet* was. But Merman is Merman, and its score hung on, and the title has ring.

In other words, it isn't feast or famine, as we have today, a *Phantom of the Opera* or *Big*. There was a valid midpoint, a means of paying the rent and giving pleasure without having to become a Craze. One could even survive a critics' attack. We've seen *"Wish You Were Here"* and *Can-Can* do so. And our next show opened in the midst of certain death—a newspaper strike—and *then* got critically attacked, yet went on to become one of the immortal titles, at that in the form of operetta, the corpse that refused to die. Well, we all know that Cinderella's reviews are written by the ugly stepsisters.

"Only five dinar for that lovely lyrical thought."

5

Kismet

A curiosity of the musical's history is that, while it reads as a gradual perfecting of form, the popularity of specific types of musical rises and falls arbitrarily.

For instance, the First Age, in the nineteenth century, is one of infantile entertainments largely heedless of the smarter European exports of Offenbach and Gilbert and Sullivan. It revels in fairy-tale "extravaganza," farces with a few songs, and burlesque (an evening-or half-evening-length spoof of some familiar literary or dramatic work). The Second Age, starting in 1900, suddenly sets to rationalizing the art of storytelling, and all the older forms die out—with, ironically, the exception of extravaganza, the least rational of all. The Second Age popularizes the revue, but what it mainly loves are, one, musical comedy and, two, "comic opera" (i.e., operetta). The one is smart and wicked, the other romantic and ultra-musical. World War One takes comic opera out, as its mainly middle-European composers are too associated with German culture.

By the 1920s, the start of the great Third Age, operetta has unaccountably made a comeback: *The Student Prince, Rose-*

Marie, The Vagabond King, The Desert Song, The New Moon, The Three Musketeers. Yet by 1930 the cycle is over. Operetta had been leading the artistic development of the integrated show; but its period settings at length seemed terminally quaint, its heroes and heroines grandiose, its very vocabulary congested. The few successful operettas of the 1930s are strictly modern-day pieces like *The Cat and the Fiddle, Music in the Air,* and *White Horse Inn.*

Yet unreconstructed operetta in its full kit of *Prince of Pilsen* decor, love duets, and ethnic pastiche had not quite given up. In the middle of the 1940s, *Song of Norway,* on the "life" and using the music of Edvard Grieg, came to New York from Edwin Lester's Civic Light Opera on the west coast, a reactionary stronghold where Johann Strauss and Victor Herbert were *derniers cris.* With *Norway's* cartoon characters, generic numbers, protagonist caught between hometown girl and turbulent opera diva, and its attempt to fill out a skinny plot with the halling, the rigaudon, a "Spring Dance," a ballroom waltz, a *Peer Gynt* ballet, and even a *Song of Norway* ballet to the famous piano concerto—all of it—*Song of Norway* was sure to bomb. It ran two years, only 30 performances short of *Carousel's* 890 that same season.

However, the musical play had already begun to absorb operetta's better qualities—the musical intensity, the confrontational drama, the passion, while demonstrating by its realism just how silly all that cornball humor, pantywaisting around in ballrooms, and dancing to concertos really was. True, two Victor Herbert shows, *The Red Mill* (1906) and *Sweethearts* (1913), were revived on Broadway in the late 1940s with success. But these were revampings in 1940s style, especially of *Sweethearts,* dominated by clown Bobby Clark. The new operettas were invariably failing with gigantic thuds.

By the 1950s, then, operetta was through. Yet there was one more, from Edwin Lester, of course, and with, once again, *Norway*-style, melodies adapted from those of a classic Name, Alyeksandr Borodin. But this show was not concerned with Borodin's life. Lester took hold of Edward Knoblock's play *Kismet* (1911), a hit with Otis Skinner and, for two years, in London with Oscar Asche, later famed as Abu Hassan in the insanely long-running *Chu Chin Chow*. Skinner filmed *Kismet* twice silent; Ronald Colman made the talkie, with Marlene Dietrich. Clearly, there was something timelessly engaging in the story: a brilliant beggar attains wealth and power and weds his daughter to the caliph inside of a single day in ancient Baghdad, all the while acknowledging that his inventiveness, his ability to seize control of his life, is nothing next to . . . *kismet!**

Robert Wright and George Forrest wrote the score, as they had done for *Song of Norway*. But where the earlier show creaked between the singing and dancing, *Kismet* crackled. For perhaps the first time since *Sweet Adeline* in 1929, an operetta sported the book of a musical comedy. In place of the stilted, faux-antique dialogue that dogged traditional operetta, *Kismet*'s librettists, Charles Lederer and Luther Davis, wrote in modern colloquial or spoofed Omar Khayyam lingo; and almost all the characters, from leads to bits, contributed to the comedy, whereas operetta's worst quality was its habit of centering all the alleged humor on one or two roles.

Most important, where the typical operetta narrative tends to lurch from one setback (to the love plot, usually) to the next, *Kismet* moves smoothly through an ever-revolving series of rash encounters among five principals, each with his own agenda. The beggar's daughter, Marsinah, and the Caliph, who she thinks is a gardener, are the soprano and tenor lovers. The Wazir (bass) is the villain, eager to manipulate the Caliph's marriage for political and financial gain and thus determined to drive the lovers apart. The Wazir's wife, Lalume, sings in a range that *Kismet* invented, the dramatic-soprano sexbomb. Lalume is somewhat incidental to the plot but the foil of, sardonically, the Wazir and, amorously, the Beggar (baritone), billed only as "a public poet, later called Hajj." Marsinah, the sole person in the story who does know his name, calls him only "Father."

In fact, *Kismet*'s protagonist is something the musical virtually never had before *Show Boat* in 1927, underwent development only sporadically in the 1930s, and began to appear regularly in the 1940s: a one-of-a-kind personality whose dialogue, music, and

---

* Turkish, from an Arabic word, meaning "fate."

overall worldview is utterly unlike those of any other personality in any other musical. First of all, the Poet (as the script terms him) is a comic. When was an operetta's hero a comedian? He is also a father, we know, and his relationship with Marsinah is very touching, especially when he determines to murder the Wazir in full view of the court because he put Marsinah in harm's way. The Poet thus calls more for a singing actor than for a romantic hero. True, he has a sort of love plot with Lalume. But this is clearly set out as an erotic and not rhapsodic duo. Marsinah and the Caliph sing "Stranger in Paradise." The Poet and Lalume duet only on "Rahadlakum," a salute to an aphrodisiac, the music marked "Rock it."

Then, too, the Poet's musical program is rather various for an operetta. True, the "Stouthearted Men" kind of hero died out in the 1930s, even if Wilbur Evans got away with a semi-revival of that kind of baritone-rousing-the-troops number in "The Big Backyard" in *Up in Central Park* (1945). Still, the Poet's songs cover a great diversity of type. Even *Carousel*'s Billy Bigelow, possibly the richest male character in a musical to this point, basically sings romantic songs and a sea chantey. But the Poet gives us the romantically comic "Rhymes Have I"; the brooding, then ecstatic "Fate"; the aggressively wheedling "Gesticulate," which starts broadly but continues as a patter song; the mock-amatory "Rahadlakum"; the lyrical "The Olive Tree"; and the finale, which—incredibly for a musical of 1953 but particularly for an operetta, at least in 1953—finds the Poet alone on the stage, quietly reprising the undulating "Sands of Time."

But what makes Kismet so special is this very multifariousness. Don't see it as a modernized operetta (though it is that), but rather as a nexus of historical developments: the Rodgers and Hammerstein drive toward more resonant character relationships; the rise of individualistic choreographer styles; the hunger for romantic melodies rather than the pop tunes that had dominated for so long; and the timeless love of a star turn.

First, let's look at *Kismet*'s book. Witty? No, but quick and funny and sure. The good old stuff that—given seasoned talent—never fails. The Poet, mistaken for Hajj, is dragged off to the tent of the ferocious brigand Jawan:

JAWAN: You know me?
THE POET: (*Hysterically*) I know no one—and nothing. I have no memory.
JAWAN: I am Jawan.
THE POET: (*In horror*) Jawan! Oh, no!
JAWAN: Ah, your memory freshens.
THE POET: (*Prattling with fear*) Well, it's a famous name . . . Jawan? . . . It strikes a chord. Let me see, you're Jawan, yes, the great astronomer.

The romance is finely turned, too. After a verse and chorus of the love-at-first-sight "Stranger in Paradise," the love line needs some extra knotting—the Caliph plans to meet Marsinah again, this time with a nuptial cortège to sweep her off to his palace—so the number's second chorus must now be given an emotional launching:

MARSINAH: You say you're a gardener. What kind of flowers should I plant along the fence?
CALIPH: I must go in a moment—will you meet me here again this evening?
MARSINAH: I thought hyacinths—but perhaps oleanders . . .
CALIPH: (*Insistently*) At moonrise? Here in the garden?
MARSINAH: (*Facing him again*) Yes. (*Simply*) Yes, of course.
CALIPH: You won't forget? You won't fail me?

And she's already singing "I saw your face," the start of the release of the most passionate number Broadway had heard since the days when Romberg and Friml roamed the earth.

A lot of the libretto concerns Lalume's strong libido, apparently a citywide joke in old Baghdad. At length, with the Wazir killed and the Caliph and Marsinah reunited, there remains no more than for the Poet to name his own fate, his kismet:

THE POET: (*To the* CALIPH) Oh, Prince of Justice, let me help you to compose this most difficult of verdicts against Hajj who, in his life, never once did right—and never wronged anyone. Condemn this scoundrel to some dreadful—oasis . . . Force him to take with him the widow of the late Wazir . . . (*aside to* LALUME) . . . and all the property she can get her hands on before the late Wazir's accounts are audited.

(To the CALIPH*)* Condemn him to lighten her sorrows, and to toil constantly to remove all grief from her heart.

LALUME: You have just sentenced yourself to a lifetime of hard labor!

As for Jack Cole's choreography, this in no small way gave *Kismet* its personality: barbarically physical and grandly ceremonial, a whirling riot at the opening of "Bazaar of the Caravans" but then a graceful *pas des femmes* in the same scene for "Baubles, Bangles and Beads" when the arrayed Marsinah enters to be heralded as the "Princess of the Province of the Moon." *Kismet* is studded with dance—yet Cole managed to do without a single scene employing the entire dancing ensemble, the kind of all-out number that Michael Kidd did in *Guys and Dolls'* "Runyonland" opening, that Jerome Robbins did in "The Small House of Uncle Thomas," or that Herbert Ross did in *A Tree Grows in Brooklyn's* "Halloween Ballet."

No, Cole usually preferred to showcase his dancers or to work them in tiers. The three noble claimants of the Caliph's heart— Zubbediya of Damascus, Samaris of Bangalore, and (as a unit) the three princesses of Ababu—each get a wooing dance (*sola, sola,* then *sole*), and the Ababus also get three earlier spots, jumping out of a wicker basket to perform a warlike parade accompanied only by percussion, then in a bluesy flirtation dance with two young men, and after that on a shopping expedition to buy a cobra.

Even the refulgent "Night of My Nights" and the urgently swinging "Rahadlakum" did not inspire Cole to fill the stage with his corps. "Nights" was a procession, more than a dance, all downstage in one, with no room to expand; and "Rahadlakum", though an eyeful of torrid delight, was danced by ten women—neat, no chaser. This never happened in any other operetta: but then all other operettas were generic. *Kismet* was novel and, better, wild, boiling with erotic heat in its very look. What other operetta had four bodybuilders in the cast, including the future king of Italian *Hercules* movies, Steve Reeves? *Kismet* was a musical feast, the only operetta of all time to throw off not hit tunes but a hit score, eventually counting eight *major* recordings. And *Kismet* was weird, an irreverent and sexy entertainment set in a culture dominated by the most pietistic and puritanical religion of all time.

That score really is a wonder in the way it has the variety of a musical comedy's tunestack but the intensity of oldtime operetta. There's nothing stale here, nothing conventional. The lovers duet but once, in "Stranger in Paradise." "And This Is My Beloved," the second act's big love song, is, unexpectedly, a quartet; the two lovers are in the number but each sings to someone else, unaware that the beloved is only a few feet away, unseen. Cleverly, Wright and Forrest planned "Night of My Nights" as a choral showpiece as much as the Caliph's wedding song, and the fourth ballad, "Baubles, Bangles and Beads," is a love song only in feeling, not subject.

The rest of Kismet is character numbers, plot numbers, exotic numbers, and even—in an operetta!—a comedy song that is actually funny: the villain's sadistic "Was I Wazir?" The Asian sensuality of Borodin, in his slithery melodies and diminished-seventh harmony, is why Kismet sounds so right, but only partly. "Based on themes of Borodin" reads the published score, but there's actually as much Wright and Forrest as Borodin here. Frequently, they utilize the Russian as a starting point, developing a number entirely on their own.

For instance, two songs were taken from Borodin's Second String Quartet. The second movement provided the main strain of "Baubles, Bangles and Beads," but, halfway through the second A, Wright and Forrest are elaborating, and by the release ("I'll glitter and gleam so") they are composing. The quartet's third movement gave them "And This Is My Beloved," but similarly the release ("And when he speaks?") is theirs. "Gesticulate" is mucho Borodin, with a first section drawn from Konchak's aria from Prince Igor, a transitional section from the opera's second-act love duet, and a main theme from the first movement of Borodin's First Symphony; all the rest is original. But "Rhymes Have I" owes to Borodin nothing but two notes (and the underlying harmony) in Skula and Yeroshka's scene in Prince Igor's fourth act. More: "My Magic Lamp" is taken almost note for note from Igor's scene with Ovlur in Prince Igor's second act, but "Bored" is a considerable enhancement of Konchakovna's cavatina from the same opera, and "Rahadlakum" is entirely original (though its orchestral intro-duction wittily quotes the "sea" motif from not Borodin but Rimsky-Korsakov's *Scheherazade*).

Wright and Forrest were no less able in their lyrics, making a virtue out of operetta's singular curse, flowery diction. "Stranger in Paradise" and "Night of My Nights" revel in metaphor and euphuism to a point that would have seemed absurd in a musical play. But then *Kismet* is not a realistic entertainment, as, say, *South Pacific* or *A Tree Grows in Brooklyn* are. They are fictions that are true to life; *Kismet* is, as the posters had it, "a musical Arabian night": fantastical, bizarre, ultra-romantic. Yet the love songs mate nicely with the hot numbers, for the Neverland magic of the verses keeps the work consistent, binds the tenderness to the sensuality. All love is sex, this show says, but also: all sex is love.

With such a rich score, even lovely numbers had to be dropped—both "Bored" and "My Magic Lamp" were cut, though they can still be heard in underscoring—and the cast was hard-pressed, in those days before body mikes, to project into the cav-ernous Ziegfeld Theatre, especially given Arthur Kay's lavish or-chestrations.

It was a great cast, headed by Alfred Drake in his first solo star billing. *Here* was a prince enthroned, *Oklahoma!*'s Curly reaffirm-ing his *Kiss Me, Kate* Petruchio as Broadway's new choice in op-eretta heroes, frisky and sensual where his predecessors were wooden, opaque. Drake truly had Hajj's one-of-a-kind personality; *Kismet* was inconceivable without him.

Lalume was Joan Diener—looks like a Valkyrie; sings like a . . . Valkyrie—and Marsinah was Doretta Morrow, Tuptim once again going Eastern in a dark wig over her blond locks. Richard Kiley somehow managed to baritone his way through the Caliph's high line (which goes to a top B flat) and Henry Calvin played the Wazir as a kind of serious stooge, funny but also threatening. Albert Marre (Diener's husband) directed, and *Kismet* opened to some very damning reviews.

Or, rather, it opened to no reviews, because of that newspaper strike. "Assembled from a storehouse of spare parts," said Atkin-son, when the *Times* finally made its reappearance; "It's the sort of show that would sell its soul for a joke," said Walter Kerr. Clearly, both men were confused by the show's odd form. The other critics were kinder, but in any case word of mouth and airplay of the immediately popular score sent the piece on a seventeen-month run. It helped, too, that Columbia recorded the show three days after the premiere and rushed the disc into stores, for OL 4850 was one of the glories of the LP revolution in the national popularization of Broadway: two very stuffed sides, with the Ziegfeld's pit players coming off as a symphony orchestra, thanks to Kay's scoring and a few extra ringers in the violin section. The disc has been available without a break ever since.

There was a movie, in 1955, and here, too, was a formidable element in the cultural aggrandizement of Broadway. Most shows toured only to the bigger cities. The very occasional phenomenon, such as *Oklahoma!*, played also to good-sized towns. But a movie went everywhere. True, hit shows had been going Hollywood since the first year of regular sound production, 1929, when the film industry, forced willy-nilly into talkies yet unsure about exactly what a talkie should be, raided Broadway for titles and talent. But, by the early 1930s, a more confident Hollywood began buying Broadway titles not to film them but to reconceive them for film.

Once again, it was Rodgers and Hammerstein who changed the rules. By refusing to sell *Oklahoma!* to a studio, with the plan to enter into partnership with a consortium giving them artistic control, they focussed attention on the integrity of composition. Then, too, by the 1950s shows themselves were popularizing this integrity by their very nature, and such works as *Call Me Madam, Guys and Dolls, The Pajama Game, Damn Yankees, Silk Stockings, Bells Are Ringing*, and *The Music Man* enjoyed quite faithful film versions.

Kismet did, too—sort of. With Howard Keel, Dolores Gray, Ann Blyth, and Vic Damone, it offers a mixture of ersatz operetta (the cluelessly effervescent Keel and the sopraninetto Blyth), pop single (Damone), and real thing (Gray, who utterly outsings Keel in "Rahadlakum" without even trying to). To the Broadway version the movie adds sand and reinstates "Bored"; from the Broadway version it extracts the sex, the fun, and the spectacle.

Still, the Hollywood transmission was a crucial event in the

maintenance of a classic's reputation. An excellent adaptation—
the Oklahoma! that finally was made, also in 1955—meant can-
onization. An unfaithful adaptation—Gentlemen Prefer Blondes,
Can-Can—confounded the history. A lack of adaptation—A Tree
Grows in Brooklyn, "Wish You Were Here"—meant obscurity.

Kismet survived MGM's deconstruction. Its London stand, in
1955 (with Drake, Morrow, and Diener, and Juliet Prowse as
Princess Samaris, in a replica of the Broadway mounting) ran
longer than the New York original in a larger theatre. After that,
its production annals are somewhat like those of Guys and Dolls:
an institutional revival (at Lincoln Center) in original style with
the original star, Drake, like Guys and Dolls' several appearances
in the City Center's spring seasons, including one with one of its
originals, Vivian Blaine; an all-black-cast Broadway staging,
though unlike Guys and Dolls in 1976, the black Kismet, retitled
Timbuktu! (1978) was something of a revision, with wholesale
changes in the script and restoring "My Magic Lamp"; and a London revival in the late 1970s, just before Guys and Dolls, too,
made a return, at the National Theatre.

The New York City Opera also got to Kismet, not happily. But
by now the piece is indestructible. It is, truly, the last operetta—
not the last to be staged but the last to succeed before the musical
play definitively absorbed its Big Music. And what has kept Kismet
so potent for so long is what its music conjures up: sheer romance,
that elusive but palpable something-or-other that was all over the
1920s and almost immediately gave out by 1930. Song of Norway
didn't have it; Song of Norway had Balanchine. But Kismet had it.
I still recall, as a very small boy, being taken to the original at a
matinee late in the run. Certain moments resonate yet: how the
dawn calls to the faithful from the towers of Baghdad were sim-
ulated by singers placed high up in the auditorium; how Cole's
dancers could slide from the tender to the savage to the gamey in
a moment; how Drake, sneaking out of the Wazir's palace at the
end of Act One, dropped his cloak on the parquet during a busy
dance-and-choral movement and hightailed it upstage and away
till the Wazir, spotting the empty cloak, gave Diener a "Where'd
he go?" look, and Diener pointed straight up as the curtain shot
to the floor.

But most of all I remember that when the lights came up in the auditorium at show's end, I noticed that I was in a sea of kids and parents, and all the kids were begging to stay and see it again. Some of the kids may have seen musicals before. But *Kismet* was something new: our first contact with the magic lamp—romance.

6

The Street, 1954

An art form, when youthful, is made up of both old and new elements, the old ones mostly retrograde, conventional, and limiting and the new ones as yet unsifted, still experimental. A good example is early silent film, so dependent on the look and behavior of the theatre yet discovering things the theatre cannot do, in the closeup, the dissolve, cross-cutting.

When mature and vigorous, an art form is made up of the former new elements, now sorted and codified but still in development, along with even newer elements, being developed in their turn. A parallel would be Hollywood in the late 1930s, when the movies had completely lost their staginess yet were still realizing their potential, reaching a kind of apex in *The Wizard of Oz* and *Gone With the Wind*, all but unproduceable five years before.

Eventually, an art form grows moribund and is composed entirely of old elements—but that doesn't concern us in this volume. The fifties musical was in its vigor and maturity, getting newer all the time. We see this particularly in its treatment of old subjects, in effect reinventing them.

What could be older than James M. Barrie's *Peter Pan?* The boy who wouldn't grow up had become, in postwar America, the play that was older than God. True, Jean Arthur and Boris Karloff had a success with it in 1950, albeit in a delightful staging (by the Old Vic's John Burrell) and after a long absence from Broadway. Still, wouldn't true rejuvenation come only in a musical transfer? The Burrell mounting had incidental music by Alec Wilder and songs by Leonard Bernstein (writing lyrics as well as music), but they were too few and slight to be more than filigree—three wistful bits for Wendy, two extremely strange chanteys for the pirates, a shadowy theme song.

A Walt Disney cartoon appeared in 1953, again in a minimusical version. Then the Civic Light Opera's Edwin Lester acquired the rights to turn *Peter Pan* into a full-sized musical. It is tempting to imagine the floperetta that Lester might have made of it, as was his wont, with Irra Petina as a tempestuous Peter and a Wright and Forrest score drawn from the melodies of Dame Ethel Smyth. But Lester was thinking more creatively, and he conceived a vehicle for Mary Martin with a score by Moose Charlap and Carolyn Leigh. This proved a touch earthbound, and the score was bolstered with songs by Jule Styne and Betty Comden and Adolph Green.

The new titles, oddly, are not exclusively the ones that so happily reinterpreted Barrie for the modern era. "Tender Shepherd," "I've Gotta Crow," "I'm Flying," and "I Won't Grow Up" are all Charlap-Leigh. What the new team did create was the indispensable new theme song, which unfortunately renamed the Neverland—as Barrie called it—in order to fill out a musical phrase. "Never Never Land" is a misnomer that has dogged Barrie ever since. Styne's gang also came up with the irresistible "Wendy," which provisioned a charming house-building sequence, by the Lost Boys under Peter's direction; the bolero-with-coloratura-soprano "Mysterious Lady," in which Peter goads and teases Captain Hook; the silly yet, given the prancing Hook of Cyril Ritchard, absolutely correct "Captain Hook's Waltz"; and "Distant Melody," a tender love song for Peter, the boy who cannot love, replacing Charlap and Leigh's "When I Went Home," a darker version of the same idea.

What really made *Peter Pan* the musical (1954) was the staging, by Jerome Robbins in his first job as director–choreographer. Matching the dances to the sets, the portrayals to the very warmth of the lighting—in other words, ruling the playing area as total auteur—Robbins made *Peter Pan* seem like the newest show yet, not just about youth but made of it.

Of course, Martin and Ritchard were grownups, but ageless ones, in their own strange way. Smee (Joe E. Marks) was old. Everyone else was a child, a teenager, or a musical comedy gypsy, spry and dancey. *Young* show. *New* show. What, after half a century?

But that's just it: the musical now had the technology to make the old stuff fresh. Note that there was no book credit on the posters: the lines were almost all Barrie's, cut down from the original by some unacknowledged hand. The adaptation as a whole was not precisely faithful; some of the emphases favored the world according to Martin and Ritchard rather than Barrie. Nevertheless, the essence of Barrie was preserved while the show was born again; and this feat was Robbins'.

Take the show's opening. *Peter Pan*'s overture is another of those razzle-dazzle flourishes that we expect of Broadway in this time. But the curtain rises on two children in antique let's-play-grownups clothes, executing a minuet. It's culture shock, the contemporary music giving way to a daguerreotype, virtually stunning us into the action.

Or take the first Neverland scene, introduced by a bunch of pantomime animals prancing and worrying; or the street-fair square dance when the Indians and Lost Boys join forces ("Ugawugga meatball!" runs one lyric); or Hook's habit of scheming to a dance rhythm provided by his crew. ("What tempo, Captain?" asks the trusty Smee, as the pirates take out their instruments.)

Clearly, it was Robbins' plan to break *Peter Pan* out of its Anglo tradition, its farouche Peters and Shakespearean Hooks, and make the whole thing American. Ritchard's Hook was of course the exception, but then Hook is the Neverland's one alien. Barrie purists thought Martin miscast as Peter, though it's hard to be miscast in your own starring vehicle. Maybe it's more like Peter was miscast as Mary Martin. In any case, Robbins let Martin shrug off the twee lines and power punch everything else; and the purists were right. It wasn't Barrie's Peter: it was Robbins', and it worked so well that a New York revival of the Barrie play without the Martin score would be hard to contemplate.*

If *Peter Pan* marks the musical's *passéiste* side, its love of old things, *House of Flowers* (1954) shows off its need for innovation: a musical written by a composer and a fiction writer, featuring a mostly black cast at a time when the musical was routinely all-white and on a subject so sexy Cole Porter and Herbert Fields would have said no. A Caribbean jaunt had given Truman Capote a colorful *New Yorker* story on the bordellos of Port-au-Prince, and a number of people told him it would make a great musical.

What? But perhaps the protean and ambitious fifties musical impressed folk as being capable of virtually anything. With Harold Arlen to compose, the show was assured of an authentic voice for what Broadway heard in the term "black music."

Who would write the book and lyrics? Capote apparently wrote the script—the preliminary one, at any rate—and collaborated with Arlen on the lyrics (mainly by phone and post in this peripatetic stage of Capote's life). At length, it became so difficult to bill each man's contribution that the producer, Saint Subber, dispensed with the usual authors' credits and called *House of Flowers* simply "Truman Capote and Harold Arlen's new musical."

He did his boys proud in the recreative staff, hiring Peter Brook to direct, George Balanchine for the dances, and Oliver Messel to design. This is a truly distinguished trio, bordering on overproduction in that, while Balanchine had indeed choreographed for Broadway, Brook and Messel were the hottest names in the British theatre world, too "good" for musical comedy. The cast sounded hot, too: veterans Pearl Bailey, Juanita Hall, and Josephine Premice, debutante Diahann Carroll, white men Ray Walston and Dino Dí Luca, and exotic dancer Geoffrey Holder as the Houngan, master of voodoo. Alas, a stormy tryout saw Brook, Balanchine, Premice, and even Capote depart. No sooner would Carroll win the crowd with a number than Bailey demanded it be

---

* One can preserve more of Barrie than the Martin version did, however. A lengthy national tour of that version in the early 1990s with Cathy Rigby troubled to reinstate a scene from the play deleted in 1954.

reassigned (to Bailey); Subber insisted that the script be rewritten around a conventional narrative; and a light and almost plotless but by all intelligent accounts gorgeous *je ne sais quoi* opened on Broadway as a kind of nuclear puff of smoke.

It was the usual story of out-of-town frenzy: stop being *special* and start being a *hit!* But Capote and Arlen had conceived something that could only work as special, a piece made not of plot but of atmosphere. Beyond the love of young Ottilie (Carroll) and Royal (Rawn Spearman) and the rivalry of Mesdames Fleur (Bailey) and Tango (Hall), *House of Flowers* had been written around gestures of culture—Madame Fleur's three *horizontales* opening the show with "Waitin'," accompanied by a busted piano; the Houngan's capers and a cockfight; the police whistle that opens and closes the overture; even the haunting poster design of a silhouetted woman bearing an enormous feathered headdress and lolling in a hammock. There was no "plot" as such here, and imposing one on the piece only humiliated its exquisite drollery. Shimmering with such ineffable ballads as "A Sleepin' Bee" and "I Never Has Seen Snow, utterly erotic in the title number—a "Let's Do It" in nuzzling jazz—and giving Bailey plenty of chances to do her lazily outspoken hauteur, *House of Flowers'* score was cabaret rather than storytelling. The glorious songs and Messel's sets and costumes gave some of the critics cause to enthuse, but mixed reviews and, frankly, the show's distinctive nature—black and devilishly erotic—led it to failure.

Balancing the old and the new was the theme of the musical, then—another piece of the science. *Peter Pan* was too old but could be renewed; *House of Flowers* was too new.* *Hazel Flagg* (1953) should have been just right: an adaptation of the 1937 Carole Lombard movie *Nothing Sacred*, a satire on how the communications media not only report on but invent American culture. Timely stuff—and producer and composer Jule Styne had a new star to offer, Helen Gallagher, virtually a Styne stylist after a small role in *High Button Shoes* and featured ones in the Styne-

---

* It remained so. An off-Broadway revival in 1968, produced by the irrepressible Saint Subber, supposedly restored the original conception (and Josephine Premice, now in Bailey's role). Very poorly sung, it closed in six weeks.

produced *Make a Wish* and *Pal Joey* revival. But was it wise to
entrust the book to Ben Hecht, author of *Nothing Sacred*'s screen-
play but out of his element in the musical? Should Styne have
assigned the production to Robert Alton, by 1953 a has-been choreographer promoted to director–choreographer status? Was Gallagher warm enough to carry a "sympathy" heroine, seduced into
posing as a victim of radium poisoning for a magazine publicity
stunt?

The musical somehow lost everything that keeps the film engaging even today—the so cynical view of humanity that finds
smalltown New Englanders even tougher than New Yorkers, the
screwball charm, the dog-race pacing. In a day when major features almost invariably ran ninety minutes or a bit more, *Nothing
Sacred* zipped itself up in seventy-five. *Hazel Flagg* is *slow*. Worst
of all, Styne's music, written to Bob Hilliard's lyrics, found him
in poor form, though anyone curious enough to investigate the
cast album will note the dynamic vocal arrangements, virtually a
Broadway jazz and very redolent of the times. They are the work
of Hugh Martin, whose arrangements date as far back as Rodgers
and Hart's *The Boys From Syracuse* (1938) and up to his own *High
Spirits* (1964).

Another flop using old material was *The Girl in Pink Tights*
(1954), though here the source was an incident in theatre history.
A French ballet troupe whose house had burned down merged
with a black-magic melodrama to create the legendary "first" musical—certainly the first musical smash—*The Black Crook* (1866).
The making of *The Black Crook* was, more or less, *The Girl in
Pink Tights*' storyline, with the French import Jeanmaire as the
ballet company's star, Alexandre Kalioujny as her dancing partner,
David Atkinson as the playwright and Jeanmaire's lover, Viennese
comic Charles Goldner as the ballet master, and Brenda Lewis as
the theatre manager and *his* lover. Sigmund Romberg and Leo
Robin wrote the score,* Jerome Chodorov and Joseph Fields
wrote the book, and Agnes de Mille choreographed.

---

* Romberg died before completing composition, so the show's orchestrator,
Don Walker, filled out the music, supposedly working from Romberg's sketches.
However, as Romberg habitually wrote the "big" songs first and was not much

It sounds like fun—old New York for a setting, the backstage worlds of both theatre and ballet for atmosphere, a little worldview war between Europeans and Americans, a fire spectacle to close Act One, and plenty of dancing. Moreover, Jeanmaire was, as they used to put it, a triple threat: a superb dancer, a rough but very enjoyable singer, and an explosive personality. The critics tumbled to a man—to Jeanmaire, not to the show. Old-fashioned they all said. Not *funny*. Brooks Atkinson, no doubt smarting at having let *Kismet* sneak to success past his authoritative censure, descried in *The Girl in Pink Tights* "a lust for mediocrity" and heard "mechanical melodies out of a departed era."

This, and Romberg's very name, may suggest an operetta, but *The Girl in Pink Tights* was in fact a musical comedy, albeit with a lot of ballet, the "operetta" version of dance since Albertina Rasch's toe-dancers in twenties operetta. *The Girl's* score demonstrates how flexible form was becoming in the 1950s, after Rodgers and Hammerstein had showed how a certain emphasis on romantic fantasy creates a *Carousel* while an emphasis on contemporary realism creates the very different *South Pacific* even though both works utilize the same structural elements—two couples, class or race as governing factors in society, mezzo-soprano earth-mother figure, lawless comic male, randy male choral number, death.

Undeniably old-hat in *The Girl in Pink Tights* was the first chorus number, "That Naughty Show From Gay Paree," in which customers line up to buy ballet tickets for prurient and not aesthetic reasons; and Leo Robin's lyrics for the comic numbers, "You've Got To Be a Little Crazy (to want to produce a play)" and "Love Is the Funniest Thing," were fit to raise groans. But otherwise this was an up-to-speed score, with the orchestrations especially designed around a contemporary flavor and Jeanmaire's "When I Am Free To Love" coming off as a saucy, here-and-now charm song of a kind unknown to operetta. *Girl* also thought up

---

of a sketch maker, it is probable that, aside from the ballads and a few other major numbers, Walker, himself a now-and-then composer, is the author of the show's music. No doubt he intended to write in the Romberg style, but by the 1950s Romberg's style was so evolved from his "Stouthearted Men" heyday in the 1920s that it would have been difficult to know what to imitate.

an unusual opening: avoiding a lump of exposition, it raised its curtain on a ballet class, thus putting forward its best feature, Jeanmaire *en pointe.*

The singing, too, was hardly of the operetta quality. Besides one semi-legit Broadway baritone (David Atkinson) and one opera soprano (Brenda Lewis), the principals were less than golden throated. Goldner mostly talked his way through his numbers, most endearingly in "I Promised Their Mothers," on his determination to keep his ballerinas chaste. ("But we nevair promiste a t'ing!" the girls conclude.) Kalioujny kept his mouth shut virtually all evening. True, the choral singing was spectacular—but that was true of many a musical comedy at this time.

And yet. Something in the antique setting, in all the ballet stuff, in Atkinson's somewhat wooden plastique, reminiscent of many a Stouthearted Man, was the feeling that *The Girl in Pink Tights* was an operetta in hiding. It didn't sound like one, no—but it acted like one.

Better than *Hazel Flagg* and *The Girl in Pink Tights* at transforming old material was *Wonderful Town* (1953), Leonard Bernstein and Betty Comden and Adolph Green's adaptation of *My Sister Eileen.* Jerome Chodorov and Joseph Fields' 1940 comedy, from Ruth McKenney's *New Yorker* stories about two midwestern sisters looking for life and love in New York City, originally offered Shirley Booth and Jo Anne Sayers. Now, with Chodorov and Fields again writing the script, it was to become a George Abbott–directed vehicle for Rosalind Russell as the smart older sister, Ruth, with Edith Adams as the pretty younger one, Eileen.*

Hazel Flagg and *The Girl in Pink Tights* were conventional shows. *Wonderful Town* was an apparently conventional show with a lot of surprises tucked away. Its opening number, "Christopher Street," establishes the setting, Greenwich Village in 1935, with a tour guide leading his charges through a series of short

---

* To understand how central this particular star was in this particular vehicle, consider that producer Robert Fryer paid Adams $175 per week. Russell earned $12,500 per week. She was worth it: her first-night notices were a sweep, and Russell became so identified with *Wonderful Town* that, when she left and Carol Channing took over, the show quickly folded.

scenes introducing Village types—the would-be artist, the prostitute (actually she gives rhumba lessons: without a phonograph), the roughing-it couple—who all have roles in the story. It's clever, no more, a typical fifties "this is what we're doing and whom we're doing it with" thing. Later, a song for the male half of the couple, a college athlete, "Pass That Football," is one of the most unnecessary numbers of the year. In the finale, after the sisters have done a turn with the "Wrong Note Rag" and an encore is demanded, Eileen asks the band for "It's Love"—a character song from the *Wonderful Town* score! This is not unlike Aunt Eller's asking Curley to entertain at *Oklahoma!*'s sociable with "I Cain't Say No."

But wait. *Wonderful Town*'s book is dependable, its picture of young people seeking self-fulfillment is heartening, and it pleases even today. Comden and Green count a highly erratic career, but *Wonderful Town* is one of its high points—one of Bernstein's, too. The three were in stronger form in their other valentine to New York, *On the Town* (1944). But that marks one of the musical's rare moments of historical accomplishment, like *Show Boat*, *The Cat and the Fiddle*, *Oklahoma!*, *The Golden Apple*, and *Cabaret* a genuine invention. *Wonderful Town* isn't an invention, but an extra-fine-tuning of an established format.

Now look at *Wonderful Town*'s quirks. You want thirties music? Here are its vamps, hooks, and angles, starting with the big-band pickup that launches the overture, its brass choirs and heavy walking bass notes, as sturdy as organ pedals in Bach. The first-act curtain goes up on an apotheosis of the *secondo* vamp of the once-ubiquitous four-hand piano version of "Heart and Soul." Genuine pre-hipster anomie pervades the dazed, late-in-the-dance-marathon brassiness of the "Ballet at the Village Vortex."

There is a lot of pastiche in the score, as if it had been *composed* during the 1930s—"Swing," that "Wrong Note Rag," the amiably thumping boogie bass of "Ohio." In "Conga," the craze for South American dance is revived. We even get an Irish clog dance, after the conga gets out of control and Eileen is arrested. Act Two starts in jail (with a lengthy book scene, a bold defiance of the rule that fifties second acts always begin with music), and the number, when we get to it, is "My Darlin' Eileen," a part-song in Gaelic style for the cops at the precinct house, to a man the slaves of their prisoner.*

We praise also Bernstein's sense of unity, as when snatches of songs turn up in other songs ("Ohio" in "What a Waste," "What a Waste" in "Pass That Football"). However, two numbers in particular set *Wonderful Town* apart. The famous one is "Conversation Piece," not a song but a musical scene depicting the awkward silences and faux pas of an all too motley group of people trying to socialize. Bernstein outlines it with a dragging shrug in the brass, rings in yet another quotation of one of the evening's available melodies, and promptly revamps this into a cute and tight texture of strings and woodwinds. But nothing takes. The draggy noise returns as, one by one, each character attempts to erect a conversation that simply will not firm up. It's a rare moment in the musical: naturalistic, descriptive, telling of something we've all experienced in life but never had deconstructed for us musically before.

The other distinctive number isn't sung—arresting in itself, for in any other musical it would been. This is "Story Vignettes," in which a magazine editor reads Ruth's submitted stories at stage right while Russell and company enact them at stage left. Like *Wonderful Town*'s score, the stories are pastiche, cheap copies of, first, Hemingway, then working-class problem drama, then *New Yorker* sophistication. There is musical underscoring but, again, not a note of song, so this is presumably bookwriters' turf; yet the section is in fact by lyricists Comden and Green. It has their paradoxical burlesque that is at once cunning and sophomoric, pointed and vulgar. Onstage, the fun lay less in the writers' version of Hemingway ("It was a fine day for a lion hunt. Yes, it was a good clean day for an African lion hunt—a good clean day for a fine clean kill") and so on than in Russell's quick-change stunt. Playing the heroine of all three stories, she had to race on and

---

* Another George Abbott story: Edith Adams was having trouble getting the laughs in the scene till Abbott told her to play it as though the jailhouse were a mansion and she its mistress. Thereafter, the scene went over. So he *did* know how to talk to actors?

off in a completely different outfit in seconds. In the third vignette, "Exit Laughing," the Dorothy Parker tone is established with the delicately euphemistic "Everyone agreed that perhaps Tracey drank too much"—so of course Russell staggered onstage sozzled blind.

What makes *Wonderful Town* special—what made it, above all, new when it *was* new—was its alchemical expertise, its revitalization of old work. *Hazel Flagg* completely lost touch with its source, and *The Girl in Pink Tights* was an old show with a new star. *Wonderful Town* was state of the art.

Let's take the measure of this art in two musical comedies with a lot in common, *The Pajama Game* (1954) and *Damn Yankees* (1955). Each was a George Abbott show based on a novel, Abbott collaborating on the script with the novel's author. Each was produced by Frederick Brisson, Robert E. Griffith, and Harold Prince, had a score by Richard Adler and Jerry Ross and choreography by Bob Fosse. (*The Pajama Game* also counted on Jerome Robbins, billed as Abbott's co-director.) Each depended on three leads: a comic and a romantic couple. And each ran a bit over a thousand performances, a two-and-a-half-year stay, extremely imposing in those days.

There are minor likenesses as well—each includes an entertainment-at-a-rally number in Act Two just for the song-and-dance of it, each had Rae Allen in the cast, and so on. What matters is how two shows so comparable in outline are so dissimilar in effect. *The Pajama Game*, from Richard Bissell's *7½ Cents*, treats labor relations in a midwestern pajama factory, where management refuses to grant the raise that has been sweeping the industry. The comic is Vernon Hines (Eddie Foy, Jr.), the factory's efficiency expert, paired with the manager's secretary, Gladys (the wonderfully daffy Carol Haney). The primary lovers are Sid Sorokin (John Raitt), the new factory superintendant, obviously on management's side, and Babe Williams (Janis Paige), on labor's: *Romeo and Juliet*. There's little more to the plot than that Sid at length gets Gladys drunk, steals her key to the factory's account book, and discovers that the crooked manager has budgeted the raise without actually granting it. The union wins and both couples unite.

Oddly, with little story to work with, the book is excellent, fast and funny but very sharp on character interaction. The score is fine, too, featuring an unBroadwaylike top forty sound in such numbers as "Hernando's Hideaway," "Once a Year Day," and the country-flavored "There Once Was a Man." Any one of these could have been written on its own as a pop tune, but the show's hit, "Hey There," was a ballad with a catch—Raitt sang it in his office while the dictaphone was running, then replayed the tape to duet with his own voice.

It's worth our while to look at *The Pajama Game*'s exposition, a notably cagey integration of words and music in this very age of integration. The show starts cute: Eddie Foy dances onstage in front of the show curtain, a mass of fabric swatches. "This is a very serious drama," he announces. "A problem play," he says. "Capital and Labor," he tells us. "I wouldn't bother to make such a point of all this," he explains, "except later on, if you happen to see a lot of naked women being chased through the woods, I don't want you to get the wrong impression." Then he assures us, "This play is full of symbolism." At last he swings into the title number, barely fifteen seconds long, then calls our attention to the Sleep-Tite atelier. "Let her go!" he cries, as the show curtain rises on the factory in full swing. Secondary principals enter, to Foy's thumbnail characterizations.* The seven-and-a-half-cent raise is mentioned, and the boss vows to fight it.

Now for the first real number, "Racing With the Clock," the men in constant motion and singing in counterpoint to the women, sedentary at their sewing machines. Solo lines emphasize the raise and discuss the new superintendant, keeping our minds on the show's through-line and readying the romance.

The music over, Raitt himself appears for an establishing scene and song, "A New Town Is a Blue Town." He's a tough, sensible guy, no frills. He shoves an impossibly lazy worker, then must face the workers' grievance committee, headed by Paige. It's love at first sight, as in all the best musical comedies, but only Raitt is

---

* Thereafter, Foy yields up his narrator status until the show's climax, when the union gets its wage hike. "I told you this show was full of symbolism," he tells the audience.

ready to admit it. Paige needs a little encouraging, so the other girls twit her in "I'm Not at All in Love," a masterpiece of denial in waltz time. Thus, some twenty minutes into the show, we know, one, what it's about, and, two, who everyone is—all seven principals.

Again and again, this is Rodgers and Hammerstein thinking: skillful playcrafting and synoptic songs even in the merest diversion of a show, the kind that used to need only hot comedy, top tunes, and splashy personality. The Pajama Game even had a dream ballet, not a Rodgers and Hammerstein invention but a form they popularized. Damn Yankees, too, is a comedy-tunes-and-personality show; but if The Pajama Game is a so-so story with an excellent book, Damn Yankees is an excellent story with a functional book, amusing but cluttered with pointless subsidiary characters and a somewhat implausible second act.

Of course, Damn Yankees is a fantasy, so it's entirely implausible: Joe, a middle-aged baseball fanatic supporting the Washington Senators, makes a Faustian pact to turn twenty-two and play as an infernal champion for the Senators, cheating the Yankees of their annual pennant. The devil (Ray Walston) is the comic; his chief temptress, Lola (Gwen Verdon, in her first, and now starring, role since Can-Can), formerly the ugliest woman in Providence, Rhode Island, and Joe's younger self (Stephen Douglass) are the couple. Douglass gets his dream come true and a sexy tamale. What more could a man want?

His wife. Damn Yankees, for all its baseball background, is a love story. This gives it its power. Though the hit tune was "(You've gotta have) Heart," though Verdon's "Whatever Lola Wants" gave birth to a national catchphrase, and though the show's identifying number was Fosse's ballet for ballplayers, "Shoeless Joe from Hannibal, Mo," the Damn Yankees music that stays in the ear comprises three love songs—"Goodbye, Old Girl," "Near To You," and "A Man Doesn't Know"—all sung by Joe about or to his wife. "Near To You" is especially poignant, as Joe sings it while literally near to her, though of course all that she sees is a sympathetic young man she scarcely knows.

So, while The Pajama Game actually makes us care about its macguffin, the seven and a half cents, Damn Yankees never interests us in whether or not the Senators win the pennant. (They do.) The show interests us in something very rare in the musical, a couple whose boy-meets-girl occurred a generation earlier. Thus, we cannot root for Gwen Verdon—despite her conversion from the hero's seducer to his supporter—though she naturally claimed some stage time with Douglass and even sang a sort of lovers' duet with him, "Two Lost Souls," another Adler–Ross pop tune.

Nor can we root for the comic, however charming Ray Walston was, with his trick entrance (evil music in the pit, old Joe looks apprehensively offstage left, drawing the public's eye as Walston slips on stage *right*, having in effect "materialized"), his straight-man setup of some fine jests (WALSTON: Have a good trip? VERDON: Perfect. The plane crashed in Cleveland.), and his deadpan comic solo, "Those Were the Good Old Days."

Nor was Stephen Douglass of much use to the love story: because he wasn't who he was. In *Carousel* (in London), *Make a Wish*, and *The Golden Apple*, Douglass had been The Man I Love. In *Damn Yankees* he was a spook. The lovers were the old guys, Shannon Bolin and Robert Shafer, because *Damn Yankees* is musical comedy turned on its side.

It doesn't play that way. It plays conventionally, because George Abbott staged it. But its subject matter and characters are not conventional. This far had the musical come: even its potboilers were mystery meat now.

The revue, however, was an empty pan. One full-scale variety evening, *John Murray Anderson's Almanac* (1953) lasted half a year, disappointing for a carefully wrought bill headlining Hermione Gingold and Harry Belafonte. Worse, most revues were now no more than one-person cabarets—Anna Russell (with a supporting cast), Ethel Waters, pianist Victor Borge's *Comedy in Music*, all in 1953; the forgotten but not gone Libby Holman in 1954; the English Joyce Grenfell (with three dancers) and the French Maurice Chevalier in 1955.

The outstanding such entry was *An Evening With Beatrice Lillie* (1952), with duo-pianists Eadie and Rack in the pit, Reginald Gardiner to spell the diva, and Lillie at her peak in old and new material. Most comics spoof the everyday; Lillie spoofed the ridiculous, which rendered her opaque and transparent at once, a genuine one-and-only. In a set burlesquing folk songs, she accompanied herself on a zither that kept snapping strings, at that for a song that was terminally quaint in the first place. One verse began, "Now, you must have seen fairies at play."

So the oldtime variety revue was dead; but opera was alive and almost well. In 1952, Charles Friedman arranged Verdi much as Oscar Hammerstein had arranged Bizet in 1943, resetting *Aida* from Memphis, Egypt, to Memphis, Tennessee, during the 1860s. But *Carmen*, lean and sexy, is almost a musical, with spoken dialogue between its numbers, and thus traveled nicely into *Carmen Jones*. *Aida*, a grand opera, may be too ceremonial to transfer to Broadway. Gian Carlo Menotti's *The Saint of Bleecker Street* (1954) did somewhat better, winning the Pulitzer Prize (in music) and the Drama Critics Circle Award for Best Musical. Still, the exemplary exhibit in the category of Broadway opera was *The Golden Apple* (1954).

This must be the most celebrated of shows that are not properly canonical. Writers praise it vastly, as did New York's critics. John McClain of the *Journal-American* called it "a milestone in the American musical theatre," Robert Coleman of the *Mirror* thought it "the most original and imaginative work of its kind," and John Chapman of the *Daily News* pronounced it "the best thing that has happened in and to the theatre in a very long time."

A resetting of the *Iliad* and *Odyssey* in America during the first decade of the twentieth century, *The Golden Apple* is yet another show that embodies fifties energies—in its experimental nature, its heavy dance component, its array of new performing talent. One odd fact: while it played Broadway, it actually opened way downtown at the Phoenix Theatre, one of New York's many attempts to institute a permanent "repertory" company—that is, without true rep's rotating schedule and fixed acting pool but at least restaging classics of a noncommercial nature. Each year, the Phoenix also tried one new musical: *Sandhog* (1954), a kind of Popular Front period piece on the men who built the first New York City river tunnel; a couple of revues; and an adaptation of *Tom Sawyer* as *Livin' the Life* (1957).

The Golden Apple was the first in this series, and the only one

that has lasted, because its glowingly tuneful music (by Jerome
Moross) is wedded to what may be the single most brilliant set of
lyrics ever written for Broadway, by John Latouche. The ingenuity
with which Moross and Latouche pursued their subject is an article of faith among the cognoscenti: Helen is a smalltown trollop,
Paris a traveling salesman who arrives by air balloon, Odysseus a
soldier-of-fortune, seeing America jump from an agricultural village to an industrial city with a can-do philosophy and a trick of
turning a fast buck anywhere it looks. The piece is through-sung
(that is, without spoken lines) but delineated in clear-cut numbers—solos, duets, ensemble scenes—giving the whole a light,
fleet quality, all the more so in that there is no single dance number though dance permeates the piece.*

As *The Golden Apple*'s first act is entirely taken up with events
leading up to the *Iliad*—the first curtain falls as Paris carries Helen off in his balloon—the second act starts with the *Iliad* proper,
the Trojan War being played as a boxing match between Odysseus
(here called by his Roman equivalent, Ulysses) and Paris. The rest
of the act transforms the *Odyssey* picaresque into a vaudeville bill,
with Calypso as a parvenue salon hostess, Scylla and Charybdis
as stockbrokers à la "Mr. Gallagher and Mr. Shean," the Siren as
a lurid showgirl, and Circe as the louche queen of Nighttown. As
Coleman put it: "A magnificent achievement! A sensational success! A superlative feat!"

Yet audiences don't take to it. Designers William and Jean
Eckart assured the Phoenix's managers, T. Edward Hambleton
and Norris Houghton, that with a series of stylized drops and
pieces they could budget the show at $75,000, which gave them
some leeway in taking time to attract a public. This allowed *The
Golden Apple* to transfer uptown to the Alvin (now the Neil
Simon), and it racked up 173 performances in all, too few to pay
off. It was recorded and it has been revived here and there. But
unlike *Candide*, the comparable fifties title that turned a succès

---

* *The Golden Apple*'s genre is, technically, the "ballet ballad," meaning a
musical-theatre piece whose constituents of words, music, and choreography are
so integrated that all three seem to be working simultaneously. The ballet ballad
was invented by John Murray Anderson in the *Greenwich Village Follies* series
of the 1920s, though Anderson did not call it by this term.

d'estime into commercial success, *The Golden Apple* remains a cult item.

Maybe it's too intelligent. Maybe the public doesn't know its Homer well enough to appreciate Latouche's gloss on him, turning a Heroic Age into an era of entrepreneurs. Maybe the "art" public heard too much pop in Moross's music and the pop lovers were bewildered by his artistry. Maybe the score's sole hit, "Lazy Afternoon," should have been a more conventionally pleasing ballad like "Wish You Were Here" or "Hey, There" instead of a sinuously erotic bit of foolery. (It is, in fact, a "duet" for Helen, who only sings, and Paris, who only dances, the whole made extra sexy but also extra goofy when Helen grabs at Paris's collar and his suit jacket comes off, leaving him half-naked in pants, suspenders, and dickey.) Maybe the fifties musical had at last become so sophisticated that it might outstrip its audience, something a popular art by its very nature shouldn't do. But then, part of the American musical's paradoxical ontology finds it eternally seeking new ways in which to entertain.

Perhaps some ways are newer than others. *The Golden Apple*'s way was to narrate an old fable in a novel way, obviously—but its score, too, comprised revisions of old forms—the patriotic march, the barn-dance promenade, the aforementioned "Gallagher and Shean" duet, the Hawaiian number, and so on. Almost everything one hears in *The Golden Apple* is an analytical reflection of something, the whole work thus assembling a view of American culture.

The Golden Apple's cast was particularly new, its credits flourishing a kind of early fifties rolodex. Kaye Ballard, Helen, had just played Rose Marie's role in *Top Banana*'s national tour. Stephen Douglass, Ulysses, is well known to us already, and his Penelope, Priscilla Gillette, had been the ingenue in another show with characters out of an ancient Greek phone book (the Mt. Olympus edition), *Out of This World*. And Paris, Jonathan Lucas, had been featured in the *Of Thee I Sing* revival. Amid all these new faces was one old one, that of Jack Whiting, a leading juvenile in the late 1920s and 1930s who, as the treacherous, oily Mayor of the Industrial Era that devours Ulysses' companions, *Odyssey*-style, was playing a part very like the one he had played in *Hazel Flagg*, as the Mayor, really, of New York City.

Except for Ballard, none of these people made stardom. The always useful Whiting had long been taken for granted, as was Douglass, the latest in a series of ingratiating baritones that the musical needed but seldom celebrated. Gillette and Lucas played their few roles, then went their way. There were just too many stars on view at this time for anyone to notice The Others, however capable they were. This seems ironic today, when the musical has lost both the ability to create stars and the talent pool from which, for example, an extravagant singer and comedienne like Ballard could be found to play a rutting but mainly zany Helen, who runs off with Paris less for romance than to do a little shopping and get her "picture in the papers."

It's hard for younger people nowadays to realize what dense and immediate fame could attach itself to making a hit on Broadway. Take Julie Andrews, a scant eighteen years old when she played the heroine of Sandy Wilson's *The Boy Friend* (1954), one of only two English book musicals to try New York in this decade, and the only one to try Broadway. *The Boy Friend*'s many principal roles marked it as an ensemble show, and the poster named none of the players. Still, the critics singled Andrews out as someone to know of, and she was the talk of the town, much as Gwen Verdon had been when she stole *Can-Can* from Lilo. Neither became a household name overnight; it was a New York thing, a theatregoer's thing. After playing *The Boy Friend* for a year, Andrews got the lead in a TV musical, *High Tor* (1956), then lucked into *My Fair Lady*, almost certainly because of *The Boy Friend*, where Andrews' porcelain English naiveté contrasted with the overstated eccentricity of the rest of the cast.

It had not been so in England, where *The Boy Friend* was staged delicately, with a whole cast of naifs. Here is yet another new-old item, a takeoff on the twenties musical that, for all its tintypes of specific twenties songs, is a completely different piece, small and tightly constructed where twenties shows were spacious and chaotic. Originally a ninety-minute insider's joke produced "for the trade" at London's Players' Club in 1953, the piece was expanded and moved to the West End the following year for a five-year run.

Feuer and Martin, producers of *Where's Charley?*, *Guys and Dolls*, and *Can-Can*, bought it for Broadway with the stated intention of remounting it *exactly* as it had appeared at Wyndham's Theatre. No . . . one thing had to be changed, the London pit of two pianos and a very, very polite drummer. Broadway would hear the score with a twenties-style jazz band in the pit. Otherwise, it would be an *urecht Boy Friend* as originally directed by Vida Hope in Reginald Woolley's designs to John Heawood's choreography.

Then Feuer and Martin became unhappy with the tryout performances, and demanded alterations. No . . . *made* them. Wilson and Hope found themselves physically barred from the theatre; actors would be fired one day and rehired the next; one song was dropped; and Hope's atmosphere of fond bemusement was turned into outright lampoon. But that's how New York liked the show. Critics even mentioned the backstage troubles as if they were part of the fun.

There's something odd here. The English musical had been influential in America around 1900 and would be again with the coming of pop opera. In the 1950s, however, it was the American musical that colonized the world. The English musical was, largely, either throwbacks or unusual but parochial ventures such as *Expresso Bongo* (1958), *Valmouth* (1958), or *Make Me an Offer* (1959). Yet this same little English *Boy Friend* recalled the public to a pageant of history: the ongoing development of characters, structures, themes, and various spare parts that claimed both a tradition and a future. This is a form in its maturity, vitality, ingenuity. Anything can happen.

7

Fanny & New Girl in Town

When the Third Age began, in the 1920s, musicals could emphasize either a vaudeville structure or a narrative one. The vaudeville format included not only revue itself but the use, in story shows, of specialty acts and extraneous scenes to fill out scrawny plot lines—a ballroom couple covering a scene change or a singer "entertaining" in a party scene.

In the 1950s, the musical had two different choices of structure: the musical play and musical comedy. Think of it as *The King and I* or *Call Me Madam*.

The two forms had much in common, but one element especially: interesting stories, untried stories, stories with an angle were what producers wanted to stage, what authors wanted to write, what performers wanted to play. It's notable that, while no twenties musical saw its script published for a reading audience in the 1920s, six thirties titles were published in the 1930s,* and

---

* A number of twenties titles were published in the 1930s and after, but only in "acting editions" for stock and amateur companies. The six thirties titles were

about fifteen were published in the 1940s. But in the 1950s virtually every successful show (and a few failures) was issued in book form.

Clearly, the scripts were getting interesting; and here are two interesting tales for you, both set on the waterfront. In one, a young man obsessed with sea travel impregnates, than abandons, the girl he loves, forcing her to wed a tolerant older man hungry for a male heir. Then the young man returns.

In the second story, a man-hating prostitute, reunited with her father, becomes rehabilitated, especially after falling in love with a sailor. Then he learns of her past and cruelly rejects her.

I've had occasion already to point out how unsuitable such stories would have been only a decade before; but the 1950s were keen. Then, too, isn't the first story, set very evocatively among the fisherfolk of Marseilles, the kind of thing that our ubiquitous revolutionaries Rodgers and Hammerstein would love to tackle? David Merrick thought so. He had been much taken by Marcel Pagnol's trilogy of films from the 1930s, *Marius*, *Fanny*, and *César*, when they finally made it to the United States after World War II, and saw in them the basis for a musical, written by Rodgers and Hammerstein and directed by Joshua Logan, that would at once found and define the producing career of David Merrick, Esquire.

Film historians differ on the quality of the three movies. The first two, based on plays, seem to some stage-bound; the third, the only one that Pagnol not only wrote but also directed, sentimentalizes. All agree that the trilogy is loaded with atmosphere, the very thing that Rodgers and Hammerstein (as in *Carousel*'s New England or *The King and I*'s Asian court) conveyed so well. Merrick actually went to France and knocked on Pagnol's door to sew up the rights; and Rodgers and Hammerstein were interested in the material. But Rodgers wasn't willing to work with Merrick, or even share producer credit with him. When Hammerstein suggested they give Merrick an "In association with" billing—as, indeed, Merrick had had on his only previous producing venture—

---

all shows with strong political content: *Of Thee I Sing*, *Let 'Em Eat Cake*, *Johnny Johnson*, *The Cradle Will Rock*, *I'd Rather Be Right*, and *Knickerbocker Holiday*.

Rodgers replied, "I wouldn't give that schmuck a glass of water if he was on fire."

Logan signed on, to direct and co-write the book (with S. N. Behrman). Astonishingly, so did composer-lyricist Harold Rome, that master of the working-class New York sound. The homeboy Rome, amid the salty Mediterraneans of Provence? Yet it was a bizarre facet of the musical play that it not only attracted musical comedy writers but inspired them. Confronted with Pagnol's two young lovers, *his* bullying father, and *her* Don Pasquale of a husband, Rome wrote music teeming with character—*these* characters—in a score made of bits, songs, leitmotifs, musical scenes, and ensemble numbers that very nearly edge *Fanny* (1954) into opera. The lovers, in fact, are tenor and soprano, and a star opera bass played the boy's father. Here was a score that had, above all, to be sung: in the boy's volatile oath of fidelity to the sea, "Restless Heart"; his guiltily ambivalent declaration of love, "(Only you, long as I may live) Fanny"; her descant to a reprise of "Restless Heart," beginning "Does He Know?"; her frantic declaration, "I Have To Tell You"; the father and son duet, "I Like You"; the father's "Welcome Home," a touching hymn to the pleasures of the sedentary life; and the buoyant marriage proposal of the man who will save Fanny from shame, "Panisse and Son."

Rome made use of a bit of ethnic pastiche suggesting the European environment, and a mandolin in Philip J. Lang's orchestrations* registered a sense of place. But Rome's main work lay in the establishing and then intertwining of character motifs— "Restless Heart," "Fanny," "I Have To Tell You," and "Welcome Home" are not only reprised but combined, torn apart, and recombined, just as the characters themselves are. Rome was growing as a technician, too: in the complex harmonic structure of the title song's release, which moves from the relative minor of the home key through a series of tortured altered chords to an aug-

---

* One of the many distinguishing marks of the Third-Age musical is its elastic view of instrumentation. In comparable golden ages—from Offenbach to Messager in France, or the time of Strauss and Lehár in German lands—one pit band resembled another. American shows seek not only unique stories but unique sound styles to fit those stories.

mented dominant seventh; or in the "Nursery Round," in which ten groups of visitors admiring Fanny's newborn each sing their own snatch of melody, all ten snatches then sounding against each other in a potpourri.*

Most notable is the way the music keeps slipping into the book scenes, emotionalizing them as if the Broadway musical's venerable alternation of dialogue and song felt too pat for a tale this charged. Marius (William Tabbert) loves Fanny (Florence Henderson), but, even more, he loves the sea, or so he thinks. After marrying the sea, he realizes that he loves Fanny more, but by then she is the wife of Panisse (Walter Slezak), and this interloper is raising Marius's son.

See how beautifully Rome builds the dramatic climax of Act Two, Marius's return. This of course occurs at the height of Panisse and Fanny's happiness, their baby's first birthday. "To My Wife," Panisse's solo, fixes the moment for us with charm. The birthday party breaks up, Panisse departs for Paris . . . and Marius appears in the window. Almost menacingly, he paces through the house, as the orchestra underscores Fanny's anxiety. Marius knows that the baby is his—the rising ninth of "Panisse and Son" rears out of the pit—and, seconds later, Marius breaks into "The Thought of You," so lyrical yet so tormented, culminating in Marius's taking over Fanny's "I Have To Tell You" as she repeatedly cries "No!" Just before the song's end, Marius and Fanny are in each other's arms, passionately kissing. But Marius's father, César (Ezio Pinza) has entered; he separates them to a crashing dissonance. A sadly ironic "Welcome Home" accompanies the embrace of father and son. Then Panisse comes back from the station, and all four principals—the two lovers and the two fathers—are alone on stage in the most intimate moment of their lives:

PANISSE: For a long time now I've been trying to go to Paris on business, haven't I, César? I've missed every train. Every time I put my foot on the platform I would say, "This is

---

* Actually, Rome had already tried out this form in the wonderful opening to *Call Me Mister* (1946), "Goin' Home Train."

the night Marius is coming back." What if he tries to take everything away from me?

More "Panisse and Son" has run through that speech. Now the orchestra is silent as Panisse politely defies Marius and leaves. Fanny follows him. "Who is the father?" Marius demands. "The one who gives life or the one who buys the bibs?" César replies, "The father is the one who loves," and the orchestra is back again, preparing for "Love Is a Very Light Thing," César's solo.

Still more comes in this chain of numbers—Fanny's "Other Hands, Other Hearts," which, again, bursts into the title song as the three realize that Marius and Fanny are the loves of each other's lives—yet the sooner Marius departs, forever, the sooner real life can continue. *The father is the one who loves.* All three male leads are fathers, all love, and all, one way or another, self-ishly destroy love. César virtually throws Marius out of the house as the stricken Fanny collapses.

How could this tale end but in Panisse's death, making it possible for Fanny and Marius at last to solemnize their love? So *Fanny* ends. Yet this frantically despairing tale was fitted with one of the most humorous books of the day. Even the finale, César visiting Panisse's deathbed, was played for fun.* A lot of this comedy was maybe just the slightest bit forced:

> HONORINE (FANNY'S MOTHER): You're going to have a child!
> Oh, my God in heaven, it's not true!
> FANNY: Oh, Mama, it's true!
> HONORINE: You dishonest girl! It's lucky your father's not
> alive—this would kill him! . . . Who was it? Marius? (FANNY
> *nods*.) Oh, that Marius, with his dreamy eyes. Now we
> know what he was dreaming about! . . . Thank the good
> Lord my mother is tucked away in her grave. Well, she
> always did sleep through every crisis.
> FANNY: Mama! Mama! What am I to do?

---

* Oscar Hammerstein did Logan the favor of catching *Fanny* during its tryout. Said Hammerstein, "It'll work if you get a good ending"—for the finale that Hammerstein saw was dreary and maudlin. Logan and Behrman rewrote it for shameless comedy that somehow enabled the audience to approve of yet regret the passing of Panisse. Pinza and Slezak hated the new script till they heard the public laughing, whereupon they began to milk the scene for yet more jokes.

HONORINE: Do? Marry Panisse!

FANNY: But Panisse won't marry me when he finds out.

HONORINE: He mustn't find out! Don't bother Panisse with details like that! . . . Besides, you can't be sure you're having a baby . . . Why tell the truth when it might not even be the truth?

FANNY: If it's not the truth, then I don't have to get married.

HONORINE: You can get married without being pregnant. Lots of girls do it.

Still, in terms of sheer character conflict, this was one of the biggest stories since *Carousel*, and Logan managed not to lose sight of it in an at times massive production. There were staging tricks both small and large: one scene change began with a blackout into which, quite suddenly, one spotlight beamed down on a near-naked Arab dancing girl, swaying to sensually exotic music, a truly shocking moment for the time. Another scene change leading to a wedding party began with a bouquet flying in the air at stage left as a girl ran in from the right to catch it. Helen Tamiris's choreography was of the non-showy sort until a gigantic "Circus Ballet" late in Act Two, and Jo Mielziner figured out a way to present Marius's ship departing Marseilles as a crowd waved farewell and César desperately called Marius's name, a spectacular sight. Merrick had done well. He still had to share producing credit, with Joshua Logan. But *Fanny*, a fourteen-month hit in New York and a reasonably solid contender at Drury Lane, did indeed put Merrick on the map.

New Girl in Town (1957), the prostitute's tale, is, like *Fanny*, from a source that could not have been considered a decade earlier, Eugene O'Neill's *Anna Christie*. This play started as a comedy called *Chris Christophersen* (1920), about a barge captain who hates the sea, finds a new value in life when he takes in his long-lost daughter, then feels double-crossed when she falls in love with a sailor.

Chris Christophersen has the usual faults of O'Neill in the 1920s—the repetitions, the outlandish use of dialect, the naturalism so blunt it seems unnatural. It has the O'Neill virtues, too—the solid construction, the old-fashioned love of a Good Scene, the expert knowledge of how relentlessly most people go about designing their own doom. O'Neill's ear may be faulty, but his psychology is so densely persuasive that, again and again, one picks up an O'Neill script expecting something antique and transitional. And one finds that: but also genius. *Chris Christophersen* folded out of town (though Lynn Fontanne played the daughter, Anna), but a revision, *Anna Christie* (1921) succeeded, with Pauline Lord making something special out of the daughter. *Anna Christie* is smaller in size, shorter in length, and harder in spirit than *Chris Christophersen*. Anna, a stenographer with middle-class English manners in the first play, is now a rough-mouthed former streetwalker, most of the comedy is gone, and the ending is ambivalent, not tragic but less happy than sort of hopeful. It has every advantage over its predecessor, particularly in the building up of Marthy, Chris's girl friend, who originally had but seconds on stage with Anna. The *Anna Christie* Marthy enjoys one of the best-known scenes in all twenties theatre—because of the chemistry between Greta Garbo and Marie Dressler in MGM's very faithful early talkie adaptation—when the two meet in a bar. ("I got your number the minute you stepped in the door," Marthy challenges; and "I got yours, too, with no trouble," Anna replies. "You're me forty years from now.")

Even a show that veered far from O'Neill would have to be a musical play, what with a bitter protagonist and a truly dodgy romance—for Anna's sailor boy friend, having taken her for an angel, is all the more abusive when he learns of her past. True, there are plenty of chances for musical comedy fun. Marthy, already a comic, has only to be expanded (in O'Neill, she disappears after the first of four acts), and the addition of the local Democratic Club's Check Apron Ball right in the middle of the action provisions a few ensemble numbers.

Still, the bulk of *New Girl in Town*—the central triangle of father, daughter, sailor—is a serious story. So it's all the more surprising that the piece was something of a follow-up to *Damn Yankees*, with the same producers, librettist–director, choreographer, and star, Gwen Verdon: musical comedy people. It would appear that the original plan was to let the enjoyable song-and-dance stuff spin *around* the three principals, leaving them with the core of O'Neill to act and with just enough character and love

songs to hold their place in the score. It wasn't a bad idea. Verdon
was a marvelous actress and not all that great a singer. But a
musical in which Gwen Verdon doesn't dance a lot is like an opera
in which Carmen doesn't sing.

And so, bit by bit, dance crept into Verdon's part, until the *New
Girl in Town* that opened in New York was something of a musical
play framed by a musical comedy. Most of Bob Merrill's score
provides atmosphere, an excuse for Bob Fosse dancing, or numbers for Marthy, Verdon's above-the-title co-star, the immortal
Thelma Ritter. Only six numbers were related to plot or character.
(A seventh, "Here We Are Again," for the sailor's reconciliation
with Anna when they meet again in the last scene, was cut.) The
rest was good-time fill—"Sunshine Girl," a kind of barbershop trio
sung to a player piano accompaniment with a prominent banjo
part in the pit; "Flings," women's comic nostalgia on the sensual
life; "At the Check Apron Ball," a Fosse coup de théâtre wherein
a line of boys and girls paraded in their dance-hall finery from
stage left to stage right in front of the traveler curtain, the line
apparently endless until the audience realized that the exiting
players were tearing back behind the traveler to stage left and re-
entering; "There Ain't No Flies On Me," the big ball number in
that it brought the first-act curtain down on almost the entire cast
doing a can-can in one great line and a second coup de théâtre
in that the second-act curtain rose on exactly the same picture,
one second later.

Maybe this was the best route for Bob Merrill to travel on his
first Broadway show. A primitive who had heretofore written pop
tunes composed on a toy xylophone ("How Much Is That Doggie
in the Window?" was his biggest hit), he nevertheless responded
well to the core action, finding just the note of C Major purity
for "Did You Close Your Eyes?," after the lovers' first kiss, when
Anna feels, truly, virginal, yet ripping into Anna's sour outlook in
the savage "On the Farm."*

---

* One curiosity of the fifties musical: its honesty in tackling adult subjects
placed it ahead of national standards of "taste," and some show scores had to
be bowdlerized when recorded. "Damn" became "darn," especially in *New Girl
in Town*; the climax of "On the Farm" was disconnected from "Vicious sons of
bitches" to "Lecherous, treacherous cousins."

New Girl in Town was a hit, though not as big a one as *Fanny*. And while *Fanny* is revivable, *New Girl in Town* probably isn't, because its success depended largely on its staging—on, really, the irreplaceable Fosse and Verdon. *Fanny* was more a grand than a great staging; *New Girl in Town* was a great staging. Its sets and costumes were functional (though Verdon's entrance, with the star kitted out in the gaudiest of Tenderloin regalia from picture hat to checked spats, drew gasps) and its direction was the typical George Abbott "keep the actors from bumping into each other" practicality. But Fosse took control about one and a half minutes into the first scene, when a bunch of homecoming sailors swaggered on to greet the ladies of the harbor and plan a little recreation in "Roll Yer Socks Up." It's a basic musical comedy number, a reason for dancing.

A proper musical play doesn't waste its first number this way. It gets right into the exposition (e.g., "When the Boys Come Home," "The Carousel Waltz," "The Hills of Ixopo") or into character ("Oh, What a Beautiful Mornin'," "I Whistle a Happy Tune") or into atmosphere ("Dites-Moi"). *New Girl in Town* isn't a proper musical play; no Fosse show could have been if it had wanted to be.

Some talents in Broadway's history have been essentially musical play talents—Jerome Kern, Oscar Hammerstein, Agnes de Mille, and Hal Prince, for instance. Some have been musical comedy talents—Lorenz Hart, George Abbott, Carol Channing. Some moved freely between the two worlds—George Gershwin, Richard Rodgers, Jerome Robbins, Alfred Drake. One was the essential musical comedy talent, and that was Bob Fosse. His look, his motion, his structures . . . all were rooted in *sexy-now* art, spoofing and grinning and pushing the edge. It's dance with a hard-on, and that's what Fosse gave *New Girl in Town*, from the erotically rollicking boys and girls of the New York waterfront in "Roll Yer Socks Up" to the dream ballet late in Act Two, a musical-play convention that Fosse reinvented as Anna's backstory of bordello inmates and hateful sex with the same man (John Aristides) who tried to force himself on her in the first act with his "Honest, kiddo, I sure seen you somewheres before." The musical play's dream ballet was psychology, and so was Fosse's—but it was also just the kind of all-the-way, banned-in-Boston Fosse wildness that *New Girl in Town* had originally thought it could do without. No way; Gwen Verdon is playing a sexually abused woman in a Fosse show and he's not going to let her tell the public what that's like?

New Girl had to dance; *Fanny* didn't need to, though it danced all the same. Their casting, too, was very different. *Fanny* was full of voice, with Ezio Pinza (his replacement was another former big Met noise, Lawrence Tibbett), along with two very impressive vocalists, Florence Henderson and William Tabbert, his high range in particular a glory of Broadway. Only Walter Slezak fielded one of those just-good-enough-for-Broadway sounds. (And even he had imposing vocal credentials, as the son of the great Heldentenor Leo Slezak.)

New Girl in Town was not full of voice. Verdon's romantic vis-à-vis, George Wallace, had a big round baritone; but there the vocal casting ended. As in any musical, certain roles called for actors whose primary function was to sing well. The bartender of whom Verdon ordered that famous "Whiskey, ginger ale on the side—and don't be stingy, baby" was Mark Dawson, the lead baritone of *High Button Shoes* and *Me and Juliet*, here merely to substantiate "Sunshine Girl" and "There Ain't No Flies on Me." There was a great deal of such casting in the 1950s—little jobs, yet in the long run considered so important that these performers could get poster billing, as not only Dawson but the comparable Del Anderson, Michael Quinn, and H. F. Green did on this one show, just for filling in on the songs in a way that neither Verdon nor Ritter nor the Chris, Cameron Prud'homme, could manage.

Obviously, good singing would be intrinsic, on some level, in the musical play: this form is what operetta turned into when operetta got intelligent. *Fanny* was loaded with it, while *New Girl in Town* depended on George Wallace and field expedients; but what really matters is that the musical play was now absorbing musical comedy talents routinely—Harold Rome, Bob Merrill, George Abbott, Gwen Verdon, Bob Fosse. Moreover, the musical play's dramatic possibilities not only led them to major work but encouraged them to revise the science of craftsmanship as they went along.

This was what was keeping the musical, in all its forms, vigorous: renovation. The lack of it was what destroyed operetta: relying on the same talents to do the same things over and over, it strangled itself with cliché. The fifties musical play, however, had seized artistic leadership, and was increasingly to provide Broadway with its greatest successes. "Is it possible that musical comedy is headed in the direction of opera?" Elie Siegmeister asked at this time, in *Theatre Arts*. "Is the old-time musical comedy form dead?"

Yes, just not yet. Give it another thirty years.

8

By the Beautiful Sea & Plain and Fancy

No, for the time being, musical comedy is secure: *Call Me Madam*, *Guys and Dolls*, *"Wish You Were Here"*, *Can-Can*, *Me and Juliet*, *Wonderful Town*, *The Pajama Game*, *Damn Yankees*, *Silk Stockings*, *Bells Are Ringing*, *Li'l Abner*, *The Music Man*. The 1950s *hosted* musical comedy.

So try this one: turn-of-the-century Coney Island setting; gauche but charming vaudevillian of the third rank romances moderately prominent Shakespearean; the midway, the rides, the fun. Plot hitch number one: her father jumps in on Brooklyn-Bridge-for-sale business opportunities, constantly throwing her finances into chaos. Plot hitch number two: he's divorced but his daughter hates the vaudevillian who would be her stepmother.

It sounds silly. It *was* silly, tricked up in lavish Jo Mielziner–Irene Sharaff designs, a tuneful Arthur Schwartz–Dorothy Fields score, and a star turn by Shirley Booth as the vaudevillian, Lottie Gibson. Well, why not? Booth modeled some terrific period costumes, threw around her slang and mutinous grammar, and wrapped that improbable voice around Fields' comedy lyrics. In short: Aunt Cissy returns.

The problem with *By the Beautiful Sea* (1954) was that all the Shirley Booth in the world can't fill a show without a story. The Herbert and Dorothy Fields book was less interested in character than in maintaining a steady tempo in moving back and forth among the three big sets: one, the backyard of Lottie's theatrical boarding house; two, the Coney Island midway of ferris wheel, Steeplechase Park, and tunnel of love; and three, the Dreamland Casino. In between, obligatory for the scene changes, were the little scenes in one. That meant that a goodly portion of the action was given over to incidentals involving singing waiters, sailors and their dates, and so on. But *that* meant that a goodly portion of the score was made of extraneous ensemble numbers—"Coney Island Boat," "Good Time Charlie," "Hooray for George the Third," "Throw the Anchor Away." Then, too, open-hearted Lottie would have a black housekeeper, not least because Mae Barnes, a dancer in twenties musicals, was lately enjoying a career resurgence in cabaret. But Barnes' two numbers—"Happy Habit" and the big second-act opener, "(If the devil answers) Hang Up"— were written to give Barnes her opportunity, not to illuminate the action.

So we have too little story and a not very integrated score. We also have Wilbur Evans as Booth's Shakespearean, trying to make sense of a role that its authors never really wrote. On his entrance, chased by local fans, he seems snobbish and affected. In other scenes, he's a good guy. He has a confusing relationship with his daughter, a come-and-go one with Booth.

Now we have a story problem, a score problem, and a love-plot problem. Worst of all, *By the Beautiful Sea* was woefully lean in comedy—what, in a Shirley Booth vehicle? Booth's big comic number, "I'd Rather Wake Up By Myself," was a dud, and as the authors had no character in mind for their lead, they couldn't give her an interesting script. It recalls that party that F. Scott Fitzgerald attended when he first made Hollywood, where all the stars were playing themselves—William Powell doing soigné Nick Charles, Joan Crawford desperate for riches, power, Life at the Top! Except without scriptwriters to give them content, they were playing, Scott thought, empty imitations of themselves. *That* was Lottie Gibson: an empty imitation of Aunt Cissy.

However. It is another of the many differences between the musical play and musical comedy that the former is an author's medium and the latter a performer's medium. True, plenty of great performers enlivened the musical play; many brilliant writers gave musical comedy their all. Nevertheless, *South Pacific* works without Ezio Pinza and Mary Martin. Read the script and play through the score: the whole show is there. But it is very difficult to reconstruct *By the Beautiful Sea* in the same way. Too much would be missing.

For instance, what of the sheer visual élan of the opening, curtain up on the boardinghouse yard filled with vaudevillians at practice and play?—a barbershop quartet rehearing "Mona from Arizona," Diablo the magician running through his hocus-pocus, acrobats, a ballerina, a sisters' singing trio wearing identical outfits, a stiltwalker passing by while promoting Steeplechase Park, the housekeeper's nine-year-old son, Half-Note, skipping in to check out Diablo's turn. Here's all the colorful surprise and delight that musical comedy traditionally provided; and the typical snap-to-it! forward motion of the show that wants to sweep you into a dream of happy fun topped off the tableau when Mae Barnes came out onto the porch to shake out an afghan. Hearing the quartet reach its climax, she called out, "All right, boys, rehearsal's over!," the tenor replied, "Wait a minute, Ruby," and the foursome surged into the song's final line, putting a musical cap on the scene. Now for some exposition:

> RUBY: All right, gimme a hand. Take those bathing suits off the fence. Half-Note, get that crate outta here! We gotta clean up this backyard! Miss Lottie'll be in before you know it!

Everybody jumped into action, an automobile horn was heard, and from offstage, in her patented plaintive-sensible timbre, Booth called out, "Ain't no one gonna come out and help me with my boxes?" The audience got ready, and on she came in the moment, now long gone, that we used to take for granted: the absolute pleasure in once more making contact with a beloved talent doing what she was put on earth to do, entertain us. It has been scarcely two minutes since the curtain went up, but we've had a lot to take in both musically and visually, all of it interlocked by timing and gesture to guide the eye, to fake an enjoyable chaos by taking expert control. This is state-of-the-art musical comedy, cleverly bringing Ruby on during the opening number so she can prompt its finish, let out a few words of tell-the-audience-what's happening, to lead right into the Star Walks In and the Show Is On.

Or consider the moment when a peddler with a portable penny arcade photo-viewer offers "Spicy pictures penny a look!" and the stage goes dark to spotlight human depictions of the pictures—"Three Drabs," "The Iceman and the Wife," and "The Snake Charmer"—switching styles with each new shot. Or there's the montage of vaudeville acts when Lottie Gibson does her turn as an appalling tyke—dancers, a tumbler, a female impersonator of the Julian Eltinge sort, act following act like shuffled cards. These are the incidentals of musical comedy, the trivially captivating touches, entirely dependent on the imagination of the staging staff—director, choreographer, and designer(s). The musical play often rose above such chance diversions as being distractingly frivolous, and it is illustrative that the one Rodgers and Hammerstein show that is unrevivable because so much of it *lived* in how it danced and looked and behaved is their one ground-zero musical comedy, *Me and Juliet*.

By the Beautiful Sea's staging team was director Charles Walters, choreographer Helen Tamiris, and, as I've said, designers Jo Mielziner and Irene Sharaff. Walters, a one-time Broadway performer who danced (with June Knight) the pas de deux to "Begin the Beguine" in *Jubilee* and introduced (with Betty Grable) "Ev'ry Day a Holiday" and "Well, Did You Evah?" in *DuBarry Was a Lady*, was by 1954 an MGM choreographer and director (of *Good News, Easter Parade*, and *Lili*, among others). He should have been just what the show needed, but somehow these Hollywood types lose their thespian smarts very quickly—Gene Kelly was completely at sea directing *Flower Drum Song* later in the decade, and, ten years after, the acclaimed Vincente Minnelli did so badly by *Mata Hari* that the show folded out of town. Walters himself folded on *By the Beautiful Sea*, leaving the show during the tryout; Joshua Logan recommended a neophyte, Marshall

Jamison, who oversaw the production through the New York opening.

Helen Tamiris possibly deserves credit for the show's *plus vite qu'ca* pacing. The book was clumsy, but at least it moved. And, every few minutes or so, there was another of those irrelevant ensemble numbers in which Tamiris could proclaim the healthy insanity of the dance.

Mielziner, too, gets credit, for a wonderful stunt involving an air balloon. Desperate for cash because of her father's feckless investments, Booth agrees to take a parachute jump from on high to earn a thousand dollars. Mielziner figured out how to send Booth skyward in the balloon, then get her safely out of the fly loft and down to the stage while a dummy with a parachute was sent crashing down. At the same time, a host of streamers was launched into the air, clouding the public's view of the "jump" and thus comically suggesting that Booth had actually taken a dangerous tumble. She, of course, was hiding behind some set piece and now appeared, groggy but unbowed, in parachute silk. Wilbur Evans, the guest artiste presenting the prize money, is bewildered and alarmed. "Lottie?" he cries. And in one of her few genuinely funny lines of the evening, Booth answers, "Well, you gotta make your own fun around here."

That line is truer than it had a right to be. Her performance, said William Hawkins of the *World-Telegram and Sun*, "is a triumph of mime over clatter." Walter Kerr called her "an easygoing Duse." She couldn't make a dull book funny but she could make it harmless. With Tamiris and Mielziner's help, she more or less herself created an enchanting show. Singing the ancient "In the Good Old Summer Time" in counterpoint to "Coney Island Boat," quoting Shakespeare, pulling those famous vibrant high notes out of who knew where, or playing a scene with Wilbur Evans in the tunnel of love that was as endearing and sad as it was comic— two oldsters uneasily trying to light that spark in cheesy surroundings—Booth was musical comedy itself: bright, fetching, unpredictable. In such a show, story doesn't matter. Talent matters. That's why it's difficult to assess a *By the Beautiful Sea* by the evidence of its written composition. It is the essence of musical comedy that, to comprehend it, one has to be there.

Plain and Fancy (1955), however, is a musical comedy that one could easily resuscitate, because its strength lies in its story and characters and score: musical comedy as an authors' triumph. The scenery was functional, the choreography (again by Tamiris) unimportant, and the parts geared to actors, not bizarro specialists like *Sea's* Booth, Mae Barnes, and all those dancers. *Plain and Fancy* had so much story that it was already narrating during the overture, for the show curtain was a map of Pennsylvania, a spotlight traveling its roads main and minor till at last the overture ended and the lights came up behind the scrim. There was the car, parked at a gas station, and there were its passengers, mild-mannered Dan (Richard Derr) and wisenheimer Ruth (Shirl Conway), absolutely lost. It seems that the two New Yorkers are on their way to Amish country—a town called Bird-in-Hand. Can someone direct them?

Came then a wonderful first number, in effect an opening chorus situated after a brief book scene. But, again, all but the most backward of fifties musicals were now delaying the first sing till a bit of plot could be spun out. Thus, the launching number could treat a certain *situation*, as opposed to establishing in a very empty way a place or time in the tradition that the musical had been thoughtlessly honoring for a century.

Plain and Fancy's situation number is "You Can't Miss It," because not only *can* someone direct them but everyone *wants* to, each by a different route and some to places other than Bird-in-Hand. A weighty grande dame kens a clover-lined valley where General Washington once slept and a kid in a spaceman outfit wants a lift (to the moon). As the song hits its climax, Dan and Ruth drive off in the car, the lights black out, and the ensemble scampers off to change into Pennsylvania Dutch costumes.

That's a clue to why *Plain and Fancy's* authors, composer Albert Hague, lyricist Arnold B. Horwitt, and librettists Joseph Stein and Will Glickman, thought "You Can't Miss It" important. A riot of color and noise, it plays as daffy, fragmented, eccentric. Scene Two begins in the evening twilight as a buggy pulls up at center stage, an Amish farmer and his daughter riding homeward: and we are thrust into another world, one that we gradually learn is all black and white, strict, conventional, uniform. From fancy we have come to plain, in this severely dressed, utterly rustic pair. There is some slight tension. The farmer (Stephan Schnabel) is fierce in his beliefs, his daughter, Katie (Gloria Marlowe), less orthodox. She is about to marry, we learn, but her character song, "It Wonders Me," says nothing about her being in love with her fiancé—in fact, she isn't. It's a love-of-life song, chaste and simple, and an ideal transition for our entry into Bird-in-Hand.

This is an American Brigadoon, an isolated, patriarchal, pre-industrial society. Dan finds it all rather friendly and fascinating; Ruth finds it unbelievable. They have come because Dan wants to look over an old family property before selling it, to that very same farmer, as a wedding gift to Katie and his incipient son-in-law. But Katie loves *his* brother, Peter (David Daniels), sent away from the community as too independent for Amish life. Though the authors don't hammer the point home, these people inhabit a kind of Fascist democracy: no one seems to be in charge yet everyone knows and obeys The Rules. Most strangely, there is no mention of religion. A reference to the coming wedding is phrased as "So in Meeting when I stand," as if these were Quakers instead of the Pennsylvania Dutch.

It's not all that far removed from the atmosphere of Shirley Jackson's "The Lottery," especially in the first-act finale, when the farmer declares that the still rebellious brother be "shunned" (i.e., made outcast) and the community, one by one, files past him unseeing, even the girl who loves him, till he is left utterly alone. There's a feeling of Rodgers and Hammerstein here, too, for their shows often deal with community folkways.

But there is plenty of leavening comedy, almost entirely from Ruth, so wonderfully vivified by the husky-voiced Conway. Again, we marvel at how constantly the fifties musical utilized "Alfred Drake as Hajj" casting virtually through the ranks, in show after show. Ruth, after all, is a stereotype: the sophisticated Manhattanite passing sarcastic remarks about the hicks while she digs into her hatbox for the scotch and wonders why her boy friend hasn't made that pass yet. Eve Arden, right? But Conway found her own approach to Ruth, perhaps because the character doesn't merely stare and remark but tries to meet the Amish on some middle ground. One set piece finds her trying to pitch in in a

crowded kitchen, dashing madly among the butter churn, the water pump, a pot boiling over, the meat grinder, and so on. It's a
hoary gag—the slicker outfoxed by the bumpkins—but a true one,
and it never fails to play.

Of course, all this story and comedy would be nothing without
that particular glory of the fifties musical, the lyrical and clever
but above all *characterized* score. *Plain and Fancy* has a fine one.
Though few theatregoers seem to have noticed it at the time, lyricist Horwitt made no attempt to duplicate the heavy Amish dialect heard in the spoken lines, contenting himself with periodic
Amish inflections ("a farm with Katie goes," "Papa says by Lan-
caster is sinful") in otherwise standard late-middle-Third-Age-
musical-comedy English. Composer Hague, likewise, sought no,
"Amish" sound beyond the hymnlike righteousness of the hard-
liners' anthem, "Plain We Live." What concerned the two was
enriching the story and characters. They did virtually nothing with
Dan, who is something of a stick. But they found music not only
for the solemn aspect of the Amish worldview but also for its
happy-farmer celebrations ("Plenty of Pennsylvania") and sense of
humor ("City Mouse, Country Mouse"). Best of all, perhaps, they
found music for Barbara Cook.

Cook played an odd role, little more than that of "another vil-
lager," cousin of the bride-to-be but not herself romantically attached. The show's two couples were, one, Dan and Ruth, and,
two, Peter and Katie. Cook's role, Hilda Miller, was something
new in the musical, a heroine without a boy friend. She does
develop a crush on Dan, who—in an arrestingly adult and finely
shaded scene—is momentarily startled by her youth and loveliness
and scams a kiss off her before beating an embarrassed retreat.

This leads Cook into a rhapsodic waltz with girls' chorus and a
full-out dance section, "This Is All Very New To Me." It sounds
like—no, it *is* a love song: for a character without a love plot.
Hilda later gets a chorus of Peter's plea to Katie, "Follow Your
Heart," so Cook had a second ballad. Later, gently rebuffed by
Dan, she sang one of those quick and tense "I'll show *him*" num-
bers that the musical exploited in this decade, from *The King and
I*'s "Shall I Tell You What I Think Of You" to *Destry Rides Again*'s
"I Hate Him." Cook's number is called, in fact, "I'll Show Him."

Still later, as an eleven o'clocker, a now forgiving Cook took comic advice from Dan and Ruth in "Take Your Time and Take Your Pick."

It was a strangely lengthy tunestack for a character with almost no part in the actual plot. Yet *Plain and Fancy* is a very tightly constructed work, pulling many elements into one seamless narrative. *By the Beautiful Sea* has few elements in a shapeless story expanded by extracurricular dance numbers. But *Plain and Fancy* ties its two couples together, *Guys and Dolls*-style, in that Dan holds the deed to the farm that we want Peter and Katie to take over, just as Nathan Detroit makes the bet that brings Sky and Miss Sarah Brown together. In all this, Hilda should be excrescent, a character "hired" for the vocals. On the contrary, Hilda is key: she helps personalize Bird-in-Hand, plays a little comedy, and embodies the innocence that counters Ruth and Dan's worldliness. What makes *Plain and Fancy* wonderful is a genuine dramatic premise: people who are living in absolute freedom of choice run into people living in The Rules. Hilda, bless her heart, humanizes The Rules for us—she won't let her father bully her into marriage, and she knows, and says, that Katie should not be shunning Peter but marrying him.

Katie finally does: not because she suddenly becomes rebellious but because Peter's brother gets drunk (on Ruth's booze), visits a carnival, gets into a fight, and is saved by Peter. Katie's outraged father now redeclares the marriage, cueing in the Big Final Chorus (more of "Plenty of Pennsylvania") and the springing of the last delightful surprise of a delightful and surprising evening, a parade of wedding guests bearing pastoral wedding presents, each one larger and weirder till Katie's father hands over to Katie and Peter the present that the entire show has quietly centered on: the deed to Dan's farm.

Clearly, this is more than musical comedy; yet it is not quite a musical play. *Plain and Fancy* belongs to a form that was seeded in the 1940s and flowered in the 1950s: the "serious" musical comedy, the "light" musical play. In this genre, musical comedy has been strongly influenced by Rodgers and Hammerstein but not actually *Carousel*-ized, shall we say. For instance, the true musical play integrates dance. *Plain and Fancy* resorts to "By Lantern Light," a prance in the dark that has nothing to do with anything, though the second act features a "Carnival Ballet" incorporating plot action. The musical play also integrates comedy, avoiding figures who relentlessly buzz the audience with quips, as Ruth does.

On the other hand, musical comedy loves a novel setting but seldom investigates it in any meaningful way. *Guys and Dolls* is utterly set in Runyonland, yet we never learn why its inhabitants live so dangerously. *Plain and Fancy* strongly articulates the Amish worldview. Moreover, musical comedy does not generally program love songs so deeply felt as *Plain and Fancy*'s rapturous "It Wonders Me," the sorrowfully urgent "Follow Your Heart," or the one hit, "Young and Foolish," so nostalgic yet so regretful. Nor would musical comedy normally cast a soubrette who sings and acts with Barbara Cook's intensity.

The musical *play* is supposed to be intense. Yet Cook, as we'll see, spent her Broadway career largely in the fun shows. (She did, however, play both *Carousel* and *The King and I* at the City Center.) Cook's importance as a heroine is crucial: she was what more artistic musical comedies like *Plain and Fancy* were inventing even as she arrived, a woman lead of musical-play powers who was comfortable in musical comedy. In other words: a naturalized operetta star, someone real who really sings. *By the Beautiful Sea* couldn't have used such a character, but then Broadway couldn't use *By the Beautiful Sea*. The empty vehicle stuffed with diversions was becoming rare; what musical comedy wanted was stories, stuffed with character and atmosphere. *By the Beautiful Sea* had atmosphere and the fabulous Shirley Booth; it would have been a hit in the 1930s, which is why I have spotlighted such an unimportant title in this chapter: to show how purified musical comedy was becoming. The public loved stars but it now wanted more from a star show—though The Street, as always, was slow to catch on. I'm going to open the next chapter with four empty star vehicles, all from this time. One bombed, two ran but lost money, and one was a smash hit. All have vanished.

9

The Street, 1956

The problem with *The Vamp* (1955) was not Carol Channing. In fact, in this era, the problem with star vehicles was never the star. There were no Lauren Bacalls or Peter Allens then. Certainly, *The Vamp*'s premise appeared winning—a takeoff on the silent movie days with Channing as the mother of all sirens. John Latouche, fresh from *The Golden Apple*, had teamed with band-arranger James Mundy to write *Samson and Lila Dee*, an updating, of *Judges* 13 through 16, to New Orleans and Chicago in the 1930s, with the Isrealite hero a prizefighter and the Philistine temptress a nightclub singer. The show itself evaporated, but its period-inflected score seemed a match for the Channing project, then called, coincidentally, *Delilah*. True, *Delilah* was set in the 1910s, but that's close enough. Expanding their core of numbers with Mundy, Latouche collaborated on *Delilah*'s book with Sam Locke.

The story was perfect for musical comedy, covering as it did the wild and crazy years of silent film—that is, *before* Hollywood, when part of the Bronx was farmland and an ideal location site. Indeed, OHO Pictures invades Channing's uncle's Bronx farm to shoot a western, and Channing, as Flora Weems, falls for OHO's cowboy hero, Dick Hicks, the Yucca Kid (Robert Rippy, originally the role's understudy, promoted when Danny Scholl left during rehearsals). Dick falls for Flora, but a triangle is created by OHO's babytalking Elsie Chelsea, the Honeybunny Girl (Patricia Hammerlee). Meanwhile, the demented director Oliver J. Oxheart (David Atkinson) decides to turn Flora into the next icon: the Vamp!

Latouche had done his homework. These are the names and types of that age—Florence Lawrence, the Biograph Girl; Carl Laemmle's IMP studio; babylike Little Mary, "the girl with the curls"; the dippy, horse-loving cowpoke; the visionary directors like D. W. Griffith; and of course the sweet kid who enacts the wicked devourer of men. Unfortunately, beyond simply reconstructing old silent days, with the tawdry nickelodeon, films being shot simultaneously side by side in total pandemonium,* the Bible pageant, and the gossip columnist (Bibi Osterwald), Latouche didn't really have a take on the movies. What was this show about, beyond the novelty of turning Lorelei Lee into Theda Bara?

Delilah was a big show, the first major musical of the 1955–56 season, one that saw in only one other big musical at all, Rodgers and Hammerstein's *Pipe Dream*, till *My Fair Lady* turned up in late winter. A lot rode on Channing's show—a $315,000 budget, the tender new career of director David Alexander and the fading career of choreographer and "supervisor" Robert Alton (who had thus teamed with Alexander on the *Pal Joey* revival and the misfire *Hazel Flagg*), and, especially, Carol Channing's reputation. Out of town, where the title was changed to the less religious-seeming *The Vamp*, the critics were almost uniformly benign, although all felt that a lot of trimming was necessary. It was a feverish tryout, with "doctors" called in, Alton's going into the hospital with appendicitis, and, strangely, the departure of the associate producer (actually a major backer) who then tried to rejoin the production and, rebuffed, threatened legal action just as *The Vamp* arrived in New York.

---

* One clever touch: after watching the shooting, the real-life audience got to see the actual "rushes" on a screen. The show also began with projected credits, like a movie.

"The loudest, fastest, and most boring musical comedy in some time," said Henry Hewes in the *Saturday Review*; "really no good at all," said Wolcott Gibbs in *The New Yorker*. The daily press was no more appreciative, and poor Channing—who won unqualified personal raves—had to suffer the humiliation of her languorously reclining likeness covering the Winter Garden's block-long billboard, right on Broadway for all to see, as *The Vamp* staggered through two months as Broadway's failure fou.

Mr. Wonderful (1956) started on an even emptier premise than *The Vamp*: Let's give Sammy Davis Jr. his big break. Jule Styne, a tireless promoter of talent, saw in Davis a versatile star who had been typed as an easy-listening singer and needed only the exposure of Big Broadway to take off. Styne did not compose but co-produced *Mr. Wonderful*, and it is odd, in these days when ghetto anti-Semitism is so virulent, to reflect that a show about a Jewish entertainer's giving a black entertainer a boost was in fact exactly that: in real time, Styne produces Davis, and top stardom then occurs as planned.

Because Davis was technically still part of the Will Mastin Trio (with his uncle and father), the singing group was starred as well, though their entrance tells us how quickly Sammy would become a single. In a nightclub setting, the three were announced and, to hubba-hubba music, the two older men entered as if attached at the sides in a kind of Arabian shuffle. They parted—and Sammy, who had been hidden behind them, suddenly jumped forward and took control of the number, the rocking "Jacques d'Iraque."

Instantly, the show was his. The story, about an unknown singer (Davis) without ambition who is goaded on by his girl friend (Olga James) and a third-rate show biz wannabe (Jack Carter), was peanuts. Chita Rivera had a featured role so extraneous to the plot that she might have been in a revue, and the complete lack of a second act was exposed when the last third of it was given over to Davis' headlining debut in a Miami nightclub, complete with drum-playing and interpolations from Davis' own act. The book, astonishingly, was by *Plain and Fancy's* Joseph Stein and Will Glickman. At least the score, by Larry Holofcener, George Weiss, and Jerry Bock, was tuneful. Sammy was fine. Still, the eleven-month run failed to pay off.

Even Ethel Merman had a financial failure, though it acted like a hit—*Happy Hunting* (1956), which ran a year, at first to sold-out houses. Here we reach the emptiest premise yet: Merman wants to do a musical to save her marriage.

Yep. The queen of Broadway since *Girl Crazy* in 1930, Merman had never really liked what she did: she only liked being top at something. Everyone who knew her will tell you that she was tirelessly committed—taking copious notes in her former-stenographer shorthand during rehearsals, intently learning lines and music, never missing or walking through a performance. Nevertheless, she didn't care about it the way her public did; she cared about it the way her producers did. She was, in fact, *Happy Hunting*'s (unbilled) co-producer, with Jo Mielziner, in a gala Return.

Merman had retired after *Call Me Madam*, seeking a new life in Denver as a mother and wife, unfortunately to Bob Six, an airline executive who, she eventually surmised, was using her fame and money to advance his career. Six's address was Denver but he lived in New York, so Merman decided to close up the Denver home and retake both husband and Broadway. Thus was commissioned another novelty act from Howard Lindsay and Russel Crouse: Stella Dallas at the Grace Kelly–Prince Rainier wedding.

The plot twist: Merman isn't invited, so she tries to upstage the "fairy tale romance" with her own "wedding of the century," between her daughter (Virginia Gibson) and an even grander noble than Monaco's Prince Ranier. She finds him in a pretender to the Spanish throne (Typical Mermanism: misunderstanding the word "pretender," she says, "I like you all the more for admitting it"), arranges the marriage, then realizes that she loves him herself. That's okay—Merman's daughter loves the family lawyer (Gordon Polk).

If we except such obscure and unpardonable misses as *Buttrio Square* (1952), *Carnival in Flanders* (1953), *Hit the Trail* (1954), *Shangri-La* (1956), *Rumple* (1957), and especially *Portofino* (1958), by all accounts the worst musical of the decade, *Happy Hunting* must have the most terrible libretto perpetrated in this time. It's a chaotic blunder filled with mystifying featured players forever babbling fey arcana. Who are these people? one keeps asking. Were they written out in Boston and refused to leave? Are they friends of Merman's?

Definitely not friends of Merman's were the authors of the score, Harold Karr and Matt Dubey. Early in rehearsal, Karr chided Merman for stylizing a vocal line, at which Merman froze, called director Abe Burrows over, and declaimed, pointing at Karr, "That man is not permitted to speak to me again." And, believe me, he didn't.

Still, Dubey and Karr took a good stab at demonstrating what decent "Ethel Merman songs" are like when Cole Porter and Irving Berlin aren't available. There was the "Hot damn, I'm Merman!" shot, right after her entrance, "(Gee, but) It's Good To Be Here." There was the uptempo strophic strut, à la "The Hostess With the Mostes'," a bit of backstory called "Mr. Livingstone (I presume)." There was the Porteresque rhythm ballad, "This Is What I Call Love," an odd novelty, "A New-Fangled Tango," and a torchy ballad, "The Game of Love." We're not done yet—there was the title number, with Merman leading the chorus, all in foxhunt blue and yellow, the confessional "I'm a Funny Dame," and even a hit tune, a duet with her daughter, "Mutual Admiration Society." Except for "The Game of Love" and "Funny Dame," these are all valid numbers, more so in "Mr. Livingstone" and downright irreplaceable in "It's Good To Be Here." The rest of the score, however, matches the book, with inane numbers for the daughter-lawyer subplot, an archaic showgirl parade (in bathing suits, on a hotel terrace) to "For Love or Money," and one of the most synthetic of scene-change numbers preceding a party scene, "Everyone Here's Who's Who."

Yet, director Burrows kept it tight and trim. He devised an unusual staging for the opening chorus, bringing a bunch of schoolgirls on in front of the show curtain (a montage of royal wedding props, including the famous Monégasque stamps with cameos of Rainier and Grace). Groups of tourists and journalists join them, and not till Burrows had a full-scale ensemble onstage did he raise the show curtain on the first set, outside the Monte Carlo palace gates. Here he gave Merman a Surprise Entrance. To cries of "Miss Kelly!" and "Please, Your Grace!," a woman came on, her face hidden under a gigantic hat, as reporters and photographers swarmed excitedly. Finally, the hat came off—and Broadway's Queen cried, "All right, all right! So it ain't Kelly under the kelly!" Later on there was a horse for Merman to play comedy with; and a fox in the hunt sequence, a puppet on a wire that suddenly appeared next to Merman. Pointing stage left, she said, "They went thataway!" And the fox literally flew off stage right.

And there was Latin Lover Fernando Lamas as the pretender, a very fifties matinee idol* and, by hap, an okay singer. Alas, Lamas got on with the star no better than Karr and Dubey had, and during the run the Merman-Lamas feud got into the performances and the papers. Then, on Mike Wallace's TV show, Lamas likened kissing Merman to "somewhere between kissing your uncle and a Sherman tank." Oddly, Merman did not have Lamas fired. On the contrary, she held him to his contract, losing him the role of Emile de Becque in the *South Pacific* movie. (Or so said Lamas. In Merman's own report, he wanted to be released to a do a club act with his wife, Arlene Dahl, and, when offered the release, backed down).

Of our four star vehicles, the only one to make money was *Bells Are Ringing* (1956). It may be a stretch to call this title "vanished," as I have done. It did leave behind a faithful movie version. But is the show itself much performed? Again, we have a premise without substance: Judy Holliday as an answering-service switchboard operator interfering in the lives of her clients. She means well. She *does* well—but attracts the attention of an ambitious vice cop, who sniffs a prostitution ring. Meanwhile, Holliday rehabilitates an imitation-Brando loser of an actor, liberates a songwriter trapped in dentistry, and reinspires a playwright with writer's block (Sydney Chaplin, another matinee idol and Holliday's vis-à-vis). Everything in the book by Betty Comden and Adolph Green is physically possible but socially unlikely, though much of the score, by Jule Styne and Comden and Green, hits the points that the book misses, creating, in effect, "Judy Holliday

---

* Does this old term need defining? The matinee idol of the very early twentieth-century stage was a looker who held his public (popularly supposed to be exclusively female; ha) more through face and form than through talent. Through overuse, the term took in every popular male actor under the age of fifty, even John Barrymore, who had looks *and* talent. I use the term *ab origine*.

songs," as apt for her as *Happy Hunting*'s are for Merman. Thus, we understand Holliday's unreasonable crush on the playwright in "It's a Perfect Relationship," her artless charming of everyone she meets in "Hello, Hello There" and Chaplin's "I Met a Girl," and her romantic self-image in "Long Before I Knew You" and "The Party's Over." She's also present for the show's hit duet, "Just in Time," and to supply punch lines for the choral "Drop That Name," not to mention her eleven o'clocker, "I'm Going Back."

The whole show was Holliday. True, those other three shows were wholly Channing, Davis, Merman. But *Bells Are Ringing* had, one, a popular score, two, Jerome Robbins in charge (with Robbins and Fosse choreography), and, three, the incredible warmth of Judy Holliday in her first musical. *The Vamp* was far more colorful, *Mr. Wonderful* more melodious, and *Happy Hunting* treated what was at the time the greatest Town Topic in Western Civilization, that Cinderella marriage. But *Bells Are Ringing* was smart showmanship with an irresistible centerpiece. It ran for twenty-seven months, with Holliday right to the end. She's in the film, too (with Dean Martin), whereas neither Channing, Davis, nor Merman filmed their shows.

Star vehicles are usually original, being built around a personality that comes more or less prefabricated. But the fifties musical was by mid-decade leaning heavily on fiction, cinema, and older plays for its source material. Original shows, once the musical's stock-in-trade, were actually becoming risky, especially if they were *Ankles Aweigh* (1955), an attempt to return to the old leggs-and-laffs formula. Technically the work of librettists Guy Bolton and Eddie Davis, composer Sammy Fain, and lyricist Dan Shapiro, *Ankles Aweigh* was really the result of producer Anthony Brady Farrell's belief that *Oklahoma!*, *Kiss Me, Kate*, and such were dull and serious. Farrell, the aforementioned Con Edison heir, bought the huge Hollywood Theatre on Fifty-first Street, got talked out of renaming it the Brafar, settled for the Mark Hellinger, and prepared to become a power on Broadway by restoring fun to the musical. ("I wish he'd go back to drinking," his wife reportedly said. "It was so much cheaper.")

Ankles Aweigh marked the climax of Farrell's reign of terror,

not the worst but the stupidest musical that ever lived. It starred
Betty and Jane Kean as sisters, one of whom is secretly married,
in defiance of her Hollywood contract, to a Navy pilot (Mark Dawson). To be with him, she disguises herself as a sailor and stows
away on his ship, which involves her with a Moroccan spy ring.
The developers of this plot managed to be farcical without being
funny—I mean, not a line—and the score remains one of the
supremely bad ones. In fact, a piece such as *Ankles Aweigh* is why
we have the term "floppo." The more common-or-garden flop is
simply any show that fails to pay off, even items as distinguished
as *Candide* or *Follies*. A floppo, however, is a show so terrible it's
inspired. I hear oldtimers murmur, *"The Girl from Nantucket,"*
perhaps *"Viva O'Brien."* Youngsters may thrill to the recollection
of *The Prince of Central Park*, the deliciously inadequate *Marlowe*,
or the house favorite, *Jekyll and Hyde*.

Ankles Aweigh* tops them all. This was not a misunderstood or
underpraised show. This was junk, filled with numbers so idiotic
that they could not have turned up in even a halfway decent musical. Floppo is lower than bad. Floppo is so mistaken it makes cli-
chés sound bizarre. The opening chorus, "Italy," stinks. The Jane-
Kean-trying-on-a-uniform number, "Walk Like a Sailor," is
moronic, yet has the the gall to try to pass itself off as bouncy.
"Headin' for the Bottom Blues," sung by the villainous siren character (Betty George) is rancid; worse, it hopes to be. "Nothing Can
Replace a Man" proposes to rebut "There Is Nothing Like a Dame"
while reassuring Rodgers and Hammerstein that "Their opinion is
simply divine." No. The sentiments expressed in "There Is Nothing
Like a Dame" do not constitute an "opinion," but rather reflect the
feelings of the characters singing the number. This kind of wooly
thinking infects every aspect of a floppo; even the music is dumb.
"Here's To Dear Old Us," a "tipsy" number, is, amazingly, the worst
yet, but only if you missed the casino number, "Ready Cash."

By then, you know what a floppo is, though Walter Winchell
didn't. His plugging of *Ankles Aweigh* in his column, and his suggestion that the critics jumped it through a lack of sympathy with
what the public really wanted, kept it going for five months. He
was dating Jane Kean at the time.

A very few Bostonians might recall Marc Blitzstein's *Reuben,*

Reuben (1955), floppo surrealism. Actually, writers of Blitzstein's caliber are incapable of creating floppos, though *Reuben, Reuben* did close in Boston. One has to call it astonishing that the piece was produced at all, for its stream-of-consciousness action suggested a dreary nightmare. A war veteran is so shell-shocked that he literally cannot speak (though he occasionally whistles) unless he is treated with great gentleness. An evil character seeks, for mercenary purposes, to hustle him into jumping off a bridge, and various eccentrics fill his day, including a young woman who befriends him and becomes his romantic interest.

Producer Cheryl Crawford gave Blitzstein an interesting cast, in hero Eddie Albert, heroine Evelyn Lear (just ahead of her notable career as an opera soprano), comic "Countess" Kaye Ballard, dancers Sondra Lee and Timmy Everett, villain George Gaynes, soon-to-be major pop singer Enzo Stuarti, and, as Gaynes' understudy, the future Wotan and Evelyn Lear's husband, Thomas Stewart. Unfortunately, the meandering story was filled with irrelevant incidentals from the many minor characters, and Blitzstein's lack of melodic inspiration did not truly recommend him for a show that was through-sung, with a few lines of underscored dialogue. Perhaps *Reuben, Reuben*'s one praiseworthy quality was its desire to create something genuinely original, with its own sound, characters, and worldview.

Fiction continued to excite authors' interest—such as John Steinbeck's *Cannery Row*, a sage, mildly horrified, but ultimately loving look at the sometimes degraded humankind of Monterey, California. Trouble was, *Cannery Row* lacked a plot, so Steinbeck proposed to fashion a text using the characters and setting but concocting a new story for them. His partners were Rodgers and Hammerstein, and Harold Clurman was the director, so the cognoscenti got ready for something new in the musical play—a spicy Rogers and Hammerstein. But *Pipe Dream* (1955) failed to deliver, at least as far as critics and most of the public saw it. One wonders what might have happened if Feuer and Martin, who originally bought the property, had gone ahead with Frank Loesser, their original choice for the score. Loesser habitually redevised his style to suit his subjects; Rodgers and Hammerstein tended to sound like themselves.

To be fair, *Pipe Dream*'s score is lovely, and it richly covers the interior contradictions of Steinbeck, ever optimistic in the most pessimistic way. "The Tide Pool," on the food chain, heaves with sadism in music as well as words; Rodgers' setting literally suggests a feeding frenzy. "All Kinds of People" is a Sunday School sampler. Nevertheless, the novel that Steinbeck wrote to provision *Pipe Dream*'s plotline, *Sweet Thursday*, is a kind of revue, loosely structured and replete with star turns and specialty acts, while the typical Rodgers and Hammerstein show is is a narrative very precisely organized. There was bound, at times, to be tension between the source material and the adaptors.

Other reasons are generally given for *Pipe Dream*'s failure. (Though it ran a full season, it had many a losing night and did not pay off.) Everyone's favorite scapegoat is Helen Traubel, the Met's Wagner star playing a bordello madam. Okay, it sounds like a mistake: think of Birgit Nilsson as Calamity Jane, Juliette Lewis as Mrs. Lovett. But Traubel was possibly the earthiest of all the big Wagner ladies; her autobiography was entitled *St. Louis Woman*. Morever, Rodgers and Hammerstein werc the smartest casting directors that ever lived, and in fact Traubel was fine. Some blame Rodgers and Hammerstein. Steinbeck was the first to, seeing his romance between a self-doubting loser of a marine biologist and a self-hating prostitute delivered of its gritty sexuality. But there was also the problem that Clurman, an alumnus of the thirties political stage, was working in a medium that he felt was synthetic; and another problem in that the author-producers decided to ban all-out choreography as being too stylized for Monterey's mañana feeling. These are lazy people, reclining figures. Still, one of the pleasures of attending the latest Rodgers and Hammerstein was seeing what new stunt they might pull off in the dancing. *Pipe Dream*'s skimpy dancing turns—slobby guys flirting with girls and throwing laundry around, some amateurish party entertainment, Traubel's cakewalk with two little Hispanic boys during "Sweet Thursday"—only teased the public's longing for something thorough from Terpsichore. In the 1950s, a musical without dance was weird and intellectual, even *Reuben, Reuben*.

In fact, *Pipe Dream* is a good show, with meaty parts for the biologist (William Johnson), the prostitute (Judy Tyler), and two Steinbeckian mugs, Mac (G. D. Wallace, Gwen Verdon's lover in *New Girl in Town*) and Hazel (Mike Kellin). Maybe Steinbeck into a musical won't go. He does well in plays and opera, but he is an over-the-top, self-definingly brilliant voice that defeats a middle-class form like the fifties musical. True, they were able to do it to Damon Runyon. Maybe what *Pipe Dream* needed was Abe Burrows and Michael Kidd.

Film, too, provided source material, though the two examples that I'll cite were (forgotten) plays first. Austin Strong's *Seventh Heaven* (1922) made a beautiful silent for Janet Gaynor and Charles Farrell in 1927 and was remade ten years later for Simone Simon and James Stewart. The tale of the Parisian sewer worker Chico, who shelters an abused girl living by her wits in the streets, *Seventh Heaven* was the kind of overwritten and overacted romantic melodrama that was already hokey when it was new. In the climactic scene, Chico returns from the war to find his Diane in another man's arms. She had thought him dead on the battle-field—no, he's just *blind*! So he cannot see his rival, who then slips out silently, that sweet love e'er more reign in Chico's paradise on the seventh floor.

You see the problem. Certainly, the authors of *Seventh Heaven* the musical (1955) did. Victor Wolfson and Stella Unger (book), Victor Young (music), and Unger (lyrics) apparently tried to give the tale a modern edge. For starters, Chico took on an almost belligerent personality, and Diane, formerly a homeless kid on the grift, was now a prostitute. ("Where Is That Someone For Me?" was her establishing song; shouldn't it have been "I Hate Men"?) Musical comedy infrastructure was applied to the building up of the part of The Rat, a charming crook, for Robert Clary, and for the addition of a dancing trio—Camille (Gerianne Raphael), Collette (Patricia Hammerlee), and Fifi (Chita Rivera). Choreographer Peter Gennaro laid out enjoyable dances, especially the "White and Gold Ballet," Chico's dream vision, from the trenches, of his and Diane's wedding, featuring a spectacular pas de deux by Rivera and Scott Merrill. And here's a real surprise: the French painter Marcel Vertès was hired to design sets and costumes that gave the show a pastel fairy-tale look, or even just the attitude of an Utrillo, as in a taxicab, moved around the stage, that looked like a child's drawing on flat cardboard.

An ominous sign was the booking of the ANTA Theatre, house of floppos, though the leads seemed promising—Hollywood's Gloria de Haven and Ricardo Montalban as the lovers, Kurt Kaszner as Boule, the cab driver, and Beatrice Arthur as Madame Suze, the *bordeliste*. The score is tunefully conventional, the book no more than functional, and the show as a whole the sort that draws very mixed reviews. *Seventh Heaven* quickly closed.

How to squeeze a smash out of a film property was left to Feuer and Martin that same year, but then they had a far more adaptable property. *Seventh Heaven* was quaint for the 1950s and the new version lost the original's charm without creating anything compelling in exchange. But what could be more contemporary during the bomb-fearing Cold War than *Ninotchka*, Ernst Lubitsch's matchless 1939 comedy (Garbo laughs!" MGM's ads tooted) about a hard-line Soviet envoy amid the capitalist temptations of Paris, trading Party-line sermonettes for the dangerous liberation of romance?

Nursing their fifth consecutive hit, Feuer and Martin commissioned a Cole Porter score, a libretto from George S. Kaufman and his wife, Leueen Macgrath, tapped Don Ameche from the movies and racy, fun-filled Yvonne Adair from *Gentlemen Prefer Blondes*, meanwhile "discovering" the German movie actress Hildegarde Knef (whom they insisted on renaming "Neff" for dull-witted Americans), and booked the Imperial, right down in the center of hot Broadway.

Silk Stockings, they called it. From the start, it had major potential. Kaufman and Macgrath envisioned not a typical girl-crazy rave-up but a romantic comedy with songs. However, the addition of Yvonne Adair's character into the *Ninotchka* story—an American movie star—gave Porter trouble. Wasn't she exactly the sort of hurdy-gurdy decoration a romantic comedy with songs didn't need? Her introductory number, "Stereophonic Sound," was irrelevant and, worse, lame, and Porter laboriously pounded out at least three numbers for her second spot, eventually filled by the idiotic "Satin and Silk." Songs for the three comic Russian agents so baffled Porter that Noël Coward pitched in on one of them; but they're all terrible, anyway.

At least the ballads found Porter in form, especially the one hit, "All of You," the melting yet swinging (who but Porter—and Hart's Rodgers—could pull off that combination?) "As on Through the Seasons We Sail," and "Paris Loves Lovers," which pits Ameche's amorous come-on against Neff's resistant patter, West meets East. Neff and Ameche were wonderful, she singing in a throaty bass as a musical comedy equivalent of what Garbo sounded like in the movie, and he utterly in his element as a singer-actor. However, Yvonne Adair suddenly turned up pregnant, the delicate Kaufman-Macgrath romantic comedy wasn't playing, and Feuer and Martin went into battle formation, hectoring, bullying, firing, and lengthening the tryout till it lasted an unnatural three months. Abe Burrows was brought in to rework the book, tinkering so grandly that Kaufman and Macgrath departed, saving Feuer and Martin from having to bar them from the theatre in their *Boy Friend* manner. Gretchen Wyler followed two interim replacements for Adair. Three souvenir-book sellers were branded. An orangeade man was shot. Feuer took over the direction, calling in Jerome Robbins for a last-minute slap-up, and *Silk Stockings* grimly roared into town, as solid a hit as Feuer and Martin's and Burrows' and Porter's *Can-Can* had been. In fact, *Silk Stockings* was a form of *Can-Can*: but now *she's* stiff and *he's* sensual, Gwen Verdon becomes Gretchen Wyler, the comic artists are comic commissars, and Paris is contemporary rather than *belle époque*.

Adaptations from straight plays had been common in the musical since the 1910s, but almost always using comedies as source material. Adaptation of serious plays was another of Rodgers and Hammerstein's innovations, and the 1950s pursued it heartily. Virtually every season boasted at least one attempt to find the music in an at-first-thought tone-deaf property—*Arms and the Girl*, *Make a Wish*, "*Wish You Were Here*", *New Girl in Town*, *My Fair Lady*, *Take Me Along*, and *Juno* are all examples—and so is *The Most Happy Fella* (1956), Frank Loesser's version of Sidney Howard's somber, radically political *They Knew What They*

Wanted. The critics loved Loesser's version. "A masterpiece of our era," said one. "An overwhelmingly inventive new musical," "A great, great musical," and "Musical magnificence," said others. Many today insist that if *My Fair Lady* hadn't opened six weeks before *The Most Happy Fella*, Loesser's show would have been the official glory of the mid-1950s.

Billed as a "musical," *The Most Happy Fella* is in fact an opera. True, unlike *The Golden Apple* it is not through-sung. But Loesser so stuffed Howard's story with music that very little dialogue (Loesser's own, *d'après* Howard) was left to utter. It's astonishing how many mundane situations tickled Loesser's muse, but then didn't he make an immortal number out of three racetrack touts doping out their sheets? A waitress's tired feet, the contents of a dinner table after a customer has departed, a postman's cataloguing the contents of his mail bag, a rancher's farewell to a foreman he hardly cares about—any situation at all seemed to inspire a song in Loesser.

And not just songs. *The Most Happy Fella* enjoys a great diversity in the structure of its music. Loesser mixes pop ("Standin' on the Corner") and legit ("How Beautiful the Days"), arioso and recit, underscored dialogue: this is a demonstration piece of how many different techniques Broadway had developed for music theatre by 1956.

Even Loesser's pop tunes are unusually well built. "Joey, Joey, Joey," the foreman's character song, is already loaded with lyricism in its almost evilly mysterious verse ("Like a perfumed woman . . ."), then presents a chorus in ABABC format even before it gets to the release ("When the bunk I've been bunkin' in . . ."), and Don Walker's scoring emphasizes lower strings, with woodwinds in thirds sinuously floating and gliding overhead, a haunting effect.

Musical scenes abound, more even than in *Oklahoma!* and *Carousel* combined, and that makes *The Most Happy Fella* unique. What makes it wonderful is how deeply Loesser dove into his characters' emotions, despite the awkwardness of the storyline. Repelled by the fat old bozo to whom she got engaged by mail, the bride spends her wedding night with the foreman. The two young people feel nothing for each other, but she and the old man grow strangely closer, not into a kind of love but into love. Then he learns that she is pregnant by the foreman.*

What other musical centers on the romance of a young woman and a distinctly unattractive man pushing fifty? Especially when the relationship is so ecstatically developed—in the title song, *Tempo di Tarantella*, as the rancher fills the town in on his courtship by post; in his nervously anticipatory waltz "Rosabella"; in a lengthy musical scene for the lovers that culminates in "My Heart Is So Full of You"; in "Mamma, Mamma," his gloating celebration of his newfound love even as *we* have just found out about her pregnancy, letting the second-act curtain fall on an irony big enough for the old Greek Dionysia; and in Loesser's capping of the third and final act's finale, a reprise of the title song, by a spoken line (after all that music!), the rancher's joyful "At's-a me!"

There are more enjoyable fifties musicals, perhaps—there are certainly more popular ones. There is only one greater score in this decade, that of *Candide*—and even *Candide* is not as emotionally elaborated as *The Most Happy Fella*. Unfortunately, like a number of other shows—*Sally, DuBarry Was a Lady, Lady in the Dark, South Pacific, Damn Yankees, Once Upon a Mattress*—*The Most Happy Fella* has been unable to field a revival cast as strong as its original one, most particularly in the role of the rancher, Tony, first played by Robert Weede. This Met baritone somehow never truly challenged his colleagues Leonard Warren or Robert Merrill at the Old Met on Thirty-ninth Street, yet away from the opera, singing and talking in Tony's Italian-English, Weede was dynamite. Bass Giorgio Tozzi, in the first Broadway revival, in 1979, was tediously genial, where Tony more typically undergoes volatile mood swings from ebullient to crushed. Back in the baritone range, Louis Quilico at the New York City Opera in 1991 may have been hampered by tight rehearsal time; the overall power was right but the details were sketchy. The second Broadway revival, from Goodspeed Opera House in 1992, found bass Spiro Malas utterly overparted in this gigantic sing of a role.

---

* It takes place in 1927, and Loesser troubled to supply a few identifying references—Douglas Fairbanks, Queen Marie of Romania, the Charleston. Yet the story is so timeless that everyone takes it for a contemporary piece.

The other characters should be much easier to cast. Yet who has retrieved the redneck allure of Art Lund, the original foreman, Joe? ("Friendly and even generous," Loesser notes in the text. But also: "cold and possibly brutal behind the smile in his eyes.") Who, playing the subplot comics, Herman and Cleo, has matched the terminally ingratiating Shorty Long and Susan Johnson? Why do ingenues consistently fail to find all the pieces of the heroine, Rosabella (whose real name is Amy, though we don't learn that till late in the show)? She's so vulnerable yet so feisty, horribly drawn to Joe in sheer animal passion, then feeling such shy warmth for Tony. Other Rosabellas may sing the notes better than did Jo Sullivan in 1956. As the original cast discs reveal, Sullivan had a delicate instrument, unsupported and faltering on the high Gs. But she *was* Rosabella.

There's an important moment in the show, at the end of the first scene, when Cleo, Rosabella's fellow waitress and roommate, has already exited. Rosabella, pondering the fabulous tip and clumsy love letter that someone (Tony, of course) has left her, stops to be touched, look into it, sing about it. It's a standard musical comedy moment: the heroine's Wanting Song. Rosabella's is "Somebody, Somewhere (wants me and needs me)," and it is where the show makes its emotional connection with the audience. Narratively, it's transitional, taking us from "the meeting" (though Rosabella can't remember what Tony looks like) to three months later, "the proposal is accepted." Technically, it's a scene-change number, beginning in the restaurant and finishing in one so the stagehands can switch the main playing area to Napa Valley. But musically, it's a heart-stopper—or, rather, it *must* be, or you have no Rosabella, no wistful little nobody who has been touched by this mail-order courtship and can show us in a single number, at the start of the correspondence, that she is so eager to believe in the somebody somewhere that she is destined to fall in love with the man who writes the letters, whoever he be. Sullivan made the connection. Who has done so since?

One flaw in *The Most Happy Fella*—though it wasn't thought so by the standards of the time—is the generic choreography (by Dania Krupska), for a wedding party and a barn dance. The main dance number, "Big D," is the one bit that doesn't really belong in the show, though it does establish the romance of Herman and Cleo and peppers Act Two with a hoedown.

As I've said, this is the decade of dance in the musical. But much of this dance was pried into stories by crowbar. Rodgers and Hammerstein's integration of dance for character and atmosphere could not be sustained by shows that didn't have much character and atmosphere in the first place, or by shows that, like *The Most Happy Fella*, were written entirely around vocal lines. *Paint Your Wagon*, to cite an exception, was loaded with Agnes de Mille's attempt to find poetry in, first, the loneliness of the mining camp, then the jubilation when the dance-hall women hit town, and at last the growing loneliness again when the gold gives out. *Me and Juliet*, as a backstager, could revel in real-life dance, in rehearsals or during show time, now "improvised" and now according to intricate design, even down to two performers cutting up in a dressing room. And *The Golden Apple*, we remember, was saturated with dance *during the vocals*.

Still, these exceptions only prove the rule. *Happy Hunting*, *Bells Are Ringing*, *Mr. Wonderful*, *Silk Stockings*, and *Ankles Aweigh* used choreography as a kind of general utility, breaking out of a lively song. For instance, in *Happy Hunting*: juvenile remarks upon ingenue's use of "if'n" for "if," they get a duet out of it ("If'n"), whose fast tempo invites the chorus, which just happens to be hanging around, to expand it into a full-out number. Or, in *Bells Are Ringing*, Judy Holliday's infectious charm turns dour New Yorkers into madcap gladhanders in "Hello, Hello There" and a dance ensues—though, since this show had Fosse and Robbins, the number had style and shape as the two used the set, a subway car, to examine the crowd-of-strangers feeling that New Yorkers take for granted. The dance was punctuated by new boosts of energy every time the car doors opened and new riders arrived, and, rather than swallow up the star, the number featured her at its climax when an acrobatic act prepared to blast the top man into a chair held aloft. The car lurched, its lights went out, and when they came up again it was Holliday in the chair.

So this was a time that didn't necessarily exalt dance but wouldn't have been without it. Of course, this would seem to be true of the musical as far back as one can go. But the uniquely tilted dance number that serves its show as it could no other—a Subway Number like "Hello, Hello There," for example—did not come along until the 1930s. It was developed in the 1940s—one instance is *Up in Central Park*'s "Currier and Ives Ballet," useful specifically for this period piece of old New York—and became a convention only in the 1950s.

Thus, there could be a show so imbued with dance that it comes most alive when dancing, more lyrical than in its vocal score and more theatrical than in the staging of its book scenes. I'm thinking of *Shinbone Alley* (1957), an amplification of George Kleinsinger and Joe Darion's one-act opera based on Don Marquis' *Archy and Mehitabel* poems,* mainly about Archie's philosophical observations and his friendship with the selfish and unreliable cat Mehitabel. With a book by Joe Darion and Mel Brooks, the piece became a musical comedy, but a weird one, with nothing but animals for characters and, as in Marquis's columns, no plot. There's a throughline: Archy wants to reform Mehitabel; she agrees but always backslides. There's no subplot, just a succession of comings and goings among the denizens of the animal underworld, a sort of carefree slum always in trouble with the law. In jail after a raid, one pretty kitty goes to pieces:

> KITTEN (Reri Grist): We're all in jail again! In jail again! What am I gonna do? What am I gonna *do*? It's the third time this week! What am I gonna say? How'll I explain? What am I gonna tell my mother? (*Louder*) *What am I gonna tell my mother?*

* It is the fashion to print this title in lowercase, because it was Marquis's joke that Archy, a cockroach, was typing the verses on Marquis's typewriter and wasn't strong enough to depress the shift bar. Indeed, when the *Archy* columns, which originated in the *New York Sun*, were collected in book form, virtually the entire volume was set in lowercase, from half-title page to the end. (One poem, entitled "CAPITALS AT LAST," breaks the rule, but Archy's paradise does not endure: Mehitabel makes a grab for him and unlocks the shift key. Till that point, the page marks the one time in the book when Archy gives up free verse for rhymed iambic pentameter.) So, while the lowercase seems correct for Marquis, it should not affect any other writer. After all, Archy is not the compositor of every book that mentions him. And Archy isn't typing my manuscript, is he? *Archy and Mehitabel.*

OLDER CAT: (Lillian Hayman) Will you shut your mouth and
go to sleep?
KITTEN: *Mother!* What are *you* doing here?

And, as a voice-over calls "Lights out," another kitten purrs out,
"Gee, I wish this place was co-ed!"

With Archy no more than Mehitabel's chum, this had to be
opera senz'amore, and indeed there isn't a single love song. The
major numbers are uptempo, socko—"Flotsam and Jetsam," "A
Woman Wouldn't Be a Woman," "Cheerio, My Deario" (one of
the few tunes remaining from the original little piece), put over
with a dead-on rightness by Eddie Bracken and Eartha Kitt. His
wondering softness and her brittle sex appeal made fine chemistry—they had to, for, beyond George S. Irving's thuggish tomcat
and Erik Rhodes' aesthetic Tyrone T. Tattersall, all of *Shinbone
Alley* was ensemble work.

It was a unique ensemble, racially mixed right down the middle
between black and white. This was unknown in the 1950s. Casts
were almost uniformly white, except for the few black shows like
Jamaica or *House of Flowers*. (There were two Asian shows, of
very mixed ethnicity in casting.) The few exceptions, such as *By
the Beautiful Sea*'s black housekeeper, *Mr. Wonderful*'s Sammy
Davis, Olga James, and the two Mastins, the occasional black
chorus people in shows set in New York City such as *Copper and
Brass*, or the romantic subplot in *The Body Beautiful* a year after
Shinbone Alley only prove the rule. Perhaps the notion of an all-
animal cast led the production to seek an entirely unencountered
look. Or maybe it wanted to exploit black dancing talent, for this
was a show hopped up on dance.

It might as well have been, with so little story to tell. Act One
had a "Dog and Cat Ballet," Act Two a "Vacant Lot Ballet" that
lasted nine minutes, the second-longest dance in the decade, just
trailing "The Small House of Uncle Thomas." Composer Kleinsinger, whose odd sound touches on traces of Gershwin, Arlen,
and Ellington, adds in Kurt Weill and Leonard Bernstein in these
two numbers, performed by some of Broadway's finest dancers
and Allegra Kent and Jacques d'Amboise of true ballet. Rod Alexander was the choreographer, and in the famous underground
tape of the show, made on the Broadway Theatre's sound system

(available on CD), the audience clearly is having a great time at both big dances.

In fact, the audience eats the show up as a whole: so why did it fail? True, the script is little more than a succession of gags, as when Tyrone Tattersall, taking Mehitabel under his protection to develop her artistic potential, directs her in a thespian improvisation:

> TYRONE: I want you to play for me . . . I want you to become . . . a young grapefruit . . . Now, show me, show me.
> MEHITABEL: Yes, maestro . . . A young grapefruit?
> TYRONE: Precisely.
> MEHITABEL: (*Tries to work into it, then stops*) Tell me one thing.
> TYRONE: Yes.
> MEHITABEL: Am I seedless?

True also, Kitt tried to fill out holes in the action with cascades of nervous laughter, and is so "ad lib" in her delivery that we worry that she might be writing a new script as she speaks. The leads never have anything to play until late in the show, when Mehitabel turns into a high-toned housecat and sends Archy packing—"Cockroaches really aren't allowed in the house," she tells him. "It's too . . . too middle class."

But then, *Shinbone Alley* isn't a plot show. Like ballet itself, it's a pageant, neither literal nor linear. It's fanciful, circular, of its own dimension. The audience we hear at the actual performance must have raved to friends, but one imagines the friends' reaction: "A musical about *cats*?"

10

My Fair Lady

Economic freedom generates cultural freedom, and it was subsidiary sales in the piano and sheet music industries, vast and very directly connected to Broadway's power in leading the trends in American popular music, that gave the musical a big-money foundation as far back as the First Age. This continued in the Second Age, when people who wanted music at home had to make it themselves or invest in the Victrola and its at the time expensive software.

However, by the Third Age, when radio popularized musicmaking by professionals while the home public sat and listened, the recording industry greatly expanded, cleverly dropping its prices at the same time. Midway through the Third Age, as I've outlined earlier, the LP came in, revolutionizing the very function of the cast album. Before 1948, in the awkward 78 set, it was a specialty item. After 1948, the year the LP was first marketed, they took down everything but *Buttrio Square*.

All right, not everything. Revues were scanted. Fast-closing flops were beneath notice. But the taste of the day so favored the Broadway sound that labels hotly competed for the rights to The

Album: a souvenir of a production from overture to finale with its cast and orchestra, maybe a taste of its dance music, and a few lines of cue-in dialogue. Hits shows created hit albums, and Decca (progenitor of the "original cast album" with *This Is the Army* in 1942), Columbia (most eager, as the firm that invented the LP), Victor (most resentful, as it had been the industry's unchallengeable maximum leader, both technologically and artistically, till Columbia seized the day with the LP), and Capitol (the poor cousin, ever saddled with flops, though it did nab *Can-Can*) filled the field. In the 1940s, the last decade of the 78, plenty of major projects* lacked full-scale cast albums—*Louisiana Purchase, Cabin in the Sky, Panama Hattie, Pal Joey, Lady in the Dark, Best Foot Forward, Let's Face It, By Jupiter, Something for the Boys, Follow the Girls, Sadie Thompson, The Seven Lively Arts,* and I quit here, less than halfway through the decade, having named not only hits but shows by Rodgers and Hart, Cole Porter, and Irving Berlin.

Compare that with the 1950s: every hit recorded, many flops taken down, and only four major projects missing: *The Vamp, Reuben, Reuben, Shinbone Alley,* and Jerry Bock and Sheldon Harnick's first score together, *The Body Beautiful.*

There was money in it, music in it, status in it. The hip bourgeois *would* have the latest cast album, if only for social reasons. After all, Broadway was at this time the Great American Music. To host a suburban evening without being able to play the latest high-class entry was to indict one's taste, knowledge, style. *Oklahoma!* on 78s had pushed an astonishing number of units; there had simply never been anything like it on the charts. Sure, certain singles—Bing Crosby's "White Christmas," say—racked up numbers in the high terrifying. But *Oklahoma!* was *six* discs at once. Even Victor's Toscanini recordings of classical tourist stops such as Beethoven's Fifth Symphony didn't rival *Oklahoma!*. Not all show albums did this kind of business. But the big ones were unprecedentedly big.

Slowly, the Corporation turned. If there is so much money to

---

* By "major project" I mean a piece that counts at least one important thespian in its credits, whether as star, author, producer, director, or choreographer; or simply anything that scores a hit.

be made, why not capitalize a hit show from the start and clean up altogether? Ticket sales, LPs, movie, international, and amateur rights. Columbia searched for a hit musical to back. Musicals were hitting like crazy in the mid-1950s, though of course the LP revolution was one reason why: hearing and liking the score, folks wanted to collect the entire show. Thus, Lieberson happened upon Alan Jay Lerner and Frederick Loewe's *My Lady Liza*, an adaptation of George Bernard Shaw's *Pygmalion*. After hearing the songs, Lieberson proposed Columbia as the show's sole backer, expecting a cleanup not only on the show itself but on the cast album as well, confident that it would be bought by everyone in the nation not immobilized, incarcerated, or living in a trailer park.

The Sunday after the renamed *My Fair Lady* opened on March 15, 1956, the cast recorded the score. The following Wednesday—*three days later*, which haste may explain the listing of one of the songs as "I Want To Dance All Night"—the LP was published. Within a few weeks, something like half the middle class of the nation had grabbed it. Everywhere one went, one heard the songs. Radio and TV were saturated with them. *Life* magazine did a feature story on one ticketbuyer's experience lining up at the box office. Herbert von Karajan's 1960 recording of *Die Fledermaus* included a starry gala in which Birgit Nilsson sang "I Could Have Danced All Night." A Maine senatorial campaign in 1958 used the slogan "[Frederick] Payne of Maine is mainly on the wane." A *New Yorker* cartoon showed a housewife examining something at a bureau in the middle of the night and crying to her drowsy husband, "I knew this would happen! This was the night we had tickets to *My Fair Lady*!"

A phenomenon. When it finished its almost seven years on Broadway, at 2,717 performances, *My Fair Lady* held the long-run record for musicals, had spun off more foreign productions than any other show, and had simply become the summoning title in any discussion of hit musicals—the *War and Peace* of musicals, the Mona Lisa, Taj Mahal, *Don Juan*, caviar, *Wizard of Oz*. The One.

However, don't the other classic shows, both before and after it, have stronger claims to greatness? *Show Boat* tells a much grander story. *Oklahoma!* has more realism, *Carousel* more feeling. *On the Town* and *West Side Story* discovered dance as not only elemental but essential. *Cabaret, Company,* and *A Chorus Line* created new forms. Why did *My Fair Lady* seem to embody the brilliance and beauty of the American musical in a way that no other title was thought to?

Critic Ken Mandelbaum says that the show's heavily English background gave it what we might call "intelligentsia control": "At the time, musicals were looked upon by some as entertainment for the tired businessman; those who felt then that musicals were not on the same artistic plane as the best plays and who were ashamed of adoring *The Pajama Game, Damn Yankees,* or *Li'l Abner* felt safe raving about *Fair Lady* because it was not just a Broadway musical but also a play by Shaw."

A British play, at that—the show's setting and characters, and five of the six main players, were all imported from England. (The sixth, though raised in America, was of English family.) American theatregoers have long nurtured a profound respect for the English stage. Then, too, the oddly low-key 1955–56 season offered only flop musicals in the ten months before *My Fair Lady* appeared. The town was starving for a hit; could that have encouraged an overreaction?

Also, shows were running longer in the 1950s, giving the impression that they must be getting better. In the 1920s and 1930s, hit musicals ran a year, very rarely a little more. In the 1940s, there were fewer musicals but more people attending them, so *Oklahoma!* and *South Pacific* ran five years, *Follow the Girls, Song of Norway, Carousel, High Button Shoes, Where's Charley,* and *Gentlemen Prefer Blondes* two years. By the early 1950s, multi-year runs were even more common, though still outstanding, and *My Fair Lady*'s all-conquering run led some to think it therefore the presumptive all-conquering title. But then, that was *My Fair Lady*'s secret, in a way: to appear very much of its kind yet the leader.

However, *My Fair Lady* is not *of* its kind, but the whole kind, sui generis. It is an outstanding show not because it is better than all others but because it is different from all others. Not as dif-

ferent as *The Golden Apple, Reuben, Reuben,* or *Shinbone Alley,*
no. But they weren't Big Broadway. *My Fair Lady* is the mainstream, state-of-the-art show that, in its sneaky way, is totally bizarre. First of all, the leading man cannot sing.

We're used to this now; it was quite a novelty then, though it
became more common as the decade wore on. Before Rex Harrison's Henry Higgins, Rosalind Russell, Hildegarde "Neff", and
Ralph Meeker were all signed to "sing" leads in musicals, though
this meant careful, indulgent composition of the songs for actors
who more or less couldn't carry a tune (and though Meeker ultimately gave up, on *The Pajama Game,* during rehearsals).* After
My Fair Lady, Ricardo Montalban, Max Adrian, Sydney Chaplin,
Jack Warden, Steve Forrest, Farley Granger, Barry Sullivan (he,
too, left before a Broadway opening), Keye Luke, Tony Randall,
Melvyn Douglas, and Walter Pidgeon all brought varying non-
abilities as vocalists to leads in musicals; and Robert Preston and
Andy Griffith could actually sing.

Keep in mind, too, that Higgins cannot ham-and-egg his way
through the score. He has full-sized parts or completely solos in
six numbers, a Merman-sized quota—and one of the six is a ballad. Moreover, two of the other six principals are non-singers as
well—Mrs. Higgins (Cathleen Nesbitt) and Colonel Pickering
(Robert Coote), who can bluster his way through "The Rain in
Spain" but does have to sustain a few notes in "You Did It," an
often embarrassing moment in *My Fair Lady* revivals.

Something else: no love plot. After all, that's how Shaw wrote
the Higgins–Eliza relationship, and virtually all their lines in the
musical come directly from Shavian text. True, one can play those
lines with an unShavian tilt, letting the sparring between Higgins
and Eliza (Julie Andrews) gradually discover a secret, tender,
vexed symbiosis. Still, there are no genuine love songs, as the two
are almost as culturally separated as Anna and the King and thus

---

* Comic players, of course, had a long tradition of talking through their numbers, but there were very few serious or romantic leads before 1950 who basically
could not sing. Here's one: Walter Huston's Pieter Stuyvesant in Kurt Weill's
Knickerbocker Holiday in 1936.

can only romance in subtext—"Just You Wait," "I Could Have Danced All Night" (the closest Eliza gets to a love song), "Without You," and finally the sole romantic utterance allotted to either, "I've Grown Accustomed to Her Face."

There isn't even a romantic subplot of the Tuptim–Lun Tha type. There is only Freddy Eynsford-Hill (Michael King, son of oldtime operetta hero and straight actor Dennis King), who falls for Eliza, supplies the show's one other romantic number, "On* the Street Where You Live," and, in Shaw's own view of it, marries Eliza after *Pygmalion* proper is over.

Most unusual of all is *My Fair Lady*'s book, because Lerner did not adapt *Pygmalion* as much as adopt it: not only Eliza and Higgins' lines, but virtually every character's is Shaw's script cut down, with music. There are a few additions. Eliza's father, Alfred Doolittle (Stanley Holloway), is given two establishing scenes he lacks in Shaw, and Lerner wrote some new bits of continuity in the play's second half, when the sets change more constantly than in Shaw.

Nevertheless, *My Fair Lady* is largely Shaw verbatim, and this is why the musical plays so oddly without anyone's noticing: Shaw's dialogue is clever in a way that even first-rate musical-comedy books never are; his *Pygmalion* characters are individualized and fascinating. Some Shavian personalities are no more than mouthpieces—not here. Even Mrs. Higgins, who in any other writer's hands might have come off as a long-suffering, vaguely sympathetic old peach, is instead as blunt and determined as her son. (Indeed, it is Shaw's contention that Higgins has never married because he already has a wonderful relationship with a brilliant woman. This one.)

Besides, Shaw's scenes are not structured as musical-comedy scenes are. The authors tried to round Shaw out by giving a big number to Doolittle in each act, by resetting Eliza's "coming out"

---

* Mistake! It should be, in the English usage, "*In* the Street Where You Live." Lyricist Lerner also lumbered Higgins with grammatical errors—"hung" for "hanged," split infinitives, and the "illiterate tautology" (in H. W. Fowler's words) "equally as," in the line about "a dentist to be drilling," further offending the language by finishing off the sentence with "than" for the needed "as."

from Mrs. Higgins' at-home to Ascot, making the Embassy Ball (published in the *Pygmalion* script, but almost never performed) the site of a Big Ballet, and taking the "de-classed" (in Shaw's terminology) Eliza on a nostalgic trip to her old flower market for a reprise of "Wouldn't It Be Loverly?" Even so, the musical's scenes play with a tightness of logic and moral argument utterly foreign to musical comedy or the musical play.

It is interesting to note that Rodgers and Hammerstein had worked on a musical version of *Pygmalion* before giving it up as undoable—yes, if you try to *transform* it. Lerner didn't make *Pygmalion* into a musical. He made a musical into *Pygmalion*.

That's why the show is weird. As one sees it in the theatre, it doesn't seem so (especially as we're all so familiar with it, not least through the ever-present movie adaptation). It's tuneful, funny, socially aware, moves with elegance, and, if well cast, gives the two leads dynamite combat to enact. Only on examination does the piece reveal its quixotic character.

For instance, midway through Act One, there's a sequence made of alternating song and dialogue that is generally conceded to be the point at which critics and public realized that *My Fair Lady* was not just very enjoyable but very special. In fact, more than one seasoned and unbiased thespian has called this *My Fair Lady*'s "danger point," so to say. For by upping the stakes from fine to fabulous, the authors would then have to maintain fabulous throughout the rest of the evening or the show would implode.

Very few musicals have tried this. The moment has to occur in Act One (by Act Two it is too late: the tenor of the evening has already been set), and, again, it has to follow the already first-rate with the promise of the consistently superb. A busy show, with a lot of characters and narrative is by nature out of the running; this is about a concentration of texture. So *Show Boat, Guys and Dolls, Candide, Follies,* and *Rent* couldn't have contained such a moment. *Cabaret* and *Pacific Overtures* do it, most daringly, in their opening numbers, which virtually announce unique staging plans that will have to thrill and bemuse without a lessening of tension right to the final curtain.

My Fair Lady put its money on what we may call the Lessons Scene, played in the show's main set, Higgins' study:

> ELIZA: The rine in Spine stays minely in the pline.
> HIGGINS: The rain in Spain stays mainly in the plain.
> ELIZA: Didn't I sy that?

Higgins tries to coach Eliza into pronouncing an "h," Colonel Pickering looking on with a remark or two. The scene builds to a climax as Eliza learns to aspirate by repeating "Ha" in front of a candle till it goes out and the stage is plunged into darkness. Now, as strings and xylophone ape the chiming of a clock, a spotlight picks up six servants who sing a ditty ("Poor Professor Higgins!"), apparently underlining the difficulty in teaching good English to a Cockney but really designed to suggest the passing of time in the music's ticking beat. The lights come up on the study again, presumably some days or weeks later, for another lesson, this one dedicated to turning Eliza's "cappatea" into "cup of tea." Blackout, the servants again, their songlet pitched one step higher for dramatic heightening, and now we have a lesson in enunciation complete with a mouthful of marbles. Another comic climax—Eliza swallows one—and another blackout bring a third servants' ditty, higher again in key and now promising rebellion at the endless, repetitious drilling. As their music fades, Higgins brings us back to the sequence's first line, a warning that closure is imminent:

> HIGGINS: (*wearily*) The rain in Spain stays mainly in the plain.
> ELIZA: I can't. I'm so tired. I'm so tired.

Working entirely originally, Lerner has shown us something Shaw skipped over: the process.* How does Higgins treat his student? How aptly does she get on? What's the Colonel's role in it all? One problem with Shaw as storyteller is that he doesn't bother with anything that he personally finds uninteresting; this can leave holes in his stories. Lerner wants to give the tale some naturalism, firming up the time line and presenting to us Higgins the tyrant and idealist, Eliza the sleeping princess. What's more, unlike Shaw, he wants ultimately to bring the two together, so he

---

* Shaw wrote one brief lesson scene, but, as the published text indicates, he laid it out for the *reader's* curiosity, and did not expect it to be staged.

must give them some point of emotional contact, something that Higgins will enjoy and then brush aside but will leave a mark on Eliza. Or even: something that he will think he did and something that she will think she did.

So this time she gets it right: "The rain in Spain stays mainly in the plain," suddenly total and true. "What was that?" Higgins asks, bolt upright even in his exhaustion. She gets it right once more. "Again," he says.

Now the orchestra slips in with her repetition, *Tempo di Haba-ñera*, though she isn't yet singing. The Spanish tune is a charmingly silly touch, a pun, and its romantic surge during the release ("Now, once again . . .") is too lovely for a comedy song. But the genius of the whole sequence is that it's all a bit errant yet perfectly centered. "The Rain in Spain" is one of the best cued-in songs in the musical's history. It literally "comes out" of the action without trying to. It's also a very short number, leaping into a dance as if in relief at getting away from all that elocution and diction. The dance itself, a bullfight thing between Higgins and Pickering while Eliza does flamenco on the couch, is logical but completely unacceptable: logical because of the Habañera but unacceptable because what do these characters know of Spanish dance styles? It's a matter of feeling, of collaboration, of pals. "Why Can't the English?," "Wouldn't It Be Loverly?," "With a Little Bit of Luck," "I'm an Ordinary Man," and "Just You Wait" uphold a high level of composition, but it was "The Rain in Spain" that defined *My Fair Lady*'s individual brilliance. Keep in mind that two and half minutes later Eliza breaks into "I Could Have Danced All Night" and immediately after that comes the scenically dazzling (and very funny) episode at Ascot, and one sees *My Fair Lady*'s secret: it is ingeniously put together out of parts that no musical had ever had before.*

The score has its quiddities, too. I should point out, for starters,

---

* "The Rain in Spain" at first did prove a worrisome coup, in that a long dance sequence relating the preparations for Eliza's visit to the Embassy, a number for Higgins entitled "Come To the Ball," and Eliza's "Say a Prayer For Me Tonight" all seemed to dispel "Spain"'s high energy level. These three numbers were dropped out of town. "Prayer," which made its way into Lerner and Loewe's *Gigi* score, can still be heard in *My Fair Lady* in the music leading into the Embassy scene, transposed into a march.

the extremely strange opening number, billed in the program as "Street Entertainers." The curtain rises on a nervous bustle, scored nervously, C Major abutting A Flat Major in a kind of food fight of a tune, as an opera audience standing outside Covent Garden seeks taxis while buskers dance for alms. It's an astonishingly empty picture for a show with a ton of sociopolitical content to unload. One envisions audience after audience, back in 1956, when this was the hottest ticket there had ever been, thinking, "What's so great?" Then a busker bumps into Eliza, not seen till this moment, and she goes on about her flowers being ruined, and someone warns her that a cop is taking down everything she's saying, and he comes out from behind a pillar, only it's not a cop: it's Higgins. There they are, the pair. The two-minute opening music and dance and the street entertainers vanish from consideration. They were never there, even. It was all a crazy way to get the curtain up on a crazy show. I can see Rodgers and Hammerstein, when they were trying it, asking each other, "But how would it start?" This way.

Moving on: Has there ever been a purer melody than that to "I Could Have Danced All Night," so C Major, so basic, so free of harmonic facetiae? (I remember thinking, as a child, how come no one thought of this tune before? It's so . . . obvious. I thought that of the title song to *Camelot*, too.) This number, too, erupts out of the action: Mrs. Pearce, Higgins' housekeeper, says, "Eliza, I don't care what Mr. Higgins says, you must put down your books and go to bed." Strings and woodwinds trip excitedly down the scale as Eliza sings "Bed! Bed! I couldn't go to bed!," and we're off in a rare case of a ballad's being played *Allegro molto* ("very quick"), wonderfully developed for plot when two concerned servants sing a duet in counterpoint to Eliza's second chorus while getting her to sack out on the couch. There's a wonderful touch, too, in the treatment of the three-note pickup to the last A (on "I only [know when he . . .]"). In the first two choruses, Frederick Loewe put a *tenuto* ("held") on each of the three notes, in the sense of pulling back, aggrandizing. But then, in the final chorus, Loewe marked the notes *a tempo* (that is, going straight on) for a sweeping, headlong effect to close the number and the scene on a note of ecstatic pleasure.

Again, it's the *detailed* expertise of the show that I wish to de-
note, the way that all the musical's arts, great and dainty, were
marshaled most particularly in this work—the frenzied *spiccato*
violin solo in the Hungarian pastiche (including quotations of
Liszt's *Second Hungarian Rhapsody*) of "You Did It"; the in fact
altogether brilliant orchestrations of Robert Russell Bennett and
Phil[lip J.] Lang, which play wonderful games under the voice in
"I Could Have Danced All Night," yet find something subtly different to do with each chorus; the smashing pageantry of the "Ascot Gavotte," Cecil Beaton's rococo black-and-white costumes for
the women (the men were in the regulation grey) against the se-
rene white and gold of Oliver Smith's set, a truly startling beauty
after the almost drab quarters in Higgins' house; Moss Hart's stylish direction, which gave the chorus striking faux Edwardian poses
and walks that imitative directors retain in revival without conviction; even the simple utter rightness of Al Hirschfeld's poster logo
of Shaw, on a cloud, working a Rex Harrison puppet working a
Julie Andrews puppet.

Columbia Records of course flourished that logo on the cast
album, which outsold every other recording of any kind, affirming
not only Broadway's majesty as the top money-spinner in American popular music but *My Fair Lady*'s majesty as the show album
that even people who didn't listen to show albums had to listen
to, or at least play, or at least own.* Business this big isn't just
art; it's culturally imperative. It's capitalism at its best.

* A note on this epochal recording. Goddard Lieberson of course produced it,
as he did virtually all of Columbia's cast albums right up to *A Chorus Line* in
1975, though in 78 days the sessions were supervised by Mitchell Ayres. Along
the way, Lieberson made some very virtuous history, as when he unprecedentedly
taped the entire score to *The Most Happy Fella* (on three discs) or insisted on
recording Stephen Sondheim's *Anyone Can Whistle* even after it had closed.
However, Lieberson had a horror of taking shows down as they were performed
and would tirelessly needle a piece with unnecessary changes—deleting lines
spoken during a song, inventing orchestral lead-ins, concocting medley finales
(such as that to *A Tree Grows in Brooklyn*, though it includes a few notes from
Johnny, who at this point in the story is dead), and so on. Thus, Lieberson
makes nonsense of the first line of "Wouldn't It Be Loverly?" Over the clarinet
arabesques leading into the chorus, a Cockney asks, "Where're ya bound this
spring, Eliza—Biarritz?," to which she of course replies, "All I want is a room
somewhere . . .": another example of how beautifully these songs relate to the

Had *My Fair Lady* no flaws? The choreography (by Hanya Holm) was ordinary, no match for the more famous compositions that de Mille, Robbins, and others blocked out for other classic shows. But that's about it—unless one deplores, along with Shaw, the "lazy dependence on the ready-mades and reach-me-downs of the ragshop in which Romance keeps its stock of 'happy endings' to misfit all stories." In short: Eliza returns, forgivingly, to the impossible Higgins.

Shaw himself wrote an epilogue to the play, in prose, outlining his notion of What Happens Next. Interestingly, while Eliza does marry Freddy, she retains her connection to Higgins and Pickering. The latter she dotes upon and the former she ever wars with. Says Shaw, "Galatea never does quite like Pygmalion: his relation to her is too godlike to be altogether agreeable."

I hear in that the cranky pamphleteer. Who is Shaw, a man who didn't have a sexual encounter till he was twenty-nine and lived for the most part ascetically after that, to discourse upon Romance? Eliza *can* like Higgins precisely because his tantrums and childish need to control render him all too mortal. Understanding him, she can love him.

It was a long-established tradition that hit Broadway shows would close in New York and then tour the whole production, packed up and hauled from city to city. Occasionally, exceptional successes would cast and launch one or more touring productions while the original was still in New York—*Oh, Boy!* (1917), *Blossom Time* (1921), *My Maryland* (1927), *Oklahoma!*, *South Pacific*. *My Fair Lady*'s tour, which opened on March 18, 1957, at Rochester's Masonic Auditorium with Brian Aherne and Anne Rogers and ran five years, was so carefully planned that it employed two

---

libretto. That is, the song's first words are an answer to a question, the spoken words invoking the sung ones. *That's* loverly. But Lieberson dropped the Cockney's question—we must hear those clarinets!—so Eliza's first line seems a non sequitur. Lieberson also made the orchestra play the "Danced All Night" tenutos on all three choruses, sapping the song's last page of its vitality, though one can hear the true ending on the London cast (also produced by Lieberson) and most other *My Fair Lady* discs. Lieberson's mania for adjustments was so perverse that he recorded the third chorus of "Danced All Night" repeating the *second* chorus' orchestrations. *Why?*

sets of scenery, one to play in and one to send on to the next date. This was a big show, built around a revolving stage—and maybe that's another reason why this title so overwhelmed the glory of other shows: it was the most elaborate production yet, even more expensive than *The King and I.*

Whatever its quality, it was without question the hot ticket of the decade. Just to have taken it in was a social feat, and here's a famous story on that matter, so famous that it's twice-told and perhaps should not be repeated. But isn't it part of the history?

Early in the run, a woman attending *My Fair Lady* with her husband notices that the seat next to them is empty. A vacant seat at the hit of the century? During the intermission, she leans over the empty seat and asks the woman across from her how this has come to be. Has her husband been called away on some vital government mission?

"I'm afraid my husband's dead," the other woman replies.

After murmuring the expected obsequies, the first woman asks, "But couldn't one of his friends have escorted you?"

"They're all at the funeral."

11

Li'l Abner

In London, generally, fifties theatregoers divided into two groups: those who frequented musicals (and plays by boulevardiers such as Noël Coward and Terence Rattigan) and those who frequented anything else. There were no equivalents among the English musicals for *Show Boat*, *The Cat and the Fiddle*, *Oklahoma!*, or *The Most Happy Fella*, or any other breakthrough American title. Indeed, the West End kept its musical scene vital simply by importing the above-named shows.

In New York, theatregoers divided into all sorts of groups—those who went only to the more audacious offerings of off-Broadway, those who followed favorite stars, and so on. But everyone went to musicals, because they were reflections of culture. Manhattan's tinhorn underworld, television, labor relations, the marketing of celebrity, baseball fever, the Cold War, Hollywood—*topics* were what the musical loved now, because its zest for social commentary was always hungry for new subject matter.

Perhaps it was inevitable that the musical would get around to Al Capp's comic strip of life in Dogpatch—a hillbilly mountain town of freaks and types—because social commentary was Capp's stock-in-trade. John Steinbeck called Capp "the best satirist since Laurence Sterne." The series, which started in 1934 when Capp left his job as Ham Fisher's assistant on *Joe Palooka*, was an entirely original one, fantastical and wide-ranging, eager to tackle anything in American life that Capp felt needed a good, solid spanking. At the center stood the gloriously stupid hunk Abner Yokum, his ridiculous little Pappy and formidable Mammy, along with Abner's eternal girl friend, Daisy Mae Scragg.*

There were plenty of regulars, mainly the citizens of Dogpatch, including bully Earthquake McGoon, curvacious but aromatic Moonbeam McSwine, aggressive Tobacco Rhoda, Marryin' Sam (who performs, rather than takes part in his ceremonies, as a deadpan god of conclusion, marriage as a crossing over into death), the hog tycoon J. Roaringham Fatback, who demanded that Onnecessary Mountain be moved because it threw a shadow over his breakfast egg, charmless Lonesome Polecat and his inseparable buddy, the hairy Hairless Joe. But much of *Li'l Abner* involved people from *outside* Dogpatch—evil plutocrat General Bullmoose, King Nogoodnick of Lower Slobbovia, the Shmoos and Kigmies and the Bald Iggle, whose gaze induces truth-telling and thus must be destroyed by the government.

Sixties social upheaval led Capp to introduce such figures as Joanie Phonie (i.e., Joan Baez) when, like many other liberals of the FDR stripe, Capp noted the destructive element in the New Left and shifted rightward. Capp himself claimed that it was the Left that had moved, not he. But in attacking leftist sacred cows, he lost his intellectual following.

Still—a *Life* cover! Capp was central in the 1950s, and a number of writers tried to adapt him for the stage. The version that came to Broadway had a book by Norman Panama and Melvin Frank, music by Gene de Paul, and lyrics by Johnny Mercer. Most

---

* The strip was so big that when Abner and Daisy Mae capped their eighteen-year courtship by marrying, in 1952, *Life* magazine made it a cover story. "At last, *our* dreams," crowed Mammy to Pappy, "an' th' dreams o' billyuns o' *other* decent people has *come* true!!" Ironically, this national event was inspired by a chance insult. "Look, don't think of yourself as another Dickens," someone told Capp. "You're a guy who's got one trick—Abner doesn't marry Daisy Mae. That's all that's in that strip."

important, it was directed and choreographed by Michael Kidd. It had to be—for Broadway had only just realized that, in certain musicals, the key player is the choreographer. Not in the musical play or the musical comedies strong in characterization, such as *Plain and Fancy*. But in a cartoon-style musical comedy, where the absurd, the picturesque, and the crazy reign, isn't the guy leading the dances the guy closest to the very spirit of the show? I'm talking energy, motion, even vision—one thespian's "whole idea" of how the finished piece should look, sound, and behave. In the 1920s, that was the producer—Florenz Ziegfeld, say. In the 1990s, that will be the director—Harold Prince, probably. In the dancing 1950s, it was the choreographer. And note that Kidd was one of *Li'l Abner*'s producers.

The director-choreographer is actually an old hand at the musical. Two such, Julian Mitchell and Edward Royce, were already at work at the turn of the century. But their choreography was of a standard cut, a series of hoofing "combinations" replicated from show to show. Much later, George Balanchine, Charles Weidman, and Agnes de Mille reinstituted dance in all its sorts, and in 1947 de Mille became the first Third Age director-choreographer, on Rodgers and Hammerstein's *Allegro*.* It happened, in a way, by fluke: de Mille had choreographed the first two Rodgers and Hammerstein shows, and the third, this same *Allegro*, was to be played largely on an open stage, scene flowing into scene rather than scene ending and then scene starting. It would be three hours of movement, and thus needed a kind of . . . what? dance guardian?

One year later, Gower Champion was the director-choreographer of *Lend an Ear*, but this bitty revue hardly needed a wizard in charge. Indeed, its tidy proportions were probably why its producers let one talent stage the entire thing himself. The true wizard would be Jerome Robbins, staging the Mary Martin *Peter Pan* in 1954. Robbins had already co-directed (but not choreographed) *The Pajama Game*, and then directed (but only co-

---

* Balanchine actually preceded de Mille on two earlier forties shows, *Cabin in the Sky* and *What's Up*, as the overall director and choreographer, though the book scenes were in fact credited to others.

choreographed) *Bells Are Ringing* in 1956. Still, clearly, a new job was being created, one that would define an entire musical by the style in which it danced. At the decade's end or so, Bob Fosse joined Robbins and Kidd, Champion returned, and a new era had dawned, in which, sometimes, production would collaborate with or even overpower composition. In a way, *Allegro* is responsible for this, as the script and score were written around a staging concept which, therefore, was in effect shaping the text, or at least tilting the authors' approach to the text.

Li'l Abner's composition, on the other hand, is very conventional in structure. There was the typical barnstorming overture with its attention-getting salutation (a rustic violin tuning up on open fifths), played to a show curtain of a fence covered with in-joke Dogpatch graffiti, the typical opening chorus (called, in fact, "A Typical Day, in which the Dogpatch locals were introduced one by one), the typical in-one, scene-change plot scenes, the typical Act One love song ("Namely You"), the typical Act Two love song, introduced when a plot hitch derails the romance* ("Love in a Home"), the typical Act One curtain full of plot suspense, the typical fifties duet for alternating voices popularized by Frank Loesser, generally used for comic effect, as here by Daisy Mae and Marryin' Sam ("I'm Past My Prime"), the typical asinine ensemble number that plays well because of the staging but gets dropped from the cast album ("There's Room Enough For Us"), the typical number that gets dropped from the *show* yet maintains an echo in a dance ("In Society"), the typical wrapping up of the plot at the very last second, immediately followed—actually, in this case interrupted—by a fast reprise by the whole cast of something noisy for a typical jubilant curtain. And so on.

Nevertheless, if the organization of the material is ordinary, the material itself is faithful to Capp's grotesquerie, and this makes *Li'l Abner* unique in characters, design, and story. The show looked like a comic strip. The plot itself is amazingly detailed even for a musical comedy. It's the kind one can follow in one's theatre

---

* Cf. "Once Upon a Time Today," "Wish You Were Here," "A Quiet Girl," "My Heart Won't Say Goodbye," "Other Hands, Other Hearts," "Why Does It Have To Be You?," "Follow Your Heart," "Two Lost Souls," "If That Was Love."

seat but, coming out at the end, could not recount for a million dollars. Roughly, and in *very* brief: Daisy Mae chases Abner; Abner resists. Instead of the typical secondary romance, there is a political subplot—the government wants to use Dogpatch as a nuclear testing site. In *another* subplot, government scientists discover miraculous salutary benefits in the tonic that Mammy brews from her yokumberry tree, and General Bullmoose wants to get his hands on it, nefariously if possible.

The three plots are ingeniously interlaced, and so propulsive that, for once, a musical's second act is not only *not* short in story but overloaded with it. Moreover, there are takeoffs on or at least cracks about everything from consumer culture, bodybuilding and Levittown to the Teamsters Union, TV quiz shows, and Congress. Add in such Cappian icons as Evil-Eye Fleagle, Stupefyin' Jones, and Apassionata Von Climax, as well as the annual Sadie Hawkins Day Race (in which the Dogpatch women chase the Dogpatch men: who's caught gets hitched), and *Li'l Abner* was rich in authenticity, not to mention Dogpatch's pseudo-redneck argot. (Unhappily greeting her bad relations, the Scraggs, Daisy Mae remarks, "We only meet at weddin's and hangin's—usally theyah own.") The show even opened the same month as Sadie Hawkins Day, on November 15, 1956, sporting a poster logo by Capp himself.

Of course, a musical based on a popular comic strip can have a casting problem, even if *You're A Good Man, Charlie Brown* and *Annie* are done everywhere all the time. *Li'l Abner's* producers were lucky that Peter Palmer happened along when he did; who else was Li'l Abner's double, sang well, and read lines in character? Edith Adams filled out Daisy Mae's wondering dimness in good faith; Charlotte Rae and Joe E. Marks were perfect as the senior Yokums; Howard St. John played a fine, smooth Bullmoose; Julie Newmar was original sin itself as the non-speaking Stupefyin' Jones. There was one piece of false casting, the amiable Stubby Kaye as Marryin' Sam, for in Capp this character is humorless and aggressive. But then, anything with Stubby Kaye in it is a happier show.*

---

* Palmer, Adams, St. John, Kaye, and Rae got featured billing, followed by eight names in smaller type, including Marks and Newmar but also a few actors

Happy above all is what fifties musical comedy was: a modern version of what Jacques Offenbach termed "le genre primitif et gai"—a quickstep burlesque that has no use for Shaw's class-conscious ironies or a leading man so stimulated by his mother that he cannot mate. Actually, *Li'l Abner* is as rich in class consciousness as *My Fair Lady* but in its own Cappian way, concentrating not on language-as-class but on the more American appearance-as-class. We know General Bullmoose is a villain because he has a big office, a gorgeous boring girl friend in fur, and flunkeys who on signal sing an *a cappella* ditty ending, "What's good for General Bullmoose is good for the U.S.A.!"

Li'l Abner has the mother problem, too. As anyone even slightly familiar with the strip knows, Abner has a powerful mom and no mating instinct whatever. Again, it's the Cappian version: Abner isn't emotionally but *nutritionally* damaged, for the yokumberries that give him his strength also stunt his romantic urge. *My Fair Lady* had to twist Shaw to bring Higgins and Eliza together; Abner has only to imbibe a "potion" (made of swamp water) to liberate his amorous faculties and claim Daisy Mae.

What about the dancing? There was a lot of it, and it's fair to say that it matched the look of the show and the sound of the show: Michael Kidd was the musical's auteur as sure as Capp was the comic strip's. Even the scenery danced. That opening number, "A Typical Day," roved through Dogpatch with the use of decor mounted on "wagons," so that new sights could be rolled on and off almost as if a camera were in charge. Marryin' Sam rode in on a donkey, Daisy Mae appeared atop a hill, and, as the hill moved off, a house and porch appeared with the Yokums, Abner napping under a newspaper.

If de Mille and Robbins were the ballet choreographers and Fosse the slick sex touter, Kidd was the stamper, the banger, the

---

whose impact on stage was frankly tiny. Again, this was characteristic fifties billing, especially in musical comedy. Apparently, the aim was to suggest shows stuffed with performing talent. But such excess could mystify, as when *The Vamp* listed Carol Channing above the title and *fourteen* names below it, or when *Me and Juliet's* Jackie Kelk, who had perhaps fifteen lines, was cited just below the title along with the show's five leads.

crasher. His kids worked harder than de Mille's, Robbins', and Fosse's, for Kidd gave them no pensive pause, no soft shoe. Kidd's Dogpatchers were ceaselessly going berserk, building numbers, shaping the line, stomping the floor as if trying to work into the basement. "(Don't that take the) Rag Off'n the Bush" was basic, a choral number that is simply an excuse for a dance. It took Kidd's corps exactly thirty seconds to get through the vocal, and then they were off on the real business of the evening: dancing. Orchestrator Philip J. Lang brought out a *concertante* feeling in the music as the view constantly changed, from the boys doing Chaplinesque tramps to the girls playing coy, to Pappy's solo, Mammy's solo, their sour-mash pas de deux, and on to the final vocal chorus, the ensemble earning its paycheck with mule kicks, a "Klondike" step, and a giant can-can line: not because the story feels this way right this moment but because the *show* does.

Kidd's masterpiece was the finale of Act One, the lengthy "Sadie Hawkins Ballet." Here the *concertante* air was supplied by the dancers, for Kidd allowed everyone at least one solo as Daisy chased Abner and boys and girls grouped and regrouped, ran, hid, got caught, escaped, got "stupefied" (by Julie Newmar: any man who sees her bodacious self freezes in his tracks), and led the plot toward the first-act curtain, a mass wedding of the captured men and victorious women and, mainly, the terrible moment when Abner got stupefied and General Bullmoose's confederate, Apassionata von Climax, took two steps, claimed Abner, and Daisy Mae stood forlorn to the strains of "Namely You."

So story did matter. Indeed, amid all the plot snarls involving health tonics and nuclear testing, it was the love plot that held the show together, just as it held Capp's strip together. Remember?—"You're a guy who's got one trick." Then why did *Li'l Abner* need a director-choreographer? Because dance was by the 1950s so important that the head "integrator" of the musical's elements might better be a dance man than a book or score man. Integrated books and scores were easy now; dance was tricky. Unruly, unpredictable. Worse yet: abstract. Who knew what a choreographer might do if he were not responsible for the storytelling as well? Letting choreographers direct was almost a bribe: to get them to respect the narrative. Robbins did it in *Peter Pan* by figuring out how a fairy tale behaves. Kidd did it in *Li'l Abner* by figuring out how a comic strip feels.

In all, *Li'l Abner* found the satiric musical comedy in fine health, which is good news for democracy. What's more free in a free society than *le primitif et gai?* At 693 performances this show remains the decade's biggest forgotten hit—despite a 1998 City Center concert staging—although a Paramount film preserves virtually the entire New York closing cast in a replica of Kidd's production, albeit shot on Hollywood sound stages. Like the film of *Top Banana* (which was shot in the theatre), the *Li'l Abner* movie brings us of today back to what a fifties musical was like as a living experience.

Actually, Paramount's decision to take down what Kidd had done with *Li'l Abner* rather than revise *Li'l Abner* for the screen tells us how imposing the director–choreographer was becoming, and why I have again given a chapter to a forgotten show: *Li'l Abner* typifies mid-fifties musical comedy in its social satire and dependence on production smarts.

Still, what the director-choreographer had yet to do, in 1956, was stage not just a hit musical but an enduring classic with the artistic weight of *Oklahoma!* or *The Most Happy Fella*. Something with the emotional resonance that, some thought, was simply beyond a dancer's comprehension.

Coming soon.

12

Candide

Each decade has its uniquely influential title. In the 1920s, it's *Show Boat*. In the 1930s, it's *On Your Toes*. In the 1940s, it's *Oklahoma!*

This decade, it's *Candide*: because of its extraordinary music, its never-before picaresque structure, its cast of every vocal possibility from tenor Robert Rounseville and mezzo Irra Petina through musical-comedy heroine turned coloratura soprano Barbara Cook to non-singer Max Adrian, its sheer defiance of the elements. After *Oklahoma!*, serious musical playmaking was possible; after *Candide, anything* was possible, because, suddenly, nothing was unthinkable. This discovery—which eventually would provision *Pacific Overtures, Rent*, and *Titanic*—was perhaps the last crucial revolutionary development in the musical's history.

If *My Fair Lady* typifies the mid-fifties musical play and *Li'l Abner* the musical comedy, *Candide* is the High Maestro Opus, musically a Blitzkrieg that seemed to originate from other climes than Broadway. Legit composers are not a novelty on The Street, but they tended to write popular—Victor Herbert, Vernon Duke,

Kurt Weill. Leonard Bernstein had done so, too, in On the Town's songs (not in its ballets) and in Wonderful Town. Here, in Candide, he wrote Total, for a Total subject that was staged extremely Totally. From its opening on December 1, 1956, Candide created controversy, and, though it is now a repertory item, it does after all come from the most controversial novel ever published, "translated from the German by Doctor Ralph." So ran Voltaire's byline. Though he was by then in French-speaking Switzerland, out of the reach of the French police, all his life he (uselessly) denied that he had written Candide; or, The Optimist Philosophy (1759).

Let's get the book down first. It's a short and relentless Bildungsroman in which a gentle young German tours the Western world, now fleeing, now invading, now adventuring, all the while learning that the then trendy "Whatever is, is right" worldview (to quote Alexander Pope) is a fraud.

Humanitarian, rationalist, and religion-hater, Voltaire was in fact going after the German philosopher Leibniz, in a fury at Leibniz's having disgraced what Voltaire believed was the philosopher's mandate: to tell truth. Leibniz's idiotic apologies for every brutality on earth incensed Voltaire. So he invented a German youth (Candide = "naive") who loves a selfish minor princess (Cunégonde) with a vain brother (unnamed in the novel; called Maximilian in the musical), all three taught by a Leibniz (Pangloss = "explainer of everything"), and showed them the world as it is. Forever victimized by man's natural bent for larceny and rapacity, they keep surging back for more. Finally, all end up in Westphalia, where they had started. There Candide, at last cured of his master's hopelessly inadequate teaching, responds to a last outburst of candy-coating the world's ills with "Okay, but let's just settle down and try to live life as best we can." The more concise original could literally be translated as "We should tend our garden."

It's a wild ride, this book. For example:

> One day, Cunégonde, while walking near the château, in the little woods that was called The Estate, saw through the bushes Dr. Pangloss giving a lesson in experimental physics to her mother's chambermaid, a very pretty and accommodating little brunette. As Mlle. Cunégonde had quite an interest in

science, she quietly observed the repeated experiments on display; she clearly saw the doctor's theorem, the effects and causes, and went home all in a state, thoughtful, filled with the need to become wise, dreaming that she could serve as a theorem for young Candide, as he could serve as hers.*

Or:

After the earthquake that destroyed three-fourths of Lisbon, the local wise men could find no better way to avoid absolute destruction than to give the people an excellent *auto-da-fé*; it was decided by the University of Coïmbre that the entertainment of people being burned alive, in a great spectacle, is an infallible secret for the prevention of earthquakes.

Or:

"Who," said Candide, "is that fat pig who so denigrated the play I so enjoyed?"
    "He's a self-hating killjoy," answered the abbé, "who earns his living by panning all plays and books; he hates whoever succeeds as eunuchs hate lovers: he's one of those serpents of writing who feed on mud and vermin; he's a hack."
    "A hack?"
    "A Fréron.†

There is no question that Voltaire was one of the world's great liberal pioneers. When new, the novel *Candide* was dangerous, democratic, and rational, and Lillian Hellman and Leonard Bernstein fixed on it as the source of a show they would write to defy McCarthyism as Voltaire had defied the hypocrites of his day. The two were especially eager to play the Inquisition that follows the Lisbon earthquake as a McCarthyite hearing. For the lyrics, they called on John Latouche of *The Golden Apple* and *The Vamp*. It would seem that Hellman had in mind a play with a bit of music, like her version of Jean Anouilh's *The Lark*, for which Bernstein had provided medieval background noises. Bernstein, however, had in mind the Great American Comic Operetta.
    Latouche died, replaced by Richard Wilbur, and Hellman re-

---

* The extracts from Voltaire appear in my own translation.
† Élie Catherine Fréron, a critic who lived to attack and attacked to live. We still have them.

signed herself to writing the book of a musical. This she did in a voice unlike Voltaire's but also unlike anything Hellman had produced before. For instance, from the Inquisition Scene, in which Candide and Pangloss are tried by a fast, sly young lawyer and two weary, cynical old priests:

> POLICEMAN: (*who has been looking in* CANDIDE's *bag.*) Germs of earthquake have been found.
> LAWYER: (*to* CANDIDE) You are charged with communication with the Devil.
> VERY OLD INQUISITOR: Oh, come on. You always take too long. Guilty.
> LAWYER: Just a minute, sir. We must observe certain legal, civil, and moral laws as written into the code of Western liberalism. (*To* CANDIDE) Death by hanging.

It's an odd voice, aphoristic and stylized, but far from Voltaire's dry synopsis, not to mention the contemporary naturalism that Hellman favored in her own works.

Hellman also chose to reduce the scope of Voltaire's tour, which covers the eighteenth century's idea of the known world. In Hellman, the wandering Candide, Cunegonde, Pangloss, and Maximilian start from Westphalia and then see only Lisbon, Paris, Buenos Aires, and Venice before returning home, meanwhile picking up the Old Lady (who suddenly appears, to help, manage, nag, and preen) and Martin (Pangloss' cynical alter ego, a pessimist, played by the same actor). Two of Voltaire's leading characters, Paquette and Candide's servant, Cacambo, were dropped. (Paquette's name was retained, for a one-line bit.) Still, the cast was huge, and the show had so many small and tiny parts that almost everyone in the chorus got something special to do at some point and the program made no attempt to list every role.

Here was another very expensive item, up there with *The King and I*, *Make a Wish*, and *My Fair Lady* in the $350,000 area. The cost of the wigs alone would have kept a lawyer happy, and Tyrone Guthrie's staging aimed at a stylish but very crowded opulence. Much of Voltaire's grotesquerie was not only respected but expanded. Hellman did think twice about the episode in which Candide kills monkeys that seem to be raping two women, then learns that they were the women's lovers: that went too far. But the

Inquisition Scene was enlivened by the Infant Casmira, a fortune-telling prodigy kept in a cage and played by a female dwarf made up *very* unpleasantly: when her arm whipped out of the cage and pulled Candide down to her eye level, Robert Rounseville cried out in such terror that the audience gasped. Later, when a freed Casmira denounced Candide to the Very, Very Old Inquisitor, *he* was so unnerved that, infirm as he was, he tried to edge off his throne and escape.

Guthrie even thought to use drag queens, in the Venice casino, where four young Englishwomen were in fact one woman and three men assuming the *physique du rôle*. But Guthrie's oddest idea was to play the final scene, when all the leads return to a destroyed Westphalia, in mostly modern dress (modern rags, actually), as if they'd come out of fallout shelters after a nuclear war. This was one of Hellman's better scenes, bitterly comic, though still nothing like Voltaire:

> CUNEGONDE: (*to* MAXIMILIAN) You deserted me in Buenos Aires. What are you doing here?
> MAXIMILIAN: Resting. I didn't desert you in Buenos Aires. (*Points to* CANDIDE) *He* killed me.
> OLD LADY: (to CANDIDE) What's the matter with you, you can't even kill a man?
> MAXIMILIAN: (to CUNEGONDE) Your lover killed me—
> CUNEGONDE: He's not my lover. How dare you talk such filth? Never been my lover—
> OLD LADY: Once they were going to give a medal to a man who hadn't been your lover. They looked and looked . . .
>
> . . .
>
> PANGLOSS: Candide has not spoken these many weeks. I think he's a little upset.
> CUNEGONDE: I've come home to die. (*Nobody answers.*) I think I'm dying.
> OLD LADY: So die.
> MAXIMILIAN: Dig me a little grave, sister. I'm so tired.
> CUNEGONDE: I'll make you curses. You stole my fortune, tore the pearls from our mother's breast and gave them to women—
> OLD LADY: Really? I never would have guessed that.

Note that business about Candide's having killed Maximilian. The musical *Candide* retained Voltaire's jest of killing off then casually resurrecting his characters. There was even a song about it—a love duet, no less, for Candide and Cunegonde—"You Were Dead, You Know." I would venture to guess that, of the playgoers idly perusing the program before the show, half came upon this title and fell in love with this musical. Half instantly hated it.

Or did they hate the lofty tone the whole thing took? After all, to attend this piece without a knowledge of Voltaire's novel must have been bewildering; and the music really did sound like an opera, not a musical. Did they resent the lack of dancing? Eight dancers were cited in the playbill, but there was virtually no dancing in *Candide*, only a mock-ballroom waltz distracted by some plot action, a fiesta tango after the Old Lady's "I Am Easily Assimilated," and a bit of this and that during "Bon Voyage." Otherwise the dancers were more like fashion models, performers who Move Well in crazy outfits. There wasn't even a choreographer listed in the very busy poster credits, just a thank you to Anna Sokolow way in the back of the program where they cite the electricians. This was the only musical in the decade to name three lyricists—Latouche, Wilbur, and Dorothy Parker (a fancy touch, though she only wrote one lyric)—and fail to name two others, Bernstein and Hellman; and Bernstein's wife, Felicia Montealegre, supplied the Spanish nonsense verse to "I Am Easily Assimilated." This is the kind of thing one calls "imposing" if one is neutral, "pretentious" if one isn't.

There is also the problem of the brittle, mannered style that Guthrie coaxed from his actors. But then, actors can hardly spend an evening in periwigs going Method. Max Adrian's Pangloss fielded a delightfully acerbic vocal tone that subtly warred with his rosy ravings, and his training on the English stage only added to his arch presentation. At forty-two, Robert Rounseville was too old for Candide—revivals now emphasize youth above all in this role—especially as his Cunegonde, Barbara Cook, had just turned a very young-looking twenty-nine. She, too, fell in with Guthrie's direction, though her work in *Flahooley* and *Plain and Fancy* was pure musical-comedy naturalism—that is, not intrusively psy-

chologized, but sincere and intelligent. What is most interesting
is how this pop-tune soubrette managed to encompass Cunegonde's sprawly tessitura, from B below middle C to Lucia di Lam-
mermoor's high E Flat, not to mention the sheer technique needed for the coloratura of "Glitter and Be Gay." Irra Petina's Old
Lady came naturally by her operatic sound, as a former Met mezzo
and the reigning queen of floperetta. But where did this Carmen,
Preziosilla, and Plentiful Tewke get her expert comic delivery
from? This was a truly distinguished cast, perhaps not as jivey as
the players that the most recent *Candide* revivals have counted
on, but a company trying to find the soul of the piece while keeping the fun percolating.

There is no question that Bernstein's advanced musicality, Hellman's dourly whimsical yet now and again hilarious book, Guthrie's baroque staging, and simply the hybris of taking Voltaire to
Broadway gave the critics a lot to chew on. The reception was
mixed. Atkinson loved it, and John Chapman called it "the best
light opera . . . since . . . *Der Rosenkavalier*." Others were high on
the music and Barbara Cook, but unsure what to make of the
whole. Walter Kerr, who generally hated the extra-musical musical
("There's something wrong with *The Most Happy Fella*"; *West Side
Story* is "almost never emotionally affecting"), really went after
this one.

Not surprisingly, folks declined to attend. Not that there was
all that much else going on. *My Fair Lady* and *The Most Happy
Fella* were the holdovers; *Li'l Abner* and *Bells Are Ringing* had
appeared, and *Happy Hunting* would open the week after *Candide*
did. It was not a big season for musicals. But maybe Voltaire
wasn't a household name. Maybe calling your show a "comic operetta" is asking for trouble.

Candide's performance total was 73. Of course there was no
tour—but here's something that is seldom mentioned: the show's
set designer, Oliver Smith, believes that a brutal argument between Hellman and *Candide*'s producer, Ethel Linder Reiner, is
what really killed the show. Because once Reiner posted "last
weeks" in the ads, ticket sales suddenly picked up and word of
mouth got voluble. The show might well have run. But Reiner

had had it with the evil Hellman, and *Candide* didn't close: *Candide* was stopped.

Hellman admitted that she was not a happy collaborator, and she greatly resented how, during composition, rehearsals, and try-outs, the interests of the director, the composer and lyricists, even the designers, would be advanced over her objections. None of her partners seemed to see any integrity in a libretto; they viewed it as a launching pad for their personal rockets. But that's what a musical's book *is*. "I'm happiest in the theatre," Hellman confessed, "when I'm alone in my room writing." *Candide* was her first musical, and almost her last play; she later claimed that this experience started her on the road away from the stage and into the literary world.

Then, too, she was angered by the universal opinion that a flop musical with a great score must have a flop book. The notion that a flop musical might have had a flop audience doesn't seem to have occurred to a lot of people. As Columbia's original cast album *Candide* sold, sold, and sold again, some of the participants began to assume that they *must* have done something wrong. Guthrie eventually denounced his brilliant production, which was simply too strange for Big Broadway. A musical with a demented dwarf and drag queens?

Richard Wilbur, too, checked in with a kind of denunciation: "The inherent fault is that it's a one-joke novel that goes on for thirty chapters. On the stage what one sees, on the other hand, is the repetition of a single joke." Does Wilbur mean that the novel is lean enough to get away with it, while the musical is big and ponderous? Some thought that the problem was a lack of consistency in the score, so Voltairean in, say, "You Were Dead, You Know" but then building Voltaire's understated final line into a tremendously feeling chorus, "Make Our Garden Grow." Was this satire, now, or romance? Even worse, was this Leibnizian—a positive end after so much cheating and murder?

Another problem: the characters are Voltaire's puppets somewhat in the novel and very much so in the musical. Even the novel's Candide, by Chapter Nineteen, defines optimism as "The mania for insisting that everything is fine when one is doing badly." Candide in the musical, however, struggles but briefly with Pangloss' preposterous teaching, on the raft heading to Venice, and he never throws off his yoke until the final scene—but then quite suddenly, as if he had appropriated someone else's lines:

> PANGLOSS: I should, of course, like a stone over my grave, and one word—teacher—carved thereon. Then, in smaller letters, add that the deceased had nine degrees, three of them doctorates in—
> CANDIDE: (*Quietly*) In lies. You were my master, and I loved you, and you taught me lies. I was stupid boy, and you must have known it. (*With great force*) A man should be jailed for telling lies to the young.

But then, Wilbur's statement does assess a certain damage in *Candide*'s reimagining from literature to theatre in that phrase "what one sees on stage." For, even if the musical's authors had kept absolutely within Voltairean bounds, still fidelity *à la lettre* is not necessarily fidelity *à l'idée*. *Li'l Abner* went easily into musical comedy because the source is a cartoon and musical comedy is a cartoon. Voltaire's novel is a cartoon, too—but one that is zany, racy, and bitterly ironic. That makes an awfully rich cartoon. However one sees it, *Candide* on stage presented a kind of debate between how weird a novel can be (very) and how weird a musical can be (not so very). It hurt the show because the audience was mystified even as it was thrilled and entertained.

Yet that cast album went on selling long after the show had closed. The staging loses a fortune and the recording earns one? However, one doesn't usually revisit a show that confuses; but one may easily play a confusing disc a second time. That's how *Candide* got its long run: in the ear, at home.

Let's take the overture first: a rondo deploying six themes from the score in what has proved to be an American concert-hall perennial but what in 1956 was a shock in a Broadway theatre. Comic it surely is—but what operetta ever had such bustling facetiae for a prelude, with shrilling woodwinds and growling brass that manage to sneer and chuckle at once?

It was the perfect introduction to what followed—except, of course, when Bernstein waxed romantic. "It Must Be So," Candide's keening reification of his assigned philosophy even after the brutal destruction of Westphalia; the wistful "Eldorado," after Candide's return from that utopia; and the ecstatic "Make Our Garden Grow" (launched by Candide, Cunegonde following, but growing into a huge chorale as the entire cast, in a thrilling coup de théâtre, joined the principals on stage in varying ruins of their former rococo glad rags) all war with the rest of the score, which is predominantly satiric. Even certain numbers war with themselves, as when "You Were Dead, You Know" speaks a joke but sings a rhapsodic love reunion, then soars to an excitingly helpless abandon that is at once illustrated and mocked when Candide and Cunegonde grab each other and break into a ridiculous waltz. Think of the *My Fair Lady* logo: but now it's Voltaire pulling the strings of Guthrie pulling the strings of Rounseville and Cook: puppets.

It is worth noting how much of *Candide*'s score is comic when even all-joke musical comedies such as *Top Banana* and *Shinbone Alley* were unable to match the hilarity of the action to a hilarious score. *Candide*'s score might easily be the "funniest" of the decade, not only in lyrics but in Bernstein's decoctions, homages, and deliberate wrong turns and dead ends—as, for instance, when the mere use of fourths and seconds in the intro to "The Best of All Possible Worlds" sets a tone that will resound through the evening for Pangloss's self-delighting quackery. Or consider the takeoff on twelve-tone music in "Quiet"—bringing up the curtain on Act Two with a Schoenbergian tone row—or the much acknowledged "Jewel Song" parody in "Glitter and Be Gay," more truly a parody of coloratura showpieces in general. Think of the first-act finale, a spoof of first-act finales, of the wicked caressing of the "in gay old Venice" waltzes, so beloved of the nineteenth century, in "What's the Use?" (whose vamp is a speeded-up taste of the most famous item in this long-gone genre, "Carnival in Venice"). Think of the Overture, a *bouffe* in itself.

Comedy songs in most musicals tend to be character numbers (e.g., "He Had Refinement") or novelty numbers ("Love Is the Reason"). *Candide* supplies comedy in any number, of any kind. Even something as stately as a procession of pilgrims heading for the "uncorrupted" New World takes on a sublime stupidity, in the

Bachian grandeur of the phrases given to the Pilgrim Father and Mother, who, along with their SATB followers, will presently be sold into slavery. Hear in particular the off-kilter harmony of their Alleluias, redoubled for fun when Candide, Cunegonde, and the Old Lady toss in a few Alleluias themselves, on the run from a double murder.

"I Am Easily Assimilated," the Old Lady's opportunistic credo, is all-basic *Candide*, Bernstein's campy genius (he wrote the lyrics) gaming with something really dangerous—the self-satisfaction of the Jewish emigrant who has no idea that Hitler is in the wings. There is nothing overt in the lyrics, nothing twentieth century. Yet Bernstein's intelligence is too encompassing not to know what the implications are. In fact, he loves them, loves all the foreign hustlers that pepper his shows, from *On the Town*'s Rajah Bimmy and *Wonderful Town*'s Mr. Apopolous to *Candide*'s Arab master of the Infant Casmira and the Old Lady herself, veering from high-toned observations to gutter grammer, so comically relentless in her asides yet so absorbed in spilling out her risible biography ("How well I remember my first Paris party. . . . You had to present proof of seven titled ancestors at the door. The was the night the Duke of Hamburg saw me and killed himself . . .")

The centerpiece of *Candide*'s score is the "Lisbon sequence," as it was originally called, for, as we know, it was the Inquisitors' scene that impelled Bernstein and Hellman to adapt Voltaire in the first place. Possibly no show in history drew more work, reworking, and new work out of its authors than *Candide*—and no part of the score was as revised as the "Lisbon Sequence." But then, the episode was central to Voltaire as well, for the Lisbon Earthquake of 1755, an unprecedented catastrophe of its kind, was the headline of the mid-eighteenth century, the reminder that reasonable men must believe not in grace but in nature. Folding the cataclysm into his fiction was Voltaire's way of naturalizing his narrative, just as Bernstein and Hellman pointed up *their* narrative with an allusion to Senator McCarthy's kangaroo-court committee. But the two authors faced many choices on the composition of this all-important scene. Should it be through-sung? Would some dialogue help root it in reality? *Auto-da-fé*, then earthquake? Earthquake first? Comic? Grotesque? Deeply repulsive?

As now performed, the scene is an elaborate mosaic following the earthquake. It starts as the chorus merrily spills on stage in search of grisly entertainment ("What a day, what a day, for an *auto-da-fé!*"), brings the Inquisitors into the music, leads up to Pangloss' extended solo on the joys of syphilis (whose very scars prove that love "makes the world go 'round"), and closes with intricately textured music treating Candide's flogging and Pangloss' hanging.

The 1956 version was much trimmer. It began on the sunniest and most untroubled of days, with a market chorus ("Look at this, look at that, what a pretty new hat!"), going on to the Arab Conjurer's introduction of the Infant Casmira, who warns of the imminent cataclysm. At one point her warning fades because, says the Arab, "her eyesight is not enough clearly." Ah, these Bernstein fakers. The cure is gold coins placed on her eyes, the coins are thrown, and the Infant foretells: *earthquake.*

The crowd laughed at her, but when she predicted the trembling of the towers of Lisbon, the scenery began to undulate. When she predicted darkness, the sky went black, then blood red. "*Listen!*" she whispered; and the crowd went crazy with terror.

In this original version, the ensuing trial of the heretics Candide and Pangloss was conducted in dialogue punctuated by shrieking brass. At an Inquisitor's statement that "The danger is over," the earthquake proper occurred in all its devastation over one tutti chord, a harmonically spectacular b flat minor over a minor over E flat.

Again, the much shorter but also more bizarre (in the Arab and Infant Casmira) and more ruthless (in the dead-on brusqueness of the hanging judges) Lisbon of 1956 marked an attempt to address the audience directly, show it something it knew: McCarthyism. It was the one moment in the evening that was not caught up in trying to balance the romantic side of the Broadway musical with the satiric side of a Broadway musical that happens to be based on a tract. The musically richer Lisbon we see today is more fun: it shouldn't be. It's silly; in 1956 it was brutal—perhaps another reason why the original didn't go over. Throwing so much music into the scene seems almost to admit that the only thing that really worked in *Candide* was the score, that the piece really should have been an opera anyway. But there was nothing wrong with Hellman's book. It was strange, but so is the score. So is the novel, for that matter. What's wrong with strange?

Despite its inconsistencies, *Candide*'s score is the best of the decade, so full of what the Italians call "fantasia"—imagination, variety, and ingenuity at once—that it made revivals necessary. Theatre music this brilliant must be heard in the theatre. London tried it in 1959, outfitted with a revised book by Michael Stewart and in a new staging by Robert Lewis. "My Love" and "Quiet" were dropped, the Venice Quartet became a duet, shorn of Pangloss' wonderful gambling spree, and "We Are Women" was newly written for Cunegonde and the Old Lady. Denis Quilley, Mary Costa, Laurence Naismith, and Edith Coates were the leads, and *Candide* flopped again.

Candide's enthusiasts would not yield. Sheldon Patinkin had tried out a concert *Candide* in Chicago with a spoken narration in 1967, and the narrator, by distancing the action from the audience, seemed to allow the romance and satire to commingle without alienating the public's perspective. Then: what if *Voltaire himself* should narrate?—as he did at Philharmonic Hall in 1968 in another concert, dedicated to Bernstein's fiftieth birthday. Alan Arkin was Voltaire and Pangloss, piling irony on Pelion, Madeline Kahn was Cunegonde, Irra Petina repeated her Old Lady, and David Watson was a baritone miscast as Candide. The libretto was Hellman–Stewart–Patinkin, its agenda to rationalize at least some of the nonsense, soothe the strangeness. For instance, Candide's climactic (though temporary) rejection of Cunegonde, "Nothing More Than This," written in 1956 but dropped as too "musical play," too emotional, was reinstated; and the Voltairean line that I quoted from the novel, on Candide's growing disillusion, was inserted into the script, defining optimism as "the passion for maintaining that all is right when all goes wrong."

Came then a radical solution to the *Candide* problem: deconstruction. Hal Prince, librettist Hugh Wheeler, and lyricist Stephen Sondheim turned this musical prodigy into a high-school variety night. Wheeler managed to get in more of Voltaire, with so many characters from the novel that, every time the lights came up on a scene, one thought, Another hundred people just got off of the train. At the same time, a lot of Bernstein was lost. A skimpy band, a gang of silly kid actors, an "environmental" set (both in Brooklyn in 1973 and a year later at the Broadway Theatre)—and, at one performance, Katharine Hepburn prankishly leaping out of her seat onto a much-too-nearby bit of scenery—convinced critics and public that *Candide* had been rejuvenated. (Well, at least those baroque perukes were gone.) June Gable's Old Lady and Lewis J. Stadlen's Voltaire and Pangloss (among other roles) upheld a professional level; the rest of the cast were no more than functional in a staging whose function was to castrate the satire and sitcom the romance. Typical of the production was its following "Make Our Garden Grow" with a gag: Candide and Cunegonde's cow keels over, dead.

Why didn't Rodgers and Hammerstein ever think of that? Next time someone revives *The Sound of Music*, as the von Trapps climb their mountain, shouldn't the Nonnberg Abbey cow keel over, dead? In fact, why didn't Prince himself think of this earlier? I bet the original *She Loves Me*, which he directed, would have run ten years if, at the finale, as the last lovely strain of "Dear Friend" welled up in the pit and the lovers embraced, Amalia's cow keeled over, dead, in the snow.

Prince restudied his production for a 1982 revival at the New York City Opera. Much of the music was redeposited, sometimes with the wrong characters in the wrong scene; and the overall atmosphere remained neither satiric nor romantic nor that elusive satiric-romantic but vacuously antic. This was substantially the version that came to Broadway in 1997, now with a starry lineup: Jim Dale, Met soprano Harolyn Blackwell, and Andrea Martin. Meanwhile, Bernstein himself, in association with Scottish Opera, had worked out a "final" version of *Candide*, one filled with as much of the music as possible, this time sung by the appropriate characters. Hugh Wheeler died before revising his book, so John Wells "recut" him, so to say. This *Candide* mark five is the first since 1956 to be worthy of what its authors—and maybe even Voltaire—had in mind from the start.

The Arab Conjurer and Infant Casmira are gone, but almost everything else in the score has found a place—maybe too much of the score. Even this genius piece has its duds, such as "Martin's Laughing Song." And does Pangloss need *two* songs on syphilis? "Dear Boy," an amusing treatise on the by-products of spirochetal development (such as tobacco and chocolate; but your nose falls off) is so intelligently delineated (by Richard Wilbur) that audiences cannot follow it and it dies on stage every time. "Ringaroundarosy," built into the now eight-minute Lisbon Sequence, troubles to name all the partners in a syphilitic module ("Well, the Moor in the end spent the night with a friend . . ."), including Pangloss's personal donor, Paquette (see page 173), who is now a lead in the show, singing mezzo-soprano.

Still, better too much of this score than too little. One wonders how Bernstein would have reacted to the notion of dropping the Voltairean narrator in a return to the original show's straight-on action, but perhaps by now it is a received intelligence that *Candide's* unique tone needs that puppetmaster of a Voltaire pulling his strings: so we don't have to worry too much? When Scottish Opera unveiled its *Candide* in 1988, director Jonathan Miller presented a *Candide* exactly opposite to that of Tyrone Guthrie's gala 1956 grotesquerie: a bare stage in the typical modern's big white box that progressively fills with toys, props, and architectural models that mount up the more the principals get their passports stamped. Toured to London and shown on the BBC, this is the true Final *Candide*. But then, when Verdi chopped and sifted to give the world Final *Don Carlos* in 1884, some of what he had first wanted to show was missing—and not necessarily because he truly wanted to discard it. Sometimes a composer makes a compromise with a sluggish public. Then, many years later, Andrew Porter discovers lost *Don Carlos* music, allowing each next production to develop the text out of a host of choices. In the end, there is no Final *Don Carlos*.

Surely it will also be so with *Candide*. Incredibly, there is even *more* music than we have heard; and the chance remains that some enterprising company or producer will persuade the Lillian Hellman estate to lift her ban on the use of her libretto. This would retrieve a truer *Candide*—not one more Voltairean, but one observing the wish of its authors to confront the culture with something entertaining yet outrageous, controversial, and, above all, thought-provoking. What *Candide* was *about* was lost, in 1956, in confusion about how *Candide worked*. That in itself made it outstanding—when before did anyone have trouble figuring out how a musical was supposed to work? Its immediately classic score, in the face of an abysmal run, was outstanding. Its lavish budget given to Tyrone Guthrie's madly eccentric vision, was outstanding. Random House published the text of this supposed bomb; *that's* outstanding.

This was an era of outstanding musicals, but *Candide* is the champ. I would even call it comparable to *Don Carlos*—another work centered upon an *auto-da-fé*—in that it was thought impenetrable when new and eventually became canonical. True, Verdi was Europe's major composer at the time of *Don Carlos'* premiere, in 1867, and worked with Paris Opéra regulars on the libretto. Heavy mainstream. By comparison, Bernstein was in 1956 one of many first-call composers, and his collaborators were somewhat out of the way for a musical.

Still, I see a parallel: between opera at its popular height utterly subverting a form (French grand opera) to change opera forever, and the musical at its popular height inventing a form (comic operetta—has there been one since? Oh, I forgot . . . *Anya*) and maybe not changing anything. Not specifically. Not in the way that *Gypsy* + *Cabaret* + Sondheim's nervous romanticism = *Follies*.

Yet don't *Don Carlos* and *Candide* remind us that, in art, there may be no single authoritative version, even by the author? Authors can be pressured, limited. They can err in guessing who their audience is. What entices more than the rediscovery of a masterpiece?

Bernstein is gone. Hellman is gone. McCarthy is gone. *Candide's* a kid still.

13

The Street, 1958

Here's an irony: Rodgers and Hammerstein inspired just about everybody on Broadway *except* Rodgers and Hammerstein. That is, the latter part of their joint career—when all Broadway was getting into the musical play and character motivation and odd song shapes—forms the less interesting half. Nothing after *The King and I* bears the tension of the Curley-Laurey or the Anna-King relationship, the music no longer startles, the choreography seems run-of-the-mill or even self-effacing.

Flower Drum Song (1958), typically Rodgers and Hammerstein in its out-of-the-way subject—C. Y. Lee's novel on San Francisco's Chinese-American subculture—was otherwise not typically Rodgers and Hammerstein at all. The author-producers made the decision to reinvigorate their style with young affiliates—choreographer Carol Haney, for instance—and to bring in musical comedy specialists such as Oliver Smith, who had never worked with them before. And what about this brainstorm?: in an age tending toward the director-choreographer, let's not merely use but *introduce* one . . . Gene Kelly, a cohort of Rodgers's from *Pal Joey*, eighteen years earlier, who had since been busy starring in and then directing movie musicals. Though Lee's novel, centering on a tug-of-war between a conservative father and his increasingly independent, Westernized son, had its dark side, the musical that Rodgers and Hammerstein were making of it was turning out breezy and colorful. Such songs as "Sunday" and "I Enjoy Being a Girl" had an almost Hollywood happiness about them, and indeed the show was the kind of thing that might have been a movie musical but for the hard sell of the all-Asian cast of characters.

In fact, the company that *Flower Drum Song* assembled was extremely multicultural: Miyoshi Umeki (Japanese) as a mail-order bride, Larry Storch (white) as her unwilling intended, Pat Suzuki (Japanese) as his girl friend, Keye Luke (the sole Chinese principal) as the patriarch greedy for control, Ed Kenney (Hawaiian) as Luke's son, who loves Umeki yet stands to lose her to Storch by Chinese community law, and Juanita Hall (black) as Luke's sister. It was a fine cast, except for the hard-driving Storch. But the real problem was Gene Kelly, for it turned out that stage musicals have a shape and tempo entirely different from movie musicals. "Pan! Pan!" he kept shouting. "Iris out!" All right, he didn't; but he *was* at a loss: in what to tell the actors, how to play to the audience's many pairs of eyes rather than to the camera lens, where to cut draggy dialogue scenes.

Some out-of-town tryouts consist of changing everything, in hysteria. Some consist of firing the ingenue and cutting two songs. This tryout consisted of Rodgers and Hammerstein's taking charge in replacing Larry Storch with Larry Blyden (also white) and building up the parts of the irresistibly charming Umeki and the pow!-voiced Suzuki, who were registering so strongly with audiences that the show's other problems didn't matter.

That put *Flower Drum Song* over as a big hit, but then it does have strong story content—the generation war and the dilemma of hyphenated Americans at once. Carol Haney made sure that the old and new ways of the American Chinese carried their battles into the dances, but her centerpiece was one of those dream ballets. We've seen the development of this absolutely basic device as one of the marks of the Rodgers and Hammerstein era, but in fact it was introduced at least as early as 1937, in two Rodgers and Hart shows, *Babes in Arms* and *I'd Rather Be Right*. By the time of *Flower Drum Song*, the dream ballet was becoming a cliché, though Haney gave it a burst of energy with an erotic paradox, confronting Kenney with stylizations of Umeki (the girl he respects) and Suzuki (the girl who's hot). Or: the girl his father wishes to impose upon him versus the girl his father resents. His father doesn't want him to enjoy sex. His father wants him to enjoy submission. The one, of course, is the opposite of the other.

Flower Drum Song is larger than the sorting out of two couples' matrimonial arrangements. Working with Joseph Fields, Hammerstein wrote one of his funniest but also wisest books. He even thought of aspects of Chinese-American life that novelist Lee missed, as when two fathers planning a wedding contemplate a new dress made for the bride, complete with that modern American convenience, breast-padding:

DR. LI: What are those things for?
WANG: All of the women over here have them.
DR. LI: At home our daughters are told to strap themselves in.
WANG: Here, they let themselves out.
DR. LI: Maybe they serve to keep people away from them in crowds.

Make no mistake, however—there is a real war under way here:

TA: (*the son*) Anytime I wanted to do anything, *you* decided it for me.
WANG: (*the father*) That is as it should be.
TA: In China—yes. But here a man is supposed to think for himself.
WANG: While you are in my house, you will live the life I have designed for you. When the day comes that you think for yourself, I will let you know!

It may be that *Flower Drum Song*'s book is better than its score. The tunes are appealing, and a few of them recall the old Rodgers and Hammerstein who would write anything but the expected—"You Are Beautiful," the first-choice ballad, wonderfully scored for mandolins in imitation of an Eastern instrument and placed, in defiance of all show-shop smarts, about two-and-a-half minutes into Act One; or "I Am Going To Like It Here," Umeki's solo, a

very shy love song made of lines interchangingly repeated but very
sparingly rhymed and climaxed with a lovely moment in which the
orchestra took over and Umeki simply wandered about the set,
acclimatizing herself with wistful abandon; or the flower drum
song itself, "A Hundred Million Miracles," with its distinctive percussion line after the first two vocal measures.

Yet much of *Flower Drum Song*'s score is ordinary, glib, like
the two numbers mentioned earlier that might have gone over in
a Hollywood musical. When did Rodgers and Hammerstein ever
write anything that easy? Or: someone asks Suzuki if her marriage
will mean moving, and Suzuki demurs. "I've got to be where the
action is," she cries. "Where is that?" she is asked, and she breaks
into song with her address: "Grant Avenue, San Francisco, California, U.S.A.," and we're off on a big musical spot that has nothing to do with anything. These people wrote *Oklahoma!*?

Worse: these people wrote *The Sound of Music* (1959). If *Flower Drum Song* was a conventional musical made of unconventional material, *The Sound of Music* was conventional to its core, albeit by the advanced standards of the late 1950s, standards that
Rodgers and Hammerstein most helped to create. Though it did
not enjoy the longest original run of a Rodgers and Hammerstein
show, it was their biggest hit in the long view of it, counting domestic and world-wide stagings, recording and sheet music sales,
and, mainly, The Movie.

In fact, that film starring Julie Andrews and Salzburg had a
success so influential that it brought on an avalanche of Big
Broadway Movie Musicals in the late 1960s, many of which rang
up such fabulous losses that the cycle ended with the absolute
collapse of the American film musical.

Why this terminal quality in such a harmless show? Why does
it not only shatter economies but raise passions? No hit musical
before the pop-opera era is more vilified by those who dislike it,
as sophisticates shiver at the concept of "a lark who is learning to
pray," at the buoyant nuns and growling Nazis and all those kids.

However, the "lark" line, not to mention those utterly inconsequential items that the heroine adores in "My Favorite Things"
("whiskers on kittens," "warm woolen mittens," even "doorbells"),
bears witness to the way Hammerstein could get into a character's

head. He wasn't writing lyrics for a sophisticate, but for a teenaged girl of extremely narrow cultural background, almost a simpleton, and a highly religious one at that. To my knowledge, nowhere else in the thirty-seven shows for which Hammerstein wrote lyrics did he refer to anything of this nature.

Then, too, *The Sound of Music*'s nuns are rather a mixed bag. One is buoyant. Another is severe. A third is loving. The main nun, the Mother Abbess, is all three put together. The rest are chorus. There's nothing cute about these nuns—and what else should Nazis do but growl? The kids are something else; either you like (or tolerate) kids in musicals or you don't. My point is that most of the legends about *The Sound of Music* are false, promulgated by those who don't like musicals in the first place.

In fact, there's nothing wrong with *The Sound of Music*. It has a slight but strong story: a young woman afraid of life's complicated emotional tugs seeks refuge in a religious hostel but is forced out by the mistress of the order, who sees something emotional, loving, needy in the girl. The true Bride of God can give love but cannot use it. This girl is desperate for it.

The Sound of Music also has a slight but extremely tuneful score. It's the least ambitious of all the famous Rodgers and Hammerstein titles, just songs; but fine ones. The book is only serviceable, but then Hammerstein didn't write it; those penetrating savants Howard Lindsay and Russel Crouse did, on commission from Mary Martin. She had seen a German film on the life of Maria von Trapp, postulant, governess, and then wife and mother as well as artistic director of the Trapp Family Singers, and Martin wanted to play Frau von Trapp on stage. Martin had a special relationship with Rodgers and Hammerstein and asked for a song or two. They said, No, let's do it as a musical.

What Rodgers and Hammerstein might have done with the material if they had signed on from the start is idle speculation. One can at least say that, generically, *The Sound of Music* is their only unsurprising show, and that may account for its somewhat disappointing position in the Rodgers and Hammerstein canon. It's just the wrong note for them to have struck in their final collaboration. (Oscar Hammerstein died in 1960, nine months after the premiere.) Why didn't we get something startling and inspiring—

something truly *final*—from them, perhaps comparable to *West Side Story* and *Gypsy*, the late fifties masterpieces that seem both to cap yet transform the Rodgers and Hammerstein construction? Why, in this dance-crazed time, did they not make the dance history we love in *Oklahoma!* and *Carousel*? *The Sound of Music* is so "play" that it has no dance—just some hoofing around a bicycle for two young sweethearts and a ballroom Ländler.

Instead, Rodgers and Hammerstein closed their career together with a Mary Martin show containing a hit parade of the most detachable numbers ever assembled by top talents in this era: the title song, "My Favorite Things," "Do Re Mi," "The Lonely Goatherd," "So Long, Farewell," "Climb Every Mountain," "Edelweiss"; one semi-plot number, "You Are Sixteen (going on seventeen)"; and three situation songs, "Maria," "How Can Love Survive," and "No Way to Stop It." Mind you, not a one of these is plopped in as baldly as "Grant Avenue" is into *Flower Drum Song*; but is any one of them irreplaceable in the manner of "The Surrey With the Fringe on Top," "A Puzzlement," or "Sweet Thursday"? *The Sound of Music* outgrossed *Carousel*; maybe that's what's wrong. We enjoy this show; but we don't enjoy seeing it overwhelm historically important titles, especially in its "final" form as a movie, owing Broadway but belonging to Hollywood.

The Rodgers and Hammerstein influence lay so powerfully on Broadway that Bob Merrill's second score—after the somewhat disconnected *New Girl in Town* songs—was the ably integrated *Take Me Along* (1959). Based on Eugene O'Neill's only sunny work, *Ah, Wilderness!*, a domestic comedy-cum-*Bildungsstück*, *Take Me Along* was also a David Merrick special, starring Jackie Gleason, Walter Pidgeon, and Eileen Herlie above the title and featuring Robert Morse, a guaranteed up-and-coming Name.

Two forces were at work here: Merrick's determination to entice the crowd with an above-all conventional piece, and the authors' wish to enjoy fifties liberation. Fat chance. Merrick believed in unconventional *English* theatre and very, very conventional American theatre. The English had the prestige; the Americans had the long runs, or Merrick would know why.

So, for instance, Merrick demanded a heard-it-all-before opening number of his writers, Merrill and librettists Joseph Stein and

Robert Russell. Their idea was a Big Overture followed by a substantial book scene—on newspaper editor Nat Miller's having won for his Connecticut town a new fire engine, to the citizens' thrill—followed in turn by the first number. As the scenery shifted to the Millers' home, the Millers would chatter excitedly as the orchestra slipped in, and "Oh, Please" would thus work its way out of the story into the score. It was to be a deft introduction to the Miller family—virtually O'Neill's entire cast of principals—and a flouting of convention.

But Merrick wanted to raise his curtain on something reassuring to audiences—noise and color and music, a *flaunting* of convention. *Ah, Wilderness!* is about growing up in a bygone America, but David Merrick's theatre was about manipulation, especially David Merrick's, of the composition and the reviews, and this not to exclude various PR didoes. So, for starters, *Take Me Along* began with "The Parade," third-rate: but what do you want when the writers are producing against their will?

Left to their own devices, they created a nice standoff between a David Merrick show and an honest and even O'Neillian piece of work. Merrill found a voice for each of O'Neill's leads—patriarch Nat (Pidgeon), his alcoholically undependable brother-in-law, Sid (Gleason), Sid's patient fiancée, Lily (Herlie), and Nat's romanticizing teenage son, Richard (Morse). Pidgeon, so drearily pompous in his endless movie career, somehow redevised himself on stage as vital and arrestingly introspective. Merrill gave him an expansive musical scene (actually two scenes, as it took a different form on its reprise), "Staying Young." Gleason was Gleason, but that works for Sid; his entrance, on a trolley car gliding in from stage right into a crowd of cheering male choristers ready for what the Italians call the *aria di sortita*, was a winner. "Wellll . . . Get a load of all the bottle babies!" cried Gleason through his applause. Then: "What is every choirboy and candy kid in town dong down here at the station?" A few more lines, and Gleason and company plunged into "Sid, Old Kid," a report on his roguish ways.

Herlie's wistful "We're Home" was of a rare tender honesty, and Morse' part was almost pure O'Neill, so determinedly self-deceived and self-dramatizing. The best number of all was given to a supporting character, Richard's friend Wint (Peter Conlow), who told of rented love to a hoochy-coochy vamp that strives to be as wicked as possible while conveying the height of naiveté.

Merrill could not, of course, leave out what we might call "the Merrick stuff"—"I Get Embarrassed" for Gleason and Herlie, a rather ribald piece, and the strutting title song for Gleason and Pidgeon, played in one as the two, heading for a picnic, progressed from stage left to stage right, Gleason throwing off ad libs, poses, and assorted other fun.

The critics mostly loved it, and *Take Me Along* settled in for a 448-performance run. It seemed like a hit at the time, yet we notice a disquieting sign of the age in that ticket sales did not turn a profit, the cast album lost money, and no movie was made.*
Ten years earlier, a thirteen-month stay guaranteed success, but production costs had outstripped the slight rise in ticket prices, holding at between an $8.05 and $9.90 top for a musical when *Take Me Along* opened in the fall of 1959.

Comparable to Bob Merrill was the team of Jay Livingston and Ray Evans, conveyors of Hollywood pop who, in *Oh Captain!* (1958), suddenly found themselves fashioning a pointed, story-telling score, and a rich one, too—eighteen numbers, not counting numerous reprises and dances. *Oh Captain!*'s source was the Alec Guinness film *The Captain's Paradise*, about a man leading a double life on a schooner plying trade between two ports—and two wives—at the Strait of Gibraltar. One wife (Celia Johnson) is English and prim; the other is Yvonne de Carlo. Edith Adams had tried to nail down the rights for a musical version, intending to play both parts. But *Oh Captain!* starred Tony Randall, in this retelling sailing the English Channel between wife Jacquelyn McKeever in a London suburb and mistress Abbe Lane in Paris.

José Ferrer directed, co-wrote the book (with Al Morgan), recorded the score (with wife Rosemary Clooney), and received shamefully fulsome billing. However, Randall was the main thing here, tossing off his musical debut with the panache of a Cyrano,

---

* MGM had already filmed a musical *Ah, Wilderness!* as *Summer Holiday*, with Mickey Rooney, Walter Huston, Frank Morgan, and Agnes Moorehead, released in 1948.

the assurance of an Achilles, and the mock-ham grandeur of an Alfred Drake. Actually, Randall couldn't sing, but you'd never have known it from the way he whipped through his numbers. He even danced with Alexandra Danilova in an out-on-a-tear-in-Paris special called "Hey, Madame," going from fake ballet into fake hoofing. The fifties musical loved to sneak ballet dancers into the line, and of course Jacques d'Amboise and Allegra Kent were among *Shinbone Alley*'s prized possessions. But Danilova got featured billing—with her name in a box—for a role that lasted no more than three minutes.

McKeever ran some nifty riffs on the housebound Maude, who wins a trip to Paris in a recipe contest and thus discovers Randall's adultery, and Abbe Lane's Bobo was a treat. (Sourpuss Walter Kerr thought her "better constructed than the plot." True, but misleading: the plot was quite well constructed, and Lane was *brilliantly* constructed.) There was also Susan Johnson as a nightclub hostess who dominated the close of Act One with her smoothly socko belt, then opened Act Two with the hushed, clip-clopping *aubade*, "The Morning Music of Montmartre."

But without Randall, *Oh Captain!* would have bombed. It lasted half a year, lost money, and has not been given since, even by the concerns specializing in lost musicals. Still, like *Take Me Along*, it didn't act like a flop, mainly because the 1950s enjoyed seeing someone come in from Outside to headline a musical. It was glamorous, surprising, a bit of Hollywood on Broadway. Robert Coleman of the *Daily Mirror* caught it just right in calling Randall a "take-over guy . . . with the know-how and the vitality to steer [the show] over dangerous shoals." What impressed everyone, really, was Randall's confidence—his ability to carry a show less on musical-comedy talent than on smarts and charm. This was a decade rich in stars who carried shows on their singing or dancing or comedy or *something*—Ethel Merman, Mary Martin, Alfred Drake, Gwen Verdon, Shirley Booth, Phil Silvers, Judy Holliday, Sammy Davis, Jr., Lena Horne. Now here was Randall doing it on sheer personality. Some in the theatre community resented him; he made it look easy.

What I find interesting about *Oh Captain!* is how well Livingston (composer and co-lyricist) and Evans (lyricist) adapted to what a Broadway musical needs. On their palette was England quaint and Paris hot, but also the Captain's hedonistic self-satisfaction versus his two women's feelings and needs. Add to this the Captain's Italian first mate (Edward Platt), a flirtatious Spaniard (Paul Valentine) who comes on to Maude, the S. S. *Paradise* and the nightclub and the tightening knot as the chaste and the earthy swirl about the Captain while his paradise evaporates in honesty; and the two songwriters took it all in and filled their canvas. Like Randall, they were new to it all, yet utterly ready.

Consider McKeever's "Surprise," a swelling two-step tickled by woodwind figures when Maude wins her recipe contest; "Femininity," Lane's ribald credo, lazy but a real jolt in its lyrics; or Randall's "Life Does a Man a Favor," heard in three versions, a music-box ditty for England, a roaring chantey at sea, and voraciously hungry in Paris. Here are anthems, confessions, joshings, accusations—a true theatre score, story songs.

Oh Captain!'s isn't a great score. It lacks, say, *A Tree Grows in Brooklyn*'s feelings, *House of Flowers*' haunting evocations. It's satisfying Broadway professionalism from men who weren't Broadway professionals, and that's intriguing. Had the American musical become so influential, so constantly played wherever music is heard, that every American songwriter now knew how its parts worked?

Certainly, that would explain how a midwestern amateur like Meredith Willson, after years of ninth and nineteenth drafts, and options and option renewals, finally got *The Music Man* (1957) on stage—at the Majestic at that, house of homers, just vacated by *Happy Hunting*. *The Music Man* was a sleeper, unheralded despite its out-of-town success. But then, whoever heard of a musical starring Robert Preston?

Here is, again, a musical comedy star vehicle for a star who'd never been in a musical—who'd never been a star, not on this level. As the Woodrow Wilson–era con man who sells instruments and uniforms to small towns on the promise of forming their kids into a band but hits the road as soon as he's paid, Preston capped an unimportant film and stage career by becoming the musical's only new male star in the decade who wasn't a one-off. He had

strong support, especially from Barbara Cook as the suspicious
librarian who resists then succumbs to him, David Burns as the
beady-eyed mayor, and youngster Eddie Hodges, discovered as a
singing contestant on the TV show *Name That Tune*, as Cook's
problem-child brother. (He lisps and too deeply mourns his dead
father; in Willson's original script he was a spastic, one reason
why it took so long for *The Music Man* to find a producer.)

The show got a superb mounting in general, from director Morton da Costa, choreographer Onna White, and designers Howard
Bay and Raoul Pène du Bois. But this really was a triumph of
composition. Maybe Willson was so much the amateur that he
ignored the conventions out of, literally, ignorance, for *The Music
Man* (great title, by the way) is stuffed with improvisations and
novelties. One number is a piano lesson, two characters wrangling
while a student executes a fingering exercise. Then the child prac-
tices her "cross-hand piece," a bit of juvenilia that accompanies
a major ballad, "Goodnight, My Someone." This, in a change of
tempo, becomes the show's theme song, "Seventy-Six Trombones." A school board of four querulous men demanding Preston's credentials turns, at his whim, into a barbershop quartet,
the four antagonists now not only harmonizing but providing
backup tunes to a gossips' chorus, a love song, and numerous
scene changes. Preston's salesman's spiel, "Ya Got Trouble," is
presented *as* a spiel, spoken in rhythm till a musical explosion at
the end that sounds like a revivalist prayer meeting going into
overdrive. There is even a conventional love song, "Till There Was
You"—the only Broadway number covered by the Beatles.

Let's consider *The Music Man*'s exposition, to demonstrate how
different it is from other expositions that we've examined
heretofore. The overture doesn't end but runs right into "train
music," during which we see one, belching real smoke. This is a
scrim, and as the lights come up behind it it rises in typical fifties
usage, revealing a car interior occupied by nine traveling salesmen, playing cards, reading newspapers, and so on. We get our
look in just as the train has stopped in the middle of a conversation about credit as an element in the salesman's economy, and,
as the conductor calls out the next stop and the train lurches into

motion, the conversation takes on a rhythmic gait in a kind of song without music. Some of the men speak in sales-talk gibberish, others in communicative English, but all fall into this locomotive, repetitive, ware-pitching tempo as the topic runs from credit to the changes wrought in the retail community to a salesman known as Harold Hill, the music man himself. The conversation slows as the train slows, stopping at River City, Iowa. One of the salesmen dismisses this Hill—he's a fraud who makes life tough for honest salesmen. One thing, though—Hill would never dare try to trick these "neck-bowed Hawkeyes." Suddenly, one of the card players pockets his winnings and jumps up, saying, "Gentlemen, you intrigue me. I think I'll have to give Iowa a try." He holds up his suitcase, marked "PROF. HAROLD HILL," and, as the train set breaks in two, each half full of gaping salesmen sliding into the wings, Hill finds himself on River City's Main Street on July 4, 1912, just in time to see a pool table delivered at the billiard parlor and to hear the locals hymn the state's essential quality in "Iowa Stubborn." At a pause in the music, one woman complains that no one visited her in the hospital: "Cousin Will never come, Aunt Bertha never come . . ." A friend reminds her that Aunt Bertha's dead. "She wouldn't a' come anyway."

The number climaxes with a tasty visual—the pool-table delivery men bring the wooden packing case frame to center stage, where a farmer and his wife come forward into the frame to pose as likenesses of Grant Wood's *American Gothic* couple, pitchfork and all: Iowa, hate it or leave it.

Now a book scene fixes Hill up with an old crony, who warns him about the local music teacher and librarian, smart and a purist in everything, likely to expose him. But Hill's got a band to sell, and he smoothes into "Ya Got Trouble," setting the plot proper into motion. Why, that pool table promises nothing less than the arrival in sin in River City! The good people of the town can only protect themselves by herding their youth into a marching band of . . . yes! Seventy-six trombones!

Okay, we've had a startling novelty in the salesmen's rap number, a mock-traditional "opening" chorus of "merry" villagers—Sigmund Romberg gone sour—and the action has kicked in painlessly, naturally. One thing's missing—the romance. No: here comes the music teacher, to prim, self-righteous "walking" music. Hill follows her, masher-style. We're on.

Clearly, one of *The Music Man*'s unique qualities is its resuscitation of a culture that, after two world wars, Hollywood, television, and Elvis Presley, had utterly disappeared. Knickers, pianola, cistern, corncrib, dime novels, "so's your old man," stereopticon slides, Montgomery Ward, canoodling—a goodly portion of the show's content had been retired to the American memory bank by the 1950s. Willson is telling a story that is all but faërie today.

Yet the story itself is a favorite in American lore, that old Fred Astaire–Ginger Rogers thing: he lightens her and she deepens him. Katharine Hepburn said, "He gives her class and she gives him sex," but in *The Music Man* he gives her sex while she gives him self-esteem. She's trying to keep order in the library; he's trying to stuff it with trombones. When he visits her there, to an insidiously aggressive piano vamp of thumping boogie-woogie, he pulls out a drawstring bag, shows it to her, sings her name—Marian—and remarks, "Marbles. Six steelies, eight aggies, a dozen peewees and one big glassie with an American flag in the middle. I think I'll drop 'em." "*No!*" she cries, finally giving him the attention he has manipulated out of her—and only then does he pursue the song itself, "Marian the Librarian," with that piano ostinato running to the end like a yokel playboy's seduction.

Marian is unmoved till she sees the revitalization of her troubled little brother when the band instruments arrive, just in time for the first-act curtain. So far, so good—till Hill's interest in Marian causes him to linger long enough to be unmasked, not only to the townspeople but to the brother, furious at the betrayal. Band? "*What* band?" he sneers. Then comes the smartest line in the whole play, maybe a sentimental fraud of a line, but a sharp one all the same. Says Hill, "I always think there's a band."

There was very nearly a greed for non-singing musical-comedy leads like Preston in these times. The extremely unmusical Jack Warden played a boxing manager in *The Body Beautiful* (1958), with a fighter (Steve Forrest) who couldn't sing, an assistant (William Hickey) who couldn't sing, and so on, right through the cast except for the two ingenues, Mindy Carson and Barbara McNair. Maybe boxers and their staff members shouldn't come off as lyrical figures, but then why do a boxing musical?

The critics compared *The Body Beautiful* unfavorably with *Guys and Dolls* in that both shows treat underworlds with their private lingo, social customs, and moral codes, *Guys and Dolls* to spectacular effect and *The Body Beautiful* in a clunky manner. Moreover, both shows are conventional in format, and both use two interlocked couples to power the plot engine. Still, the comparison seems unfair, if only because *Guys and Dolls* finds beauty and even glamor in its underworld, yet so lightly, finely, that it comes off as a fantasy. *The Body Beautiful* is earthbound, gritty, realistic, with a mixed-race cast, as the boxing background made necessary.

Still, it's a terrible show, witless and plodding. The book, by *Plain and Fancy*'s Joseph Stein and Will Glickman, never catches fire, and the score is notable only in that it marked the first collaboration of Jerry Bock (one of *Mr. Wonderful*'s authors) and Sheldon Harnick (who had been contributing to revues). Yet Hal Prince heard enough in the Bock and Harnick songs—maybe in the bouncy release of the title song, or in the thrill-seeking flight of "All These and More"—that led him to tap the team for Prince's next musical. We'll hear from them to advantage presently.

Why were so many producers hiring non-singing male leads for musicals? Had the emergence of strong storylines called for strong leading men—that is, actors as opposed to singers? *Goldilocks* (1958), a look at early American silent film in the same period as that of *The Vamp*, centered on the love–hate duel of a reluctant star and an obsessed director. The star was Elaine Stritch, who after critically acclaimed singing spots in the revue *Angel in the Wings* (1947) and the revivals of *Pal Joey* and *On Your Toes* was ready for her closeup. But the director was Barry Sullivan, a minor movie lead who chanced to notice, during the Philadelphia tryout, that he couldn't get through his songs and left the show. (Actually, sudden marital problems overtook Sullivan as well; his numbers themselves were of the post–Rex Harrison sort, patter songs rather than legato rhapsodies.)

Don Ameche took over for Sullivan—and, excuse me, but why wasn't Ameche hired in the first place? Hadn't *Silk Stockings* revealed how well this guy took to the stage, how persuasively he sang and acted? After Cole Porter's amiable Steve Canfield, *Goldilocks's* Max Grady was a challenge: tight and tense, "a common, on-the-make hustler," as Stritch calls him during one of their many set-tos. Musical comedy was used to bickering lovers, but these two were a real case, dangerously tough on each other, though even a neophyte theatregoer could guess that the good-natured socialite (Russell Nype) whom Stritch was engaged to would ultimately have to step aside. Curiously, the ingenue (Pat Stanley) with whom Nype could have been paired off as a consolation prize was not developed romantically, as if librettists Walter and Jean Kerr were trying to naturalize their tale.

Nevertheless, *Goldilocks* had, like *The Body Beautiful*, an old-fashioned two-couple structure with a colorful background, more concerned with the comic and absurd than with the natural. Its burlesque of moviemaking in 1913 is very funny, especially when Ameche directs Stritch in a frenzied western while Stritch makes sarcastic comments. (Told to send a telegraph message during an Indian attack, she pauses over the apparatus, and, when Ameche shouts, "What are you waiting for?," replies, "I'm trying to keep it under ten words!") Agnes de Mille worked up some nostalgic dances, and Peter Larkin's sets expertly guided the eye back in time, from the opening, a theatre facade that broke into halves and then rode offstage, revealing the finale of a musical called *Lazy Moon*, to the last scene, a spectacular stepped Egyptian terrace recalling D. W. Griffith's Babylon.

Best of all, the score, composed by Leroy Anderson to lyrics by Joan Ford and the Kerrs, is delightful. It is not the kind that throws off hit tunes, perhaps because Anderson's forte was the orchestral novelty piece, often with a gimmick, such as "Blue Tango" (with a prominent flatted, or "blue" note), "The Syncopated Clock," "Bugler's Holiday," or "Clarinet Candy." Anderson was so unused to songwriting that on his only previous Broadway assignment the decision-makers replaced him at the last minute. (The show was *Wonderful Town*, and the replacement, obviously, Leonard Bernstein.)

But *Goldilocks*'s score pleases yet today.* That opening, a chorus number that is also called "Lazy Moon," is a clever replica of "Shine On, Harvest Moon." Thereafter, the pastiche generally retires, even in a big dance number, "The Pussy Foot." There is a profusion of character songs—Stritch's "Give the Little Lady (a great big hand)," "Who's Been Sleeping in My Chair?" (sung to and danced with a man in a silent-movie bear costume), and "I Never Know When (to say when)"; Ameche's lowdown "There Never Was a Woman (who couldn't be had)" and frantically upbeat "I Can't Be in Love." Nype sang the ballads, and Ameche's cohort, led by Nathaniel Frey and Margaret Hamilton, handled the best of the comedy songs, "Bad Companions" and, in one just before the Egyptian finale, "Two Years in the Making."

It's a fully integrated score supporting a fast and funny book, the whole given a stylish production. True, the story becomes somewhat attenuated amid all the Ameche–Stritch wrangling, but their growing attraction for each other is rationally developed, and the Kerrs were careful to give Max Grady a genuine love of cinema and a belief in the historical importance of his Egyptian epic. One could say that *Goldilocks* must have been conceived to reach ultimate completion in a camp version of Eastern antiquity: but one could say that of this era of American silent film as well.

In fact, *Goldilocks* was everything that *The Body Beautiful* wasn't—zany, flighty, ballet-dancey, pert, and a little angry. It had personality, a key musical-comedy quality. Yet while *The Body Beautiful* bombed in a two-month run and *Goldilocks* held on for a respectable but losing five months and got a cast album out of the deal, the two are about equally forgot today. But let me tell you about a show no better than *Goldilocks*: another old-fashioned two-couple concoction, but this one lacking a story or characters as intense as Max Grady and his Goldilocks.† Yet it ran over six-

---

* As do Anderson's own orchestrations, in collaboration with Philip J. Lang. It used to be a truism that only Victor Herbert and Kurt Weill scored their own music on Broadway. But in this decade alone Bernstein, James Mundy, George Kleinsinger, Morton Gould, and Marc Blitzstein, along with Anderson, did their own orchestrations, either solo or with assistance.

† The reference, of course, is to Little Mary: the Girl with the Curls. Stritch's character's name was Maggie Harris.

teen months. This was *Jamaica* (1957), with an Arlen-Harburg score and Lena Horne in the lead. It, too, is forgot today.

Everyone in show biz tells the same joke—if God had really wanted to punish Hitler, He'd have sent him out of town with a musical. And, says *Jamaica*'s director, Robert Lewis, "it should have been *Jamaica*."

The trouble was that the show had been written for Harry Belafonte. The score was reworked for Horne, and plenty of fine talent supported her, including Ricardo Montalban as her boy friend, a simple Caribbean lad who deplores Horne's wish to move to sophisticated Manhattan. But the book had not recovered from the Belafonte-to-Horne transfer, and, during tryouts, librettists Harburg and Fred Saidy refused to let producer David Merrick bring in a doctor.

"I'll close the show," said Merrick, with That Look in his eyes.

They gave in, Joseph Stein arrived in Boston, and Stein immediately spotted the flaw: *Jamaica* had, one, no book, and, two, too much of it. He simply cut the text down to bring out the score, the performers, and the dancing (by Jack Cole, the only member of the de Mille-Robbins-Kidd-Fosse generation who missed out on the fame that he deserved). This solution wouldn't have worked for *Candide* or *New Girl in Town*; story shows can't be stripped to their performer spots. At that, this was one of the decade's few hit shows that had a lot of detractors. Said Walter Kerr, "Can you make a whole show out of sheet music?," a reference to the richness of the tunestack more like that of a revue than of a book show, but lush with satire in "Napoleon" (on the transitory nature of power), "Leave the Atom Alone," "Push De Button" (on modern technology), and "Incompatability" yet not forgetting the all-important Arlen super-ballad in "Coconut Sweet." As for the cast, many critics mocked the relentless exposure of Montalban's torso, and Noël Coward thought the featured Josephine Premice "carried on like a mad spider."

Still, there was something irresistible in 1957 about a musical of any quality starring Lena Horne. Broadway wanted it. It was simply: who better to star in a musical? Modernists disgusted by corrupt social agendas may see *Jamaica*'s triumph as one of political expediency; on the contrary, this was not a happy time for black musicals.* *House of Flowers*, we know, got no preferential treatment, and, the same year as *Jamaica*, *Simply Heavenly*, a realistic look at Harlem culture by David Martin and Langston Hughes, couldn't attract media attention or business.

Another minority group came under scrutiny in the show that broke Feuer and Martin's string of smash hits—five till *Whoop-Up* (1958). Based on Dan Cushman's novel *Stay Away, Joe* (the source as well of an Elvis Presley film, by the novel's title, ten years later), *Whoop-Up* is set on an Indian reservation in Montana. With a script by Feuer, Martin, and Dan Cushman and a score by Moose Charlap and Norman Gimbel, the work is that rare item made almost entirely of floppo numbers, floppo lines, floppo characters, and even some floppo actors: those who had seldom worked before, would seldom work again, or were Danny Meehan. Here is the really fascinating instance of a musical comedy that failed because it was strange. Not coarse like *The Body Beautiful* or just a bit underpowered in a lively season like *Goldilocks*. Strange: having a mean story (part-Indian rodeo star and *Pal Joey* type lets everyone down), a stupid book, and an unbelievable score.

No, I mean truly unbelievable. Some have their *Hazel Flagg*, others their *Ankles Aweigh*. For me, the true fifties horror show is *Whoop-Up*, so conventional in, say, the first number, "Glenda's Place," a celebration of saloon-owner Susan Johnson's hostelry, or ingenue Julienne Marie's "Never Before," then so, well, implausible in the abrasive tom-tom pounding of "Chief Rocky Boy" or the rock-and-roll runoff " 'Caress Me, Possess Me' Perfume." What are we to make of Romo Vincent's intensely pinched high notes in "Nobody Throw Those Bull (like my boy big Joe)"? Or hero Ralph Young's ludicrously erotic "Love Eyes," a paean to the charms of a performer billed simply as Asia? Lilo, a Feuer and Martin loyalist ever since *Can-Can*, was heard to stir audibly in her seat during this number on opening night, and took the first

---

* Ricardo Montalban, though playing a black character, was of course not black, a clear case of miscegenative casting. No one seemed to notice. Yet, seven years later, when white Alan Alda played opposite black Diana Sands in *The Owl and the Pussycat*, there was *crise* on Broadway. Go figure.

opportunity to leave the theatre. And those who collect outstand-
ingly sinful lyrics will want to trade the "lark who is learning to
pray" for the climax of Sylvia Syms' torch song, "Sorry For Myself," when, beset with frustration, "I howl and I stomp like a crazy
Cree." The compleat floppo, *Whoop-Up* left the theatre almost as
quickly as Lilo had.

The revivals that were so common from the mid-1940s into the
mid-1950s suddenly stopped coming in the late 1950s. One reason may have been the City Center's annual spring season of replica stagings of relatively recent Broadway hits, along with the
perennials *Show Boat* and *Porgy and Bess*. *Oklahoma!*, *Carousel*,
Finian's Rainbow, *Brigadoon*, *South Pacific*, *Guys and Dolls*, *The
King and I*, *Wonderful Town*, and *The Pajama Game* were regular
visitors, each for a two-week run at "popular" prices with, generally, starry or near-starry casts. Interestingly, the twenties operetta
canon of *The Student Prince*, *Rose-Marie*, *The Desert Song*, and
such was utterly ignored.

Similarly, television discovered the musical for a national audience. In, usually, ninety-minute slots with the few and brief
commercial intervals typical of the day, an *Anything Goes* with
Ethel Merman and Bert Lahr, a *One Touch of Venus* with Janet
Blair and Russell Nype, a *Bloomer Girl* with Barbara Cook and
Keith Andes, a *Lady in the Dark* with Ann Sothern could reach
millions. Note, too, that these were somewhat cut down from the
original but otherwise unadorned, unrevised. Emphasizing the
shows of the 1940s and appearing almost routinely (despite being
termed "spectaculars"), the TV musical had perforce to seek out
new possibilities—a *Pinocchio* with Mickey Rooney, a *Marco Polo*
with Alfred Drake and Doretta Morrow and a score drawn,
Kismet-style, from Rimsky-Korsakov by Clay Warnick and Mel
Pahl, the lyrics by Edward Eager. (My readers will anticipate a
big ballad drawn from the slow movement of *Scheherazade*. Right
you are: "Is It You [or the sun in my eyes?].") Cole Porter, too,
went Eastward, for *Aladdin*, his last score, with Sal Mineo, Anna
Maria Alberghetti, Cyril Ritchard, and Dennis King. Arthur
Schwartz and Maxwell Anderson adapted Anderson's thirties fantasy *High Tor* for Bing Crosby and—five days before the New York
opening of *My Fair Lady*—Julie Andrews. Jule Styne tackled *Rug-

gles of Red Gap, Schwartz and Howard Dietz John Hersey's novel A Bell for Adano, Richard Adler The Gift of the Magi. There were two-hour specials, TV's equivalent of Big Broadway: Mary Martin's Peter Pan, Alfred Drake and Patricia Morison recreating their original roles in Kiss Me, Kate, Rosalind Russell in Wonderful Town, and the biggest gun fired in the entire series: Rodgers and Hammerstein writing a Cinderella for Julie Andrews, with a viewing audience of 107 million people.

That's fetching; but television was by the late 1950s Broadway's despair. All that free entertainment was keeping potential ticket-buyers home. Video was no longer silly, limited, spotty, tiny. The technology had expanded with frightening speed to enlarge and clarify the screen, amplify the networks with local channels, and perfect such fledgling genres as sitcom and the talk show. By 1960, ninety percent of American homes had at least one TV set.

And yet the revue—Broadway's most vulnerable form, so easily duplicated on TV—tried to flourish. It was a last stand. There was the theme revue in The Girls Against the Boys (1959), Bert Lahr and Nancy Walker mired in poor material and a two-week run. There was the club-acts-thrown-together variety night in The Next President (1958), with ranting comic Mort Sahl, dancer Anneliese Widman, and a folksinging group for another two-week run. There was an attempt to revive the Ziegfeld Follies—two attempts, even. The first, in 1956, closed out of town, though it was a genuine essay in restyling Ziegfeld's format for moderns with plenty of spectacle and talent: comics David Burns and Elliott Reid, dancers Matt Mattox and Carol Haney, singers Joan Diener and Mae Barnes, ensemble hopefuls Bea Arthur, Larry Kert, Sheila Smith, Julie Newmar, and, absolutely starring, Tallulah Bankhead. Oddly, a horribly cheesy Ziegfeld Follies came in the following year, closing so fast it felt like a drive-by. It looked like one, too, with plenty of cheap nothing topped by, surprisingly, Beatrice Lillie.

Perhaps it was typical of the day that the sole hit revue was a one-off completely out of the American variety tradition: virtually no music, no stars, no specialty acts, and almost all the sketches in pantomime. This was La Plume de Ma Tante (1958), a confection from Paris via London. The title, of course, recalls a standard French-grammar phrase ("The pen of my aunt . . ."), and a sign outside the Royale Theatre read, "English Spoken Inside." But of language there was next to nothing: no puns, no doubles entendres, no lyrics. The capocomico Robert Dhéry appeared in the show with his wife, Colette Brosset; but star players were as unnecessary to the event as language was. Typically, the most commented-on act was that of the bell-ringing monks, in which four of Some Order begin by pulling on but end by ecstatically riding upon and dancing with their metal charges.

What, in the face of TV's lively variety tradition—scarcely a decade old but already supreme—could the American revue do but grow small, *intime*? A prophetic event was *A Party with Betty Comden and Adolph Green* (1958), the two running through a retrospective of their career. Some of it was engagingly fresh, such as "The Baroness Bazooka," a spoof of oldtime operetta. Some of it was simply the Comden-Green songs we already knew well from their shows. But this was, for good or ill, the jumping-off place for all the authors' anthology revues that were to proliferate in the 1970s, 1980s, and 1990s.

There was but one revue that, to my mind, respected the ideals of the Great American Variety Show, Leonard Sillman's *New Faces of 1956*. Daringly, Sillman tapped drag queen T. C. Jones as his interlocutor, but otherwise it was the mix as before: many contributors wrote and newcomers performed an evening's worth of spoof, songs, tiny operas, and so on. As always in the *New Faces* series, dance was not a major factor, and one superb talent was wasted (Carol Lawrence in 1952; Maggie Smith in 1956).

The rest of the show was smartly conceived. Jane Connell's trick soprano melted the cobalt grandeur of "April in Fairbanks," on the charms of the Alaskan north. ("I'll never leave it," Connell averred, "alive.") There were takeoffs on the film *The Blackboard Jungle* and the play *A Hatful of Rain*. The reinstituted *Ziegfeld Follies* demanded burlesque and got it in the first-act finale, a showgirls-sauntering-down-the-staircase number by Marshall Barer and Dean Fuller called "Isn't She Lovely?" This featured an increasingly flatting tenor (actually baritone John Reardon), fabulously overbuilt costumes—one, made of oranges, kept losing pieces at every step—and the showgirls' air of "Who did this to me?" Japanese cinema, a hot topic among the intelligentsia just then, was married to the American western in the sketch "A Broken Kimona," and the eleven o'clocker went to T. C. Jones as one Hope Diamond, an idiot film star trying to sing and dance in "She's Got Everything."

There was one goof. Sillman's sister, June Carroll, and Arthur Siegel liked to write ironic *guignol*, musical scenes of pathetic content, and Sillman indulged them. *New Faces of 1952* had "Time For Tea," about two spinster sisters looking back on their social debut fifty years earlier, which ends with one of the two dully calling, "Here, kitty, kitty, kitty, kitty, kitty, kitty, kitty." *New Faces of 1956* offered six-foot Inga Swenson playing the adolescent heroine of "A Doll's House," lonely and neglected but snobbish around a bizarre urchin (Suzanne Bernard) who wants to play with the elaborate doll house. This then came to life as the dolls, enacted by Jim Sisco, Virginia Martin, Dana Sosa, Franca Baldwin, Rod Strong, and Billie Hayes, went into a stylized pantomime. If you liked it, you called it artistic; if you didn't like it, you called it grotesque. Nevertheless, *New Faces of 1956* really was the last vaguely successful attempt to shape a space for spoofy variety on Broadway.

On off-Broadway, the musical was a form without portfolio. Off-Broadway concentrateed on noncommercial serious new plays, European titles, and revivals of Broadway shows, from O'Neill to Williams, that demanded a second chance. In the musical, off-Broadway was strictly a way-back machine, devoted to revivals. Jerome Kern's *Leave It To Jane*, Noël Coward's *Conversation Piece*, *Lend an Ear*, and *The Boy Friend* all were revived downtown in the late 1950s—but then, the early 1950s had hosted Kurt Weill and Bertolt Brecht's *The Threepenny Opera*, in Marc Blitzstein's expert translation. The silky abrasiveness of Carmen Capalbo's production, typified by Lotte Lenya's Jenny, spurred the Kurt Weill Revival, and the show's 2,706-performance run at the Theatre de Lys seemed to introduce a novelty. No: this, too, was a resuscitation, for the piece had been seen, very briefly, on Broadway in 1933.

One new show actually made a hit: *Little Mary Sunshine* (1959), Rick Besoyan's campy review of oldtime operetta at the Orpheum on lower Second Avenue. *Little Mary* was, paradoxically, a small version of what had been capacious shows. Twenties operetta casts often numbered well over sixty, and the decor was elaborate as a rule. Besoyan's show had nine principals, a chorus of twelve, and an orchestra of two pianos. But then, his approach was to cut to the heart of operetta: the virile baritone and wiry soprano lovers, the good-guys-versus-bad-guys morality, the boys in uniform and loyal girls cheering for them, the European something in the air.

The setting is the Colorado Rockies, where the ever-optimistic Little Mary runs an inn. The rest of the cast are Indians, Gentlemen of the U.S. Forest Rangers, Young Ladies of Eastchester Finishing School, a retired Viennese opera star, a retired General (to match nostalgias with the opera diva), and Little Mary's mischievous maid, Nancy Twinkle. At the finale, three couples look forward to marriage—Little Mary (Eileen Brennan) and Captain "Big Jim" Warington (William Graham), Nancy (Elmarie Wendel) and Corporal Billy Jester (John McMartin), and Madame Ernestine (Elizabeth Parrish) and General Fairfax (Mario Siletti). This is not to mention the suddenly affianced rangers and young ladies, who of course sing an ensemble number, "Tell a Handsome Stranger," modeled on the *Florodora* (Double) Sextet, even unto duplicating the original's "strolling" vamp and "endless melody" structure of ABCD.

Most of *Little Mary Sunshine* was modeled on something—mainly *Rose-Marie* in "The Forest Rangers," the "Colorado Love Call," the setting, the Mounties-like Rangers, and Big Jim, *Rose-Marie's* hero. The General and Madame Ernestine's "Do You Ever Dream of Vienna" is deliberately ersatz Kálmán, and her "In Izzenschnooken on the lovely Essenzook Zee" recalls "In Egern on the Tegern See" from *Music in the Air.*

Musical comedy also gave Besoyan some source material. Nothing as lively as Nancy Twinkle ever turned up in an operetta, and her duet with Billy, "Once in a Blue Moon," in which he sings the refrain while she interjects "response" lines, is pure Jerome Kern Princess Theatre style. The General's flirtatious "Say Uncle" is a tintype of "All the Girlies Call Me Uncle" from Rudolf Friml's prototypal musical comedy *The Firefly.*

The idea, then, was to conjure up a vanished experience rather than a specific vanished form: to recreate the carefree time one had at a musical before *Show Boat* and *Oklahoma!* changed the musical's purpose. *Little Mary Sunshine* is a pastiche, an evening-length burlesque, but it is more: sheer entertainment. Brooks Atkinson thought it "a subtle satiric idea," but Walter Kerr saw the history in the event when he felt "pain that I almost never see anything so easy and foolish and delightful on Broadway any more."

What *Little Mary Sunshine* was saying—certainly, what Walter Kerr was saying—was that the musical was getting too intelligent to be fun.

14

Redhead

This show starts with a murder.

Or no—this show actually starts about fifteen years before the murder, in the mid-1940s, when Dorothy and Herbert Fields got interested in Madame Tussaud's waxworks in London. They thought it would prove a dandy setting for a musical murder mystery, with a spinster heroine who at last finds romance. In time, producers Robert Fryer and Lawrence Carr optioned it, and sought a star for the lead, now Ethel Merman, now Bea Lillie, now Celeste Holm, now Gisele MacKenzie. Each one would have tilted composition in a different direction, so all the show was at this point was an idea, a script that knew it was doomed to be rewritten, and a title, *The Works*. In any case, everybody turned it down.

Not until Gwen Verdon was consulted and her husband, Bob Fosse, invited to direct it in a package deal was the show finally set. Sidney Sheldon was to have doctored the Fieldses's book for Verdon, but Hollywood lured him away, and Irwin Shaw's brother David was brought in. Then Herbert Fields died, and the distraught Dorothy felt unable to touch her brother's work, leaving it all to Shaw, though she did collaborate with composer Albert Hague on the score.

Now to the murder. The curtain rises on an actress making up, oblivious and happy and humming a dippy little tune. The tympani quietly beat out suspensefully as a figure slithers out of the shadows, flourishing a purple scarf—caressing it, loving it—with which he then strangles the actress. A spotlight picks him out— a saturnine redhead with a great red thing of a beard on him. Blackout.

Now the orchestra, in a ghoulish Bob Fosse irony, merrily takes up the murder victim's humming tune as the stage bustles with activity in front of the show curtain, an antique advertisement for the Simpson Sisters Waxworks. We're in Victorian London, in the grip of "murder fever," for everyone wants to know more about the strangling of Ruth Larue—especially who did it. Over the "bustle music," Howard Cavanaugh (William Le Massena), manager of a music hall, serves, temporarily, as interlocutor, just as Eddie Foy, Jr., did in *The Pajama Game*. Howard points out to us the Sisters themselves (Doris Rich, Cynthia Latham), two old maids who, in a running gag, always disagree on everything; his prize comic, George Poppett (Leonard Stone), and Inspector White of Scotland Yard (Ralph Sumter). White is accompanied by three undercover policemen in hopes of snaring the murderer, who might be attracted by today's unveiling of an exhibit depicting the murder of Ruth Larue:

INSPECTOR: All right. (*To first man*) Fotheringall, post yourself at the Exhibit. (*To second man*) Pickett, you cover the Hall of Horrors.

FIRST MAN: *I'm* Pickett.

INSPECTOR: Right, Pickett. (*To third man*) Now, Fotheringall—

THIRD MAN: I'm Marlingston.

INSPECTOR: Right. Well, anyway, you all know your positions. It's just possible that curiosity will draw him to this exhibit.

ALL THREE: Right! (*Exeunt*)

INSPECTOR: (*To fourth man*) And you, Smythe, I'm counting on you most of all.

FOURTH MAN: Oh, I'm not a policeman.

INSPECTOR: Right. (*Exits*)

"Well, anyway," Howard concludes, "it promises to be quite a day at the Simpson Sisters' Waxworks"—and the ensemble breaks into the first number, "At the Simpson Sisters' Door," a lively bit of nothing about the sights and sensations of this museum of the bizarre.

Why so conventional an opening? Sure, the murder was a jolt, particularly for its erotic plastique; the purple scarf was brought in as if it were a love toy. But that ham-handed narrator figure! The corny "clueless inspector" bit! The asinine choral number! The following book scene was similarly dorky, proposing the ooh-la-la Verdon as Essie Whimple, a hapless younger version of her aunts, unnoticed and unloved. *Verdon* unnoticed? Pardon me, but get real. Then comes the entrance of the hero, Richard Kiley, brawling and shouting because he resents this exploitation of La-rue. (He's another of Howard Cavanaugh's stars, an American strongman act.) The script becomes almost infantile at this point.

But it was Fosse's idea, I surmise, to create a musical so sharp and tense and sexy that he didn't want a strongly written show: he wanted a show that he could *stage* strongly, a presentation piece, Fosse as super-director. Given the extraordinary number of changes that the script went through as it was peddled to diva after diva—or, more likely, the changes that were promised *if* the star signed—it could not be called a piece with any real integrity. It was, if you will, the opposite of *Oklahoma!*: something beyond the black and white of the script and the score. Something, in fact, whose script and score would be used as a point of departure.

Fosse had a Platonic conception of the piece from the start. One, in an absolutely open playing area right to the back of the theatre wall into which sets could be dropped but which could also be left open: a ballet stage, in short, all for dance and nothing else. Two, in an overall feeling of "performance" about the action, so that much of the story would be self-consciously depicted, like the murder, or like Verdon's audition number for the music hall, or her comical destruction of a music-hall ensemble number, part-ly out of inexperience but partly because she has spotted the red-bearded murderer in a stage box—that is, sitting right along with the audience of the Forty-sixth Street Theatre in a box overlooking stage left. Three, in a manipulation of the score to provide Fosse with numbers serving not the story but the talents of Fosse's hand-picked corps de ballet.

Not that the show entirely lacked story. Verdon's character is subject to visions, and in one she sees the murderer. We saw him in the show's first seconds, of course, but we meet him again midway through Act One. It's Sir Charles Willingham (Patrick Horgan), Ruth Larue's erstwhile fiancé. Naturally, he wants to get to Verdon. At the end of Act One, alone on the empty music-hall stage—that open playing area—Verdon tries to phone Scotland Yard for protection but is cut off. At the very rear of the stage a door opens and someone enters, casting a gigantic shadow. Verdon turns: it's the murderer!

> SIR CHARLES: Miss Whimple? I understand you know who murdered Ruth.

As he slowly advances, the curtain falls.

Besides the whodunnit, there was of course a romance, between the shy but hopeful Verdon and the doubting yet increasingly enthusiastic Kiley. There was no second couple; how could there be, when the ingenue had been strangled in scene one? But then, this was a show with very little plot at all, just enough to get Fosse from effect to number to effect. Effect: Kiley and Stone encourage Verdon to reinvent herself from drudge to siren in a beguine, "Just For Once," that erupts in a dance much as "The Rain in Spain" had done, though it is Fosse's joke that these three people are flesh and blood, with real appetites, and that came out in a dance purposely designed to make "The Rain in Spain" look maidenly by comparison. Number: the "Uncle Sam Rag," a music-hall special, takes up that great open stage with groups of two or three or four, moving toward and away from each other in a ragtime double chorus. Effect: Verdon and Kiley's first date is supervised by the aunts, looking on in limbo, not physically present in real time but nevertheless "correcting" the couple's behavior.

Here's a combination from Act Two, when many musical comedies have run out of plot. Fosse had run out of plot early in Act

One, but *Redhead* was about making a hit musical out of nothing but imagination and fun. Effect: trying to elude Sir Charles in London's Tenderloin, Verdon slips into the roughest of pubs, which gets raided. The set flies up to reveal the empty playing area once more, leaving Verdon and some of the girls standing stage center. Instantly, a square of prison bars crashed down in front of them in one of quickest, tightest scene changes of the decade. Number: Verdon must now flirt with the jailer (Buzz Miller) and steal the key to the cell. She was winsome, unknowing in Act One; now, she's what men get arrested for. All hips and eyes, Verdon snaps her fingers to a Latin beat. The girls snap with her. The jailer is noticing. Verdon continues to undulate and snap. "Did you know," she asks him, "that I'm [snap! snap! orchestral chord] Spanish?"

Thus begins the "Pickpocket Tango," the ultimate in Fosse sleazy-pretty dances, climaxing when Verdon rips off the jailer's shirt, gets very friendly with him, palms the key, and frees her friends.

The evening was almost over by then. But there was one major effect and one major number left. The effect: good old friendly George, about to rendezvous with our heroine, has a moment in his dressing room, unseen by us. When he emerges, he is made up in a red wig with a red beard. So *he's* the murderer—Ruth Larue's castoff lover, now to kill the interfering Verdon!

And so the number: a great gala chase through the waxworks, involving not only the villain and the heroine and her hero and the two aunts and Howard and the Inspector and the cops, but also the jailer (who breathlessly tells Verdon, "I just can't get you out of my mind!"), the real Sir Charles (so we never know whether the redhead *we* see at any given moment is good guy or bad guy), and everyone else in the cast, a whirlwind of jokes and tricks till the murderer is caught and Fosse lines his cast up—on the big bare stage—for a last go-through of the "Uncle Sam Rag."

The open playing area, previously used only in Rodgers and Hammerstein's *Allegro* in 1947, was already unusual. But Fosse was truly revolutionary in the way he pumped dance through *Redhead*'s action. Way back in the Second Age, dance tended to "follow" song. That is, someone would sing and then someone (the singer or others; it didn't matter) would dance to the same music. Big ensemble dance numbers were not common till the 1920s, when the stage was expected to erupt in a "Clap Yo' Hands" or "Doin' the New Low Down," not to mention the gigantic constructions popularized by the *Follies*, *Scandals*, and *Vanities*.

In time, the notion of a player or two singing and then dancing seemed risible, offensive to narrative flow. True, a dancing star such as Ray Bolger would make a meal out of his solos, and the secondary romantic couple could be counted on to mask a scene-change with a ditty and a dance. But by the 1950s, the choreographer's genius was bent almost as a rule to group dance, showing off the corps. Think of *Guys and Dolls*—"Runyonland," the Havana sequence, the "Crapshooters' Ballet" before "Luck Be a Lady," the Hot Box floor numbers. Think of *Wonderful Town*, so filled with everybody for "Christopher Street," "Conquering New York," "Pass That Football," "Conga! (which starts with Rosalind Russell and a half-dozen Brazilian naval cadets but eventually subsumes the entire Village), "My Darlin' Eileen" (an Irish jig for cops), and the "Ballet at the Village Vortex": no solos, not even a duo.

Imaginative choreographers would, of course, vary the recipe, and there are plenty of notable dance moments for two or three— Judy Holliday and Peter Gennaro in *Bells Are Ringing*'s "Mu-cha-cha," say, or Carol Haney, Buzz Miller, and Gennaro again in *The Pajama Game*'s "Steam Heat." Still, the fifties musical liked ensemble dancing. *Redhead*, however, marked a kind of retrospective conclusion to the history of dance in the musical: it was a sampling of all the kinds of choreography there had ever been, including a dream ballet, a comic ballet, a solo dance star goes for it, a play-within-the-play number, a duo, a trio . . . here was everything. Verdon of course soloed, intimately, soulfully, in "Merely Marvelous" and on display in her audition for a music-hall job, " 'Erbie Fitch's Dilemma," a trick number in that it was supposed to be terrible and make the character look bad, but still had to be a great number that made Verdon look wonderful. She did it in male drag, topped by a derby. The duo was of course the "Pickpocket Tango" and the trio followed "Just For Once," as reported. "Two Faces in the Dark" was Fosse's version of Victorian ro-

mance, as sentimental as a doily, though drolly skewed by the
tenor's heavy Cockney accent. This is the number that Verdon
ruined when she saw the murderer—so we think—in the audience, and she had yet another ensemble job in the "everybody's
drunk" number "We Loves Ya, Jimey."

You would think that, playing the lead and doing a fair amount
of singing and all this dancing, Verdon had already earned her
paycheck. But that dream ballet, "Essie's Vision," topped everything as the longest and most elaborately structured of all its kind,
not only choreographically but musically as well. It is built on a
theme-and-variations form, the theme being the heroine's "Merely
Marvelous." Again, the stage is big and bare (the Forty-sixth Street
Theatre, now the Richard Rodgers, has one of the widest prosce-
nium openings in New York), a pure dance place. After an introduction with *concertante* moments for every desk in the orchestra
we get Variation One, a can-can: psycho Offenbach. A change in
costume and attitude gives us a flowing pas de deux, followed by
another change for the Gypsy Dance, complete with foot stamps
and allusions to Liszt's Hungarian Rhapsodies. Last comes a
marche militaire, "Merely Marvelous" now trumpeted in the glory
of Essie's vision of herself as something tremendous, for the usual
musical comedy reason: somebody marvelous loves her.

Compare the weight of Fosse's own vision of how his show
should play with the weight of the silly script and only adequate
score and we realize that *Redhead* was a triumph of musical comedy performance. When Richard Wagner proposed the *Gesamtkunstwerk* (literally "the piece that integrates all the arts"), he
meant "a great staging of my operas." Bob Fosse's *Gesamtkunstwerk* was "a great staging of my stagings." *Redhead* was a museum of the grotesque, sex and tricks and murder: but stupendous
fun.

It ran long out of town, where Fosse dropped three songs—
"Doesn't Take a Minute," "You Might Be Next," and "Don't Mention It"—replaced Kiley's wishful-thinking celebration of his break
with Verdon, "Going Solo," with "I'm Back in Circulation," and
thought up "The Chase." The show came in on a huge advance
and won the raves usually given a piece that is brilliant itself rather than made brilliant by someone other than its authors.

But that's musical comedy: put Fosse and Verdon together with no one in their way and history gets made. A limited history: for though *Redhead* was a smash moneymaker, breaking even just five months into its thirteen-month run and sweeping the Tonys—it took Best Musical, Best Director and Best Choroegrapher, Best Composer, Best Librettist, Best Actress, Best Actor, Best Supporting Actor, Best Designer, and Best Production—it then disappeared from sight, hearing, and memory.

There was no movie, and, though Verdon planned to make her London debut in the show—with Fosse as the murderer—the project never came through. (Fosse had wanted to play the part from the beginning, and was dissuaded only because of the huge job in getting *Redhead* on stage.)

So the show ends here, an unrevivable triumph: for what's Redhead without Fosse and Verdon? In *The New Yorker*, Kenneth Tynan figured out how Verdon was unique, and why she cannot be replaced:

> The amount of physical activity in which this frail-seeming creature indulges is perfectly flabbergasting; spinning, prancing, leaping, curvetting, she is seldom out of sight and never out of breath. Yet beneath the athletic ebullience is something more rarified—an unfailing delicacy of spirit . . . Verdon invests the stereotype [of the man-hungry spinster] with so much tact and finesse that even when she is making her boldest advance . . . she appears to be shrinking from the consequences.

That was musical comedy in the 1950s. With so much talent going on, it took talent for granted.

Genius, too.

15

The Street, 1959

The end of the 1950s was much like the start, the same only more so. The musical play continued to crowd musical comedy; the revue had become ever scarcer; television kept more and more theatregoers at home. There was one notable difference between 1950 and 1959: Ethel Merman started in *Call Me Madam* and ended in *Gypsy*. Otherwise, this was in essence, in all its years, the decade that followed *Oklahoma!*, *Carousel*, and *South Pacific*.

For instance, Harold Rome continued to develop his versatility in *Destry Rides Again* (1959), which gives us a chance to consider yet another star vehicle superintended by a director-choreographer. Based on "the story by Max Brand," as the program had it, *Destry* was of course the 1939 James Stewart–Marlene Dietrich western as a musical: those characters, that storyline. The 1939 version was the outstanding one of four film adaptations, the first in 1932 with Tom Mix and Claudia Dell, the third (retitled after the heroine as *Frenchie*) in 1951, with Joel McCrea and Shelley Winters, and the last in 1954 with war hero Audie Murphy and baroque, peerless Mari Blanchard. Rome's librettist was Leonard Gershe; his stars were Andy Griffith and Dolores Gray; his director-choreographer was Michael Kidd; his producer was David Merrick; and Merrick's great publicity stunt on *this* one was slugfests involving Kidd, Gray, and Gray's mother. The headlines made Merrick's year, but the show still lost money, on a year's run.

It was a good show, the kind of thing that should have clicked: strong story (a totally corrupt and violent town gets a pacifist sheriff who won't tote a gun), pre-sold title, the sheer novelty of a musical shoot-'em-up, and two very capable and perfectly cast leads. Griffith in particular was in his heyday, vastly liked for his Will Stockdale in *No Time for Sergeants* on television, stage, and screen but also an intellectual's darling because of his protagonist in Elia Kazan's anti-fascist film *A Face in the Crowd*.

Maybe the lack of a hit-parade title was what hurt *Destry*. "Wish You Were Here" and *Fanny* enjoyed helpful airplay, but Rome's tuneful western produced but two titles—"That Ring on the Finger" and "Every Once in a While"—that were suitable for pop presentation. In the end, only "Ring" attracted (a little) attention.

Perhaps another problem was the shortage of dance. Bob Fosse conceived *Redhead* as the ultimate dancing show, but Kidd treated *Destry* as if it were a musical play, too serious for zany hoofing or crazy ballet. "The Social" was, predictably, in the lusty rustic style that Kidd had invented for the MGM musical *Seven Brides for Seven Brothers*. Bordello ladies and their customers got some nicely tender mileage out of "Rose Lovejoy of Paradise Alley," a dreamy waltz on a naughty idea. This was Kidd at his most inventive. But the utterly irrelevant "Every Once in a While" was a vaguely rock-and-roll rave-up of no value. Critics praised the "Whip Dance," in which three bad guys menace the Social until the resourceful Destry disarms them. But this was not dance in any real sense, just a trio of male gypsies going all leather-and-western on us.

Maybe Kidd simply respected the material too much. Fosse knew that *Redhead* was a meretricious piece of goods whose only virtue was its protean quality: it was so insubstantial that it could be turned into anything that its director needed it to be. Earlier, Rodgers and Hammerstein might have made *Redhead* a musical play emphasizing English class structure, with a fully delineated secondary couple and, say, Stephen Douglass and Barbara Cook in the leads. Later, Hal Prince, with, perhaps, John Kander and Fred Ebb, might have made it a concept musical using the wax museum as a metaphor for the inevitable falseness of life, a chorus of lurking wax figures, and an opening-and-closing frame of a number entitled, "Give 'Em the Works!"

Michael Kidd, however, viewed *Destry* as a work of integrity that had no need of development. He simply staged what was written—not a bad idea, at that. For starters, it had one of those slick, tight, and confident openings, as a lone cowboy shouldering a saddle in one sang a slow, apparent paean to *Destry*'s locale, Bottleneck. As he reached the end of his stanza, he suddenly changed tone and warned us off. Three other cowhands with saddles ran on, supporting his critique ("You don't know the true meaning of trouble," they insist, "till you've come to Bottleneck!"). To gunshots, the backdrop turned translucent in the familiar fifties way and rose on the show's main set, the Last Chance Saloon, as a bunch of dance-hall girls and burned-out gunslingers sang the chorus ("Don't Take Me Back to Bottleneck").

Then it was the work of a moment for the bartender to introduce "the flame of New Orleans," as Dolores Gray paraded out in dress-to-slay sequins to honky-tonk keyboard. Gray's *aria di sortita* was "Ladies": really two numbers, the first a front-parlor waltz and the second, with les girls and to a completely different melody, a trashy march. From diva to whore: just as Destry goes from pacifist to killer. Max Brand's tale gets its power not from its classic battle of saint (he) and sinner (she), but because she turns saint and he turns sinner, donning the hated guns at last to take on the bad guy (Scott Brady, in an absolutely non-singing role), though in the end it is Gray, the bad guy's girl, who shoots him to save Destry.

Here's another problem. Personality is essential in the casting of the leads, for this is inescapably a two-person story. One reason why the 1939 movie is so familiar is that the other versions' leads are so poor in personal chemistry. (Chemistry? Yeah, chemistry.) Claudia Dell? Audie Murphy? In the musical we had that amiable southern guy who is just so bewildered by fancy manners and the high-strung Broadway queen who needs a hit so very badly . . . It should have made a hot chemistry, but Griffith and Gray never really interlocked. Gray, at least, had the part of her career, the vocal compass so deep that it counts the E and F below middle C (Wagner's Erda doesn't sink lower) on important notes, and in "I Know Your Kind," when Gray rises merely to A above middle C, she makes it sound like Brünnihilde's top C. Moreover, Gray was costumed to the nth, played the doxie, the vamp, the heroine, the dea ex machina. She had one of the great all-time show-off spots in "Fair Warning," when she planted herself between Griffith and Brady and did a floor number whose theme was independence and whose subtext was "Don't mess with me, boys." She had *nine* numbers—more than even Merman had in all but two shows.* Yet Gray's coldness infected the action.

Okay, this is a tough character. It's a tough story. Two good guys—one of them Destry's sidekick—are killed, and Destry brings down the stark first-act curtain in a boldly threatening scene in which this advocate of nonviolence shoots out all the lights in the saloon with fastidious marksmanship, telling everyone just how good a shot he can be if he be driven to it. It's Destry's fair warning. Or consider the second-act curtain, when the men of Bottleneck, one by one, drop their guns, willing to submit to the rule of law in an epic moment not unworthy of *Oklahoma!* But if no one could have sung a better Frenchy (as the show spelled it) than Gray, someone else might have played a Frenchy that touched the heart. Gray's most believable moment was when she slapped Michael Kidd in rehearsal.

Now let's ponder the "musical play," again in an adaptation with two stars, Marc Blitzstein's *Juno* (1959). Unfortunately, Sean O'Casey's *Juno and the Paycock* is not a presold title. It's a great play, set in Dublin in 1922 during the war between the British and Irish rebels but centering on the collapse of a family. The mother devoted but the father dissolute, the Boyles see their son murdered for suspected collusion with the Brits and their unmarried daughter pregnant; at length, mother Juno leaves the vain-

---

* Merman had eight numbers and her personal reprise of "There's No Business Like Show Business" in *Annie Get Your Gun* and nine numbers in *Happy Hunting*, heavy vocal structures in the day before pop opera.

glorious "Captain" Jack and takes their daughter to seek a new life. As the curtain falls, the Captain is expounding obliviously away to his mooching yes-man, Joxer Daly.

It was a dubious project for a Broadway musical, but the story was not that much darker than those of *The King and I, A Tree Grows in Brooklyn*, or even *Fanny*. The political context, with the cries of "Up the rebels!" punctuating the patrols of the British Army, had an appeal for the leftist Blitzstein that it would not have had for, say, Rodgers and Hammerstein, who might have tackled O'Casey's play out of a fascination with the family relationships; and, after all, the highly political 1960s were just a year away. Perhaps Blitzstein thought the time was right, especially because he had the intention of treating O'Casey (other than moving the action from 1922 to 1921) with the utmost fidelity.

Indeed, *Juno* is the musical that O'Casey himself might have made of *Juno and the Paycock** had he been a composer and lyricist. The book, by Joseph Stein, simply opened up O'Casey's single set to include the places where the Boyles go when they aren't at home—the street, Foley's Bar, a public square, the yard behind the house. A full cast of characters filled out the Boyles's social life, and Blitzstein in effect created two scores, one derived from lines in O'Casey's text to delineate the Boyles ("I Wish It So," "Song of the Ma," the quarrel duet "Old Sayin's," Juno's tragic soliloquy "Where?") and the other to build up the social and political background in ensemble numbers ("We Can Be Proud," the quartet of whining women "You Poor Thing," "On a Day Like This," "Music in the House").

A sharp musical dramatist but a longtime dud as a melodist, Blitzstein composed, for once, a truly memorable score, from love music to carmagnole. Everything comes logically out of the story, yet there are imaginative stunts as well, for instance the Dubliners' anthem, "We're Alive," which opens the show as a cockeyed hymn and is suddenly interrupted by the murder of a young rebel

---

* O'Casey's heroine is named after the month of June, but the playwright refers also to Juno, the Roman goddess who watched over marriage and especially the rights of married women. Her favorite animal was the peacock, here rendered in Irish dialect spelling and alluding, of course, to the vainglorious Captain Boyle.

to become a funeral march. Then, as the second-act finale, it takes on a terrific irony as Juno and her daughter walk out on their private tragedy while the Dubliners continue to defy British rule.

Another great scene found the Boyles, in a short-lived burst of prosperity, buying a gramophone (as in O'Casey). With full-sized musical forces at his disposal, Blitzstein turned *Juno*'s gramophone scene into a block party: with the playing of a song entitled "It's Not Irish," the Captain's cronies impulsively joined in, and then the following disc, "The Liffey Waltz," so swept the party up that the set of the Boyles's flat broke apart and revolved to take in all Dublin, all dancing, all joyous. This, too, was suddenly interrupted, this time by the mother of the slain rebel, heading for his funeral with an escort of IRA soldiers who terrify Juno's son. As the party breaks up, the scene changes to a drab street where the son reveals his anxiety in a haunted, remorseful, hopeless dance. He'll be killed soon.

Juno was the grimmest of the decade's musical plays, but bound into a highly artistic presentation, like *The King and I*; and offering a wealth of soothing melody, like *Fanny*; and even starring Shirley Booth, like *A Tree Grows in Brooklyn*. Melvyn Douglas was her Captain, Monte Amundsen their daughter, Loren Driscoll her suitor, the unique Tommy Rall (like Driscoll an opera-weight tenor but also a fine dancer who had appeared with American Ballet Theatre) the Boyles's treacherous son, Jack MacGowran Joxer, Jean Stapleton, Nancy Andrews, Sada Thompson, and Beulah Garrick the four gossips, and Gemze de Lappe Rall's only friend.

De Lappe, an Agnes de Mille stalwart, tells us who staged the musical numbers, and de Mille was at her best here, working out not only the expected jigs and clogs but a dramatic ballet for Act One, "Dublin Night," and the big second-act gramophone sequence. De Mille did not direct, however. José Ferrer did, and there the problem may lie, for Ferrer took over during tryouts from Vincent J. Donehue, whose only credential was that he was Mary Martin's favorite director. Apparently, Donehue was unable to blend Blitzstein's two shows into a satisfying whole. The potential was there and the cast distinguished, but with such a dark subject the piece needed raves from the critics, and not one of them was enthusiastic. They all liked the dancing and the cast, but each review found something different at fault, which sounds like poor direction to me. *Juno* lasted 16 performances but may have been a near-miss. *The King and I*'s Jerome Robbins, *Fanny*'s Joshua Logan, or, I have to say, even *A Tree Grows in Brooklyn*'s George Abbott might have saved it.

Another failure, though not so quick a one, was *First Impressions* (1959), to this date the sole attempt to put Jane Austen on Broadway with music. (After the rash of Jane Austen movies in the mid-1990s, one wonders how long before we will see *Emma!*, or perhaps *Mansfield Park: The Musical*.) The sole attempt to put Jane Austen on Broadway at all was Helen Jerome's *Pride and Prejudice* (1935), so Janeite in conception that Jerome endeavored to use, as much as possible, nothing but lines from the novel. Producer after producer turned the script down as too literary, but, in that typical good old Broadway saga, it finally found a taker (Max Gordon) and met with stunning success. MGM filmed Jerome's script with Laurence Olivier and Greer Garson to even greater success as a two-hour special in 1940. Unfortunately, Abe Burrows was not content with even greater success when he turned Austen-Jerome into the book for *First Impressions*. Burrows did the unthinkable and rewrote Jane Austen. Worse, he rewrote Helen Jerome, who had at least figured out how to reduce a brilliant novel to theatre-evening length without sacrificing what made the novel brilliant: the words.

Some might say that what Burrows sacrificed in Austen he gained in Hermione Gingold. As Mrs. Bennet, mother of five unmarried girls in a town suddenly inhabited by two wealthy bachelors, Gingold was Everymother—pushy, unreasonable, critical of all her daughters' potential rivals, and ruthless in manipulating an opportunity. The uncontrollable Elizabeth Bennet was Polly Bergen, her undemocratizable antagonist and, finally, suitor, Fitzwilliam Darcy, was Farley Granger. The second of the five daughters was Phyllis Newman and her eventual spouse, the other rich catch, was Donald Madden. The list of supporting roles is too great to detain us, for here was a most crowded stage—it had to be, if Austen's social comedy of village politics, genderism, and social consciousness was to enjoy even partial representation.

Still, Gingold was the main thing here, dismissing, exhorting, arranging, flattering:

> MRS. BENNET: (*pointing to a painting*) Mr. Collins, who is that?
>
> COLLINS: That is my dear patroness' late lamented husband, Lord Alistair de Bourgh. A great nobleman.
>
> MRS. BENNET: How long has he been . . . ?
>
> COLLINS: A few years. He died wearing His Majesty's uniform. Lord de Bourgh was in London watching the triumphant return of Nelson's fleet and he fell out the window of his club.
>
> MRS. BENNET: (*with the dementedly confidential tact of which she was the unique mistress*) A hero's death.

I thought Gingold the funniest thing that ever lived and *First Impressions* a classy and lively show, even given that Burrows had ravaged it of Austen's voice. The score, by Robert Goldman, Glenn Paxton, and George Weiss, managed to suggest the era without trying to revive it, though Bergen sang the relatively Georgian "Love Will Find Out the Way" to harpsichord accompaniment, and though Christopher Hewett's comic courtship number, "Fragrant Flower," smacked robustly of the antique.

No, most of *First Impressions* sang in standard late-fifties style, especially in Elizabeth's establishing number, to counterpoint by her fondly scolding sisters, "I'm Me," in Farley Granger's Henry Higgins-like "A Gentlemen Never Falls Wildly in Love," in Phyllis Newman's "I Feel Sorry for the Girl," though it does slip in a "fee-fi-fo-fum" refrain as in scatting in Austenese. Most successful were Gingold's numbers, written for the actress rather than the character: her amusing lament, "Five Daughters"; "Have You Heard the News?," a choral number with a delightful, prancing orchestral accompaniment as Gingold ran from person to person heralding Darcy's arrival and raising the amount of his income with each report; her anthem, "As Long as There's a Mother"; her catty asides in a choral scene, "Wasn't This a Simply Lovely Wedding?"; "A House in Town," in which she reveals what we've known all along, that she thinks the whole story is about her; and her eleven o'clocker with Bergen, the waltzing "Let's Fetch the Carriage."

It was a commendable score, if lacking the dramatic tones that Harold Rome heard in Marcel Pagnol. However, if one didn't go for Gingold and wanted less of Burrows and more of Austen, *First Impressions* had nothing. Richard Watts, Jr., of the *Post* thought Gingold "was acting the wicked stepmother in a British Christmas pantomime," calling it "a savage caricature." In Austen, Mrs. Bennet is silly, selfish, and vulgar. In *First Impressions*, she is a devouring beast. Maybe that sounds wrong, but we're going to meet just such a mother a few pages hence—and not in a comic version like Gingold's Mrs. Bennet—in *Gypsy*.

Now, what about sheer unapologetic musical comedy, without gunslingers and concerns about translations from the Georgian, the kind of thing George Abbott would do. In fact, how about a George Abbott show itself, *Once Upon a Mattress* (1959)?

What a no-no title. But this was in fact a relatively innocent work reviving an old form, burlesque. We've seen *Little Mary Sunshine* using this to spoof operetta, but *Mattress* actually preceded it by six months and, like the pure burlesque of old, it did not spoof the conventions of an old form but rather retold a familiar story with lots of contemporary fun. This kind of thing was common way back in the First Age, in such titles as *Evangeline* (1874) and *Hiawatha* (1880), both by Edward E. Rice. *Mattress's* subject is *The Princess and the Pea*, which it retells first in its basic form in a lovely opening, "Many Moons Ago," narrated by the Minstrel as, behind him, the Princess, Prince, and Queen mime the tale with exquisite grace. Then the Minstrel steps forward for a characteristic fifties blackout-and-scene-change-behind-the-performer-addressing-the-audience. It seems this version is "the prettiest" but "not quite accurate." The Minstrel knows what happened because he was there: "It was a small kingdom ruled over by a talkative queen and a mute king." A bit more of this and the stage proper is set and the lights come up on just about the entire cast as the Minstrel steps back into the action, a newcomer on the scene. This allows the Lady Larken to fill him (and us) in on some helpful expository details during the testing of the latest princess.

Because this was 1959, just after the notorious television quiz show scandals, the "test" is conducted very like the *Sixty-Four*

Thousand Dollar Question, complete with "You have now reached the seventh plateau," the tricky question in several parts, the testee asking for the repeat of a question, and so on. The final question is so ridiculously difficult that the princess fails and is hustled away by the overbearing Queen, to the court's despair. No one can marry till the Prince does, and the Queen clearly won't allow him to.

An amusing ensemble number, "An Opening for a Princess," warns us how clever the evening is going to be, first of all in its punning title—the "opening" refers not only to the position they want filled in the royal family but also to the number itself, the equivalent of an "everyone onstage for the opening" song and dance. Second, the number covers the Prince's exit, but lets *him* launch the vocal as he crosses the stage on his way out, an unusually fluid touch in narrative kinetics. Finally, the scene closes with Lady Larken telling her boy friend, Sir Harry, that she is pregnant with his baby, so the ensuing duet, "In a Little While," puts a wicked little edge on the typical subplot couple's first-act ballad.

The show continues in that vein, filling out *The Princess and the Pea* with all sorts of modern devilry. The book is by Jay Thompson, Marshall Barer, and Dean Fuller, who, like *First Impressions'* Goldman, Paxton, and Weiss, somehow never got the repeated chances to firm up an oeuvre; but the music, to Barer's lyrics, is by Mary Rodgers, daughter of Richard—so here's some lively history.* The style of Rodgers *cadette*, interestingly, sounds genetically comparable, though different. It's not Richard Rodgers's sound, yet it's . . . well, related to it. Certain moments, as when the harmony becomes wonderfully dangerous in the trio section of "Normandy," recall the senior Rodgers, whose chord relationships could grow quite complex, especially in the releases of ballads. Other moments seem to pull away from the Father, almost to deny Him. Rodgers himself thought so, unhappily, of

---

* The only other instance that I can recall in which an American score was composed by the offspring of a composer is *Floyd Collins* (1996), by Adam Guettel: Mary Rodgers's son.

the release to "Yesterday I Loved You," when the stately tempo
suddenly zooms. "I wouldn't have done that," he said. "Write your
own show," Mary (may have) replied.

Like *Little Mary Sunshine*, *Mattress* started off-Broadway, but
at the Broadway-sized Phoenix, like *The Golden Apple*. And, like
The Golden Apple, *Mattress* moved uptown: and *kept* moving. Theatre after theatre welcomed it but then sent it packing to honor
a prior contract. Union economics prohibit such tactics today, but
in 1959 a show could move a few blocks for a couple of closing
weeks—for even a single week—and profit. But this endless bum's
rush hurt *Mattress*, in that people knew it was there, but where
exactly? Then, too, the smart and lovely score, so distinctive in
the house and on disc, never threw off a hit single, so useful in
these days when Broadway music was the national music, when
radio and television maintained a vigorous relationship not only
with the old standards but, hungrily, with new work.

The *cast* threw off a hit single: Carol Burnett. Among a host of
debutants and seasoned pros, Burnett made *Mattress* her personal
jumping-off place just after some one-off TV spots and just before
her regular stint on *The Garry Moore* [TV variety] *Show*. One more
Broadway musical, *Fade Out–Fade In* (1964), and Burnett was
thoroughly invested as one of America's most popular entertainers, less worshipped than beloved, in the way Will Rogers and
Lucille Ball were. So the Julie Andrews–*Boy Friend* thing was still
operating at the end of the decade: there was something tremendous about making a hit in a musical *at that time* that outdid every
other talent auction in show biz, whether in straight theatre, pop
music, or film. A Broadway musical was not the only route to
stardom; it was the most sensational. Of course, it was nothing
to be stupendous in a musical if it flopped. In the curious thinking
of show-biz managers, then and now, if it succeeds then *you the
actor* made the success. If it fails, *you the actor* made the failure.
Writing? Directing? That's no more than dress design. The star
did it all.

Thus, even a modest personal success in a hit could start a
performer on a star's career—but beware the maladroit follow-up
vehicle. Critics and intelligent theatregoers saw the stars of *West
Side Story* as the authors and Jerome Robbins. Scouts, touts,

agents, and other finaglers fingered the onstage talent and found the Maria, Carol Lawrence, to be a likely prospect. (In fact, though she left the production when it toured, she rejoined it when it played a New York return, the only one of the original leads to do so, and thus earned an I think misleading star billing. *West Side Story* has no star parts.)

Anyway, Carol Lawrence was ripe for a let's-see flotation: humdinger looks, pleasing voice, top dancer. Then *Saratoga* (1959) happened.

This brings us to musical-play territory, the serious stuff with class, sex, race, historical Americana, fortune hunters-versus-robber barons, all based on an Edna Ferber novel—and you know what the last show based on an Edna Ferber novel turned out to be: *Show Boat.*

But Ferber's *Saratoga Trunk* is very unlike her *Show Boat*, tight and angry and really about two people, two only, where *Show Boat* is about many people, and the theatre, the Mississippi, and America. *Saratoga Trunk* should have been much easier to adapt than *Show Boat*. It had made a splendid film for Gary Cooper and Ingrid Bergman in 1945. The story is there, the romance is there, the historical color that Ferber was always eager to exploit was there: cowboy Clint Maroon wants revenge on the money bosses who destroyed his father. Young beauty Clio Dulaine wants revenge on the fancy family that destroyed her mother. They team up as business partners *only* and of course fall for each other like greased dominoes. The nineteenth-century setting ranges from Paris to New Orleans to Saratoga in its socialite heyday; the heroine's entourage takes in an old cocotte of an aunt, a black maid, a combative dwarf; and she will ultimately throw over her aristo engagement for the cowboy by appearing at a ball in blackface.

You can *see* the smash show that will come of this material—Harold Arlen and Johnny Mercer for the score and Oscar Hammerstein for the book. Except Hammerstein was busy with *The Sound of Music*, and in any case wouldn't have worked without Richard Rodgers. No, *Saratoga*'s book was by Morton da Costa, a sometime actor and then director who hit a flash success in the mid-1950s. He staged a sleeper (*Plain and Fancy*): a hit. He staged an expansion of a TV drama that no one cared about (*No*

Time for Sergeants): a smash. He staged a potential sure thing that, for some reason, no other director could figure out logistically, because of its all-over-the-place scene plot. If it didn't get on, gay life as we knew it would have ceased to exist, da Costa figured it out logistically, and it came in (Rosalind Russell in *Auntie Mame*): a triple smash. He staged another musical sleeper (*The Music Man*): instant classic.

By 1959, da Costa could name his fee and billing. But *Saratoga* confounded everyone: producer Robert Fryer, songwriters Arlen and Mercer, Carol Lawrence and her co-star, Howard Keel, featured player Jane Darwell—the former child star and Shirley Temple nemesis and later Josephine the Plumber on TV commercials, playing Sophie Bellop, a penniless aristo who befriends Clio at Saratoga—and especially da Costa.

First, he began with a grave flourish, in the Parisian exile of Clio's mother and suite, in a darkened room where the mother keens for her lost love and lost New Orleans and dies. It's an interesting idea, the beginning of a play rather than of a musical. Perhaps da Costa had the notion of making *Saratoga* into, literally, a musical play: a big, bold adventure only peppered with songs.

Certainly, as with Gwen Verdon's Anna in *New Girl in Town*, Carol Lawrence was going to *enact* Clio, not turn her into a dancing lady of Broadway. Arlen and Mercer would encompass Ferber's vision of America in which heroic women manage beautiful but erratic men with music of bold gesture—Clint's bitter look at society in "Dog Eat Dog," tender and cynical love songs in "Love Held Lightly" and "(Love is) A Game of Poker," which will then be sung together, in counterpoint, for irony, a bunch of millionaires on a resort hotel porch smugly rocking as they sing "The Men Who Run the Country."

Isn't this great stuff? There would be a powerful first-act curtain when Clint avows his love to Clio in full flouting of their agreement as she coldly reminds him that they are in it for the money only. The calmly intense Ferber adventurer! No love songs for her! To which Clint replies, not using these words, "I'm going to have you all the way!" as the curtain falls. As for dance, there was to be a jivey strut of street vendors in New Orleans, "Petticoat High," and, when Clint and his toughs tangle with the minions of the railroad honchos, a "Railroad Fight" in slow motion. This is creative, dramatic, musical, brilliant.

But everything went wrong. The book was wordy and heavy. The score found both Arlen and Mercer in erratic form, good stuff side by side with okay stuff, even dull stuff. The production was extremely lavish, with sets and costumes by Cecil Beaton that pushed the budget to a record $400,000. But all that money so obviously spent by Fryer ran precisely against the one thing that Ferber made sure Clint and Clio learn: that money is destructive, not creative. Money gives hypocrites the power to disguise their character. Money destroyed Clint's father and Clio's mother: so what's it doing taking over this show?

Saratoga was obviously headed for tryout hell. Da Costa's prologue in Paris was cut, and "Bon Appetit," a lengthy ensemble number in Begué's restaurant in New Orleans in which Clio makes a big deal of herself and Clint can't make out the French menu and a chorus of waiters sings and runs around, was dropped. It was pure musical comedy, a show-off number rather than a useful one. Another show-off number, Clio's "The Parks of Paris," a waltz of sublime dreariness, went out. The droning "You For Me," Clint's first-act curtain avowal to Clio, was replaced by the slightly hungrier "You Or No One." It was decided to let Clio dance in "Petticoat High," though it seemed to contradict her desire to pass herself off as French nobility—more musical-comedy thinking. In fact, a lot of what was wrong with *Saratoga* was that musical-comedy people were writing it as a musical play that was afraid not to be a musical comedy. Too much of it was show-off, standard-make rather than distinctive.

Remember, the essential quality of the musical play as developed by Rodgers and Hammerstein is its unusual take on an unusual story, yielding a show *the like of which you never saw before.* Not just new tunes and new characters: a new way of telling a story. *The King and I*'s "March of the Siamese Children," or that clobbering gong stroke that heralds the King's guards dragging in the recaptured Tuptim. *A Tree Grows in Brooklyn*'s Johnny spinning out his worthless dreams while Katie goes on scrubbing. *Fanny*'s confrontation of fathers. *Plain and Fancy*'s shunning. Anything in *Candide*.

Saratoga told its unusual story conventionally; that sunk it. At some point in the tryout, Arlen decided that he was ill and decamped. (He never composed another Broadway score.) Jane Darwell left, too, after her one tiny solo, "Al Fresco," also went missing. Edith King replaced her.

Meanwhile, Johnny Mercer, that sometime composer, decided to write, on his own, a number to replace "Lessons in Love," a dud of a duet for Clio and her Aunt Belle (operetta veteran Odette Myrtil). Noting the potential in the song's cue line, spoken by the maid Kakou (Carol Brice)—"Gettin' a man and gettin' a husband is two diff'rent things"—Mercer wrote the racy "Gettin' a Man," now a duet for Belle and Kakou and an out-and-out show-stopper. It brought back the superb old style of two colorful personalities stepping to the beat as they cross and recross the stage, in this case while handing out Mercerian gems on man's unwillingness to commit marriage. ("They understand the Promised Land," Myrtil remarked, "but buying the property—*no!*")

That duet was the only thing that really worked in *Saratoga*, the moment when sturdy composition and thoroughbred performers got up some entertainment. *Saratoga*'s problem was that the very grandeur of the novel, and the lingering example of *Show Boat*, suggested that all Edna Ferber musicals must be *Show Boat* in weight.

However, a major show did not by its nature have to be a musical play. Da Costa's own *Music Man* was pure musical comedy. Did he seek a promotion? But musical comedy, too, was undergoing advantageous evolution, to the point where it could be as "important" as the musical play.

Fiorello! (1959), on New York City's Depression and wartime mayor Fiorello La Guardia, could easily have been a musical play: in which case it would have flopped as badly as *Saratoga* did. *Fiorello!*'s subject was no Billy Bigelow, no King of Siam. He was a jabber, a mover, a fast-talking, prejudiced, and self-righteous but impeccably honest politician: a man with the very style of musical comedy in his skin.

Fiorello! does manage to fold him into a love plot, but it sees him as being centered more on public than on private life, fighting for the downtrodden, cadging an unwinnable nomination, winning it, agitating for the extremely unpopular position of American participation in World War I (asked how he'd feel if his proposed Draft Act "applied not only to people but also to Congressmen," Fiorello replies, "I enlisted this morning"), winning World War I (singlehandedly, as we see in a newsreel), taking on the absolute corruption of New York's Tammany machine, and finally losing, so bitterly that he retires from public life until his faithful cohorts manage to rally him as the curtain falls on Fiorello's decision to try another mayoral campaign. (In a clever staging coup, the story was finished during the curtain calls, when a redeemed Fiorello, rolling in on a revolve, is seen taking the oath of office, one he in fact held for twelve years.)

Fiorello!'s book was by Jerome Weidman and George Abbott, its score was by Jerry Bock and Sheldon Harnick, and its cast was all young debutants or Broadway journeymen. In effect, all the show's leads were drawn from a pool of supporting players. This had long been a trademark of *Fiorello!'s* director, George Abbott, but this show had a star part, the title one. Tom Bosley, putting forth an eccentrically sweet soul with a brusque manner in his search for a portrayal to bridge legend and stagecraft, claimed only the first name cited *below* the title. But it is hard to imagine this show enjoying its two-year run without Bosley's mercurial powerhouse of a performance.* Just his delivery of the name "Marie"—that of his silently adoring assistant—was breathtaking in its mixture of shyness and confidence: a short, unimposing guy who thinks he's got it, but isn't sure who else has noticed. Bosley truly held the story together as this difficult but lovable man, so self-righteous yet so . . . well, right.

Here's another weird show that is so beautifully put together that it played as the latest first-class but neither challenging nor

---

* Casting the role was a major headache, especially because Griffith and Prince started with the idea of nabbing an out-of-the-way star. The new tradition of Hollywood names on Broadway led them to Mickey Rooney; the trend toward giving vocal coaching to non-singer actors suggested Eli Wallach. Ironically, *Fiorello!* made Tom Bosley's career, though he did nothing of consequence thereafter, including another George Abbott musical dealing with immigrant life in New York City, *The Education of H*Y*M*A*N K*A*P*L*A*N* (1968). What finally made Bosley a star was his role as the father on television's *Happy Days*.

troubling show. Maybe I'm wrong and George Abbott really was a genius. Maybe novelist Weidman brought something realistic yet utopian to this saga of a politician without politics. Maybe Bock and Harnick, freed from the trivial novelties of *The Body Beautiful*, suddenly realized that, like *Fiorello*, *they* had it, and sat down and used it. For *Fiorello!* boasts one of the great late-fifties scores. It's not a classic one by any means; it may even be a forgot one. But it is so characterful and various and plot-oriented that I have to rate it as comparable to *The Music Man* in its sheer vivacity of invention. One very odd thing about it, to start: the protagonist has no numbers.

Well, he does have two, both political rather than emotional and deeply cut into the story, one his exhortation of striking garment workers ("Unfair") and the other a campaign montage ("The Name's La Guardia") in which the scene changes periodically during the number and snatches of dialogue between verses advance the plot action. "Unfair" shows us La Guardia's emphatic, even obsessive social conscience; "The Name's La Guardia" shows his charm and savvy in addressing the great mass of people. He even changes language as his stumping changes neighborhoods—Yiddish included. (La Guardia was half-Jewish.)

But Fiorello has no emotional numbers, an arresting proposition for the title character in a thirteen-number score. This show is constructed more *around* its protagonist than *through* him. Much of the book, the score, and the overall feeling of the show is not who he is but how his associates and constituents regard him. The overture begins with a fire-truck siren, recalling Fiorello's fondness for riding to the scene with firefighters, and the curtain rises on another piece of Fiorello nostalgia, his reading the funnies on the radio during a newspaper strike. But the first number is given over to the minor functionaries of his Greenwich Village law office literally gushing over the man in "On the Side of the Angels." Clerk Neil (Bob Holliday) sees him as purely heroic; office manager Morris (Nathaniel Frey) thinks him a bit opportunistic. Yet Fiorello does ignore the fancy dans for the charity cases: "Each poor soul I see there could be me there." A considerable amount of book ensues, then Marie (Patricia Wilson) enters, and here's the so-to-say "other" principal in the show, Fiorello's vis-à-vis if only he knew it. When he wants her, he just comes out of his office and points at her, she comes, and, as the scene draws to a close, "On the Side of the Angels" surges up again, this time with Fiorello's would-be clients singing in counterpoint to the main strain, held down by Marie: steadfast, invaluable, and ignored.

Well, Fiorello is something of a user, for all his idealism. One of the odd things about this score is how it spreads out through all its characters, seeping, penetrating. There is no singing lead, no musical center; the songs come where they need to. Who gets the ballads? Thea (Ellen Hanley), Fiorello's first wife, launches the World War I "farewell" waltz, "Till Tomorrow," and has a smashing musical scene at the start of Act Two, "When Did I Fall in Love?," marked by a bizarre harmonic dissonance on the second beat that resolves on the fourth beat yet keeps returning, as if questioning this beauty-and-beast mating.

So Thea is the singing lead? No: she enters late in Act One and dies early in Act Two; she is no lead in any real sense. Her friend Dora (Pat Stanley) and Dora's eventual husband, Floyd (Mark Dawson), who illustrates the corruption of Jimmy Walker's administration in his rise from beat cop to gang-connected businessman, account for another number ("I Love a Cop," first a solo, then a duet-with-chorus reprise). Fiorello's campaign manager, Ben Marino (Howard da Silva), controls three further numbers, perhaps *Fiorello!*'s best, "Politics and Poker," "The Bum Won" (a dazed crossover, stage left to stage right, of the Party henchmen the day after Republican Fiorello takes the unwinnable D. C. House seat from a Democrat), and "Little Tin Box," a comic review of the Seabury Hearings on municipal corruption. Still, these three songs register so strongly as, again, political instruction that they don't establish Ben Marino as anything more than an ensemble player.

Fiorello! is, then, something really strange, a musical without a lead—at least, a lead as the musical had known it. Even the big dance number, the sole all-out ensemble display piece, seems excrescent, as if this show wanted to spin out its history without dance, without all that . . . that musical-comedy stuff that takes one nowhere. "Gentleman Jimmy" simply revels in the worthless appeal of dapper James J. Walker, and its Charleston rhythm does affirm the twenties setting. Perhaps the number's very emptiness is meant to suggest the vapid allure of a personality candidate like Walker, as opposed to the moral substance of a La Guardia. But in order to get "Gentleman Jimmy" on, the authors have to introduce a character named Mitzi (Eileen Rodgers) who has no existential reality other than as the singer hired by Griffith and Prince to put over the number. She doesn't even dance it. After a verse and chorus, she discreetly gets the hell off the stage while the dancing girls do what they do.

Perhaps Marie will supply some centralizing energy. She has two very personal numbers, both motivated by Fiorello's taking her for granted ("Marie's Law" and "The Very Next Man"). But two songs out of thirteen doesn't quite centralize her; besides, she sings them both to Morris, as if *he* were her opposite.

No. In all, this is a score surrounding the protagonist, revealing him by quizzing his cohorts on how they react to him. He's an angel. He's a bum and a winner. He's unlovable but the love of my life. This is an extraordinary notion—as if *Call Me Madam* had been filled with various numbers *about* Ethel Merman sung *by* Paul Lukas, Russell Nype, Galina Talva, and so on. But then, musical comedy had traveled so far in ten years that it could take any form at will, bend the score, the scene plot, the choreography into a fresh sense of unity every time. Two couples, a bet, a Salvation Army mission. Two sisters, the thirties, youth, ambition, cops, the conga. New York smarties, repressed farming community, a farm for sale. Victorian London, murderer on the loose, spinster heroine Knows Who. Each show was different. Not musical-play different, because all musical plays were different: *Carousel, Brigadoon, Lost in the Stars, Paint Your Wagon, Fanny, My Fair Lady, New Girl in Town, West Side Story. Musical-comedy* different, because musical comedies were finding distinctions of their own. Musical comedy could absorb death, traditionally limited to the musical play, and deal *seriously* as well as satirically with politics. Political musicals were *Of Thee I Sing, I'd Rather Be Right,* or *Call Me Madam*: fantasies. But *Fiorello!* was realistic: *Fiorello!* had actually happened.

Could anything better inform us that musical comedy had

joined up with the musical play in the evolution of popular musical theatre? Because Rodgers and Hammerstein's form was (largely) the musical play, we expect more of it and less of musical comedy, for decades an essentially frivolous and conventional genre. But the latter was now often as questing as its big brother. In fact, the two very separate terms of identity began to come together in the 1950s. Certain musical comedies (for instance, *Damn Yankees, Plain and Fancy,* and *House of Flowers*) and certain musical plays (*Paint Your Wagon, Fanny, West Side Story*) each billed themselves simply as "a new musical."

This is what it is: at the start of the Third Age, musical comedy and the musical play (operetta, as it was usually but not invariably called then) were separate. *Show Boat* married them, blending the one's energy and the other's intensity. Nothing happened for fifteen years. Finally, *Oklahoma!* married them again, and *then* it started. The two have been teaching each other ever since.

Thus, our last two shows offer, one, musical-play material treated as dance opera, and, two, musical-comedy material treated as a musical play. This is the kind of evolution you get when everything's happening at once and the talent is keen and the audience so turned on that no LP sells better than a hit show's cast album.

Two hits coming up.

16

West Side Story & Gypsy

Some call these vastly different shows the culmination of an era in that their vitally story-oriented artistry tops off the epoch of Rodgers and Hammerstein. Others see the pair as the start of the next era, in which the musical play breaks *away* from the Rodgers and Hammerstein model into new structures—*West Side Story* all magicked up with dance and *Gypsy* so lean it virtually has a cast of three—that point toward *Cabaret, Company, A Chorus Line.*

West Side Story owns an especially dispiriting gestation story, because it very nearly never happened. It started as an updated *Romeo and Juliet* called *East Side Story*, about friction between Jewish people and Catholics. It was Jerome Robbins' idea, and, from the start, Leonard Bernstein was to write both lyrics and music to Arthur Laurents' book. But in fact there was no story there, for the Jewish East Side of memory had vanished long before—and where, today, in New York, was there a Jewish-Catholic hostility? On the contrary, the cultural assimilation of Jewish and Catholic immigrants and their issue was a New York success story.

Years passed. The gang wars of Los Angeles made the headlines just when Bernstein and Laurents were in southern California in the early 1950s, and suddenly the abandoned show reinstated it-self: a *west side* story about a gang war between native-born kids and Puerto Rican newcomers. Ziegfeld jumped at *Show Boat*, and the Theatre Guild itself got the idea for *Oklahoma!*, but many a producer drew back from *West Side Story*. What, in our ambitious, dancing 1950s? But then, as Robbins pointed out in a *West Side Story* panel discussion in the *Dramatists Guild Quarterly*, "It's not surprising that people said, 'I don't understand what that's about' in the case of a work in the embryo stage that was quite radical in its time. They hadn't heard Lenny's score, they hadn't read the script, they certainly hadn't seen what was going to be danced."

Stephen Sondheim had no problem visualizing the show's po-tential, and agreed to collaborate on the lyrics with Bernstein when it became clear how much extra work the ballets would cost the composer.* Bernstein and Laurents may have seen Sondheim and themselves as a trio with a marvelous power exalted by an invincible Robbins: for surely they knew that they had something genuinely innovative. But Cheryl Crawford, co-producing with Roger L. Stevens and unaccountably dissatisfied with Laurents' lean, clear, and highly evocative book, pulled out six weeks before rehearsals were to start, leaving the production in jeopardy until Robert E. Griffith and Harold Prince agreed to take over with Stevens. As I say, it very nearly never happened.

The usual swamis continued to predict disaster as *West Side Story* set about casting. This proved especially difficult, for the customary three-tiered ensemble of principals, singing chorus,

---

* Just which verses are Bernstein's and which Sondheim's is one of history's best-kept secrets, for early in the tryout Bernstein had his co-lyricist credit re-moved out of deference to the importance of Sondheim's work. We know that Sondheim wrote "I Feel Pretty" and "One Hand, One Heart" because he never misses a chance to rip them to shreds, especially "Pretty," whose elaborate rhyme scheme, he says, suggests a character of lofty cultural background, not a shel-tered Hispanic girl. True, a heavy rhyme structure does suggest education or urbanity. But the song seems carefully to choose simple rhymes—"bright" and "tonight," "joy" and "boy." Above all, the lyrics project innocence and excited anticipation. What could be more accurate for this character at this moment? Besides, if these lyrics truly were incorrectly conceived, Bernstein would have demanded a rewrite. In any case, among theatrical memorabilia, *West Side Story* posters from the first leg of the tryout, with Bernstein's name still nudging Sond-heim's under "Lyrics by," are considered intensely collectible.

and dancing chorus would not work for *West Side Story*'s sharply delineated crew of the Jets and their girls, the Sharks and their girls, and the adults. These last are strictly speaking roles, but the kids inevitably had to sing, dance, and act with a versatility that the musical had seldom asked of anyone except the most gifted stars—Gwen Verdon immediately comes to mind, but who else? Ethel Merman never had to dance in any real sense (nor act, till *Gypsy*), Mary Martin was less into portrayals than into delightful self-presentation, and Alfred Drake was another non-dancer. Shirley Booth? Gertrude Lawrence? Robert Preston? Aren't these more charmers than all-around musical-theatre experts?

West Side Story couldn't use stars, in any case. It is a paradoxical piece in that it *feels* romantic but *behaves* with absolute realism (except, of course, in the second-act dream ballet). To have the leads sing the vocal section of a number and then more or less vaporize while the dancers took over and the singing corps hung around upstage trying to look lively would sabotage *West Side Story*'s unity. Sure, *Call Me Madam* did it. *A Tree Grows in Brooklyn* did it. *The Most Happy Fella* did it. *Flower Drum Song*, which opened over a year after *West Side Story*, would do it, blatantly. Why not?: that's how it was done. Why should a capable dancing line have to sing, too? Why should singers dance? Why ask principals to do what the chorus does? But those who conceived *West Side Story* had in mind a structure that would flow rather than jerk, whose narrative could move from book into music and then dance without anyone's noticing the joins. This would be something very rare, Broadway's equivalent of Richard Wagner's *Gesamtkunstwerk*, all the talents consolidated, all the parts fused. A show as rich as a festival and as pure as a pane of glass.

The adults were easy to cast, at least. They are Doc, owner of a congenial drugstore, the Friar Laurence figure; Schrank, a police detective, loosely modeled on the Prince of Verona; the cop Krupke, immortalized by that musical moment of virtually Shakespearean comic relief during the aftermath of the fatal rumble between the gangs; and Gladhand, who supervises the dance at the gym.

Then there were the ten Jets, the female wannabe Jet Anybodys, and the four Jet girl friends; and the eight Sharks, the head

Shark's sister, Maria, his girl friend, Anita, and five Shark girl friends. Not only must they all support Robbins's demanding regime, they must be young, too young to be the seasoned recruits that their duties require.

In the event, only Chita Rivera, the Anita, had had even relatively prominent Broadway exposure, and she was only twenty-four. The Shark's leader, Bernardo, went to Ken LeRoy, the one senior of the kids at thirty; Mickey Calin, as Riff, the Jets' leader, was twenty-two. The lovers, Larry Kert as Tony and Carol Lawrence as Maria, were respectively twenty-six and just barely twenty-five. Rivera was the most gifted all-arounder of the group, an extremely strong dancer but also a powerful singer and actress, radiating the earthy personality that sets Anita apart. Rivera was also authentically Hispanic, a native of merengue-loving, tropical Washington, D.C.

Calin and Lawrence were fine dancers, Kert and LeRoy not on that level; but they moved well. Certainly, all seemed perfectly cast, and the Jets, to a man, supported the highly individual roles that Laurents wrote for them. (Their girls have but a few lines each, and the Sharks, except for Riff and Chino, Maria's betrothed, do not get the stage time that the various Jets do.) Perhaps because of their youth, the kids fell easily into Laurents' nervous, allusive, here-and-now yet neither-here-nor-there dialogue. They have nothing to do and all their lives to do it in, which makes them explosively eager yet without a goal other than to find people very like themselves and win fierce dominion over them. A mixture of real ("gassin', crabbin'," Anybodys complains on her entrance) and invented ("frabbajabba," "cracko jacko") slang sets them off as almost futuristically contemporary; one envisions a way-out production of *West Side Story* somewhere, that is placed in some nameless city after a nuclear attack without a change of word: a go-everywhere text that is time-specific and place-specific. But then, again, this is a lyrical piece embedded in the methods of hard naturalism:

DOC: Why, when I was your age—
ACTION: When you was my age; when my old man was my age; when my brother was my age! *You was never my age,*

none a you! The sooner you creeps get hip to that, the
sooner you'll dig us.

The lyricism obtains not only in the fervent love of Tony and
Maria but in the tragedy inherent in the waste of so much youth
and energy. "You couldn't play basketball?" Doc asks. No: because
their back-alley upbringing has neglected them, led them to develop a tiny subculture beyond basketball. There's no there in the
place they live in, no work-leisure schedule, no thought, art, hope.
A number written out of town but never used, "Kids Ain't"—a trio
for the least important of the Jets, Baby John, Arab, and Anybodys—hit on this in a jazzy and comical but, all the same, plain-
tive way. The little they know about is everything they don't have.
Tony, the most mature of the gang, so much so that he has all
but retired from it, articulates this in his first scene: "Every single
damn night for the last month," he tells Riff, "I wake up and I'm
reachin' out." He doesn't know what for. "It's right outside the
door," he believes. "Around the corner. But it's comin'."

This scene with Riff is a particularly sad one: for Riff. Tony,
his best friend—"womb to tomb," runs their private oath, "sperm
to worm"—is drawing away from him. Replacing him. The text is
not overt here, or anywhere else in the play. Nothing suggests that
Riff's interest in Tony is, however repressed, erotic. However, Riff
maintains a strangely perfunctory relationship with his girl, Vel-
ma, while his opposite, Bernardo, is highly involved with Anita.
Also, we learn that Riff has been living not with his own family
but with Tony's for *four and a half* years, at an age at which one
is capable of forming passionate attachments. In the cramped
quarters, of the tenements in which *West Side Story's* kids live,
Riff is almost certainly sharing Tony's bed.

These are, after all, the counterparts of Romeo and Mercutio.
It is by now an accepted academic reading that Shakespeare's duo
are lovers, or something in that limitless Shakespearean universe
precisely yet vaguely akin to lovers, and that Mercutio must die
not to feed the Montague-Capulet feud but to free Romeo to complete his pubescent rite of passage out of guiltless, childish love
into sexual, sinful love, with Juliet.

Thus, it is Riff's tragedy that he himself arranges for Tony to attend the dance at the gym (i.e., the Capulets' Ball). For there Tony meets Maria. And the love born that night will lead Tony to attempt to stop Riff from killing Bernardo, Maria's brother. "Hold, Tybalt! Good Mercutio!" And when Riff pauses, heeding the only voice that matters to him, Bernardo thrusts forward with his knife, and that is the end of Riff—and then Bernardo and, ultimately, Tony. Maria, unlike Juliet, survives, though at one point the authors considered killing her off as well. Richard Rodgers advised them not to. After all that she has been through, he explained, "She's dead already." The Lesson of the Master.

It was possibly the knowledge that *West Side Story*'s first-act curtain would fall on a stage decorated with two corpses, at that in the extremely unromantic surroundings of a deserted, fenced-in yard under the West Side Highway, that had so many of the in-crowd hostile. What *hybris*, to take on a subject of sweat, slang, and blood in a form meant to delight and exalt. What pop impudence, to denude Shakespeare of his glitter.

Or are these excuses for those who simply couldn't get *West Side Story* even after hearing Lenny's score, reading the script, seeing what was danced, to go back to Jerome Robbins' explanation of why the *idea* of *West Side Story* gave pause. For some, the *fully-realized West Side Story* was a problem, mainly because some lazy, self-righteous ears simply couldn't absorb the music. (Sondheim later had this problem when he began composing.)

This is Bernstein's most deviously brilliant theatre score. Like *On the Town* and *Candide*, it is centralized in an ur-theme, the upward-or downward-moving tritone, immediately resolving a half-step up, that we hear (in its purest form) in the first three notes of "Maria." This is anticipated in the first three notes ("Who kno-ows?") of "Something's Coming"; repeated in this form at the start of the dance at the gym as the now famous curtain of streamers drops to the floor; and then reappears, now rising again, in the Cha-cha when Tony and Maria meet. It launches "Cool," defines the fugue theme of the "Cool" dance, and nudges along "The Rumble."

West Side Story folds and refolds its melodies into itself, as when the lower woodwind sound the main strain of "Somewhere" during "Tonight," when "Maria" sneaks into "One Hand, One

Heart," or when the nervous, syncopated chords that open the first scene become the striding, combative accompaniment to the "Jet Song." Two little facts are relevent here: one, *West Side Story* sounds like no other musical, and, two, it was written at the same time as *Candide* and even shares some of its music.

What? The most satiric musical in Broadway's history co-owned melodies with the most romantic? Strange but true: the music for "Gee, Officer Krupke" was conceived, on the lyric entitled "Where Does It Get You in the End?," for the spot that was finally held in *Candide* by "What's the Use?"; the first notes of "Tonight" can clearly be heard in the music that, in the original and certain other productions, underscored Candide's dazzling re-entrance as a millionaire after his Eldorado adventure; "One Hand, One Heart" was composed in somewhat different form for *Candide*; and the underscoring before "One Hand"'s vocal sounds like something more suitable for *Candide*'s impish rhapsody than for *West Side Story*'s anguished lyricism.

In the end, all of *Candide* is absolutely *Candide* and almost all of *West Side Story* is *West Side Story*. Imagine the music of "America" in *Candide*, "Glitter and Be Gay" in *West Side Story*. I can't think of two shows less alike—especially in the intellectual confidence that *Candide*'s enthusiasts need, confronted as they are by a very course in Western Civ: Voltaire, the Lisbon Earthquake, Leibniz, McCarthy, German grandeur, French wit, and the very meaning of pastiche as an energy of satire. It's college in every scene. Then there's *West Side Story*'s tight little tale, demanding nothing—not even the knowledge that it is drawn from Shakespeare.

Still, in the long run, *Candide* is a comedy and *West Side Story* a tragedy, and the latter will always be easier to play but harder to sell. I have pointed out many a great first-act curtain for you in these pages; here's a great second-act opening. After the gang fight that leaves Riff and Bernardo dead, the action recommences *chez* Maria, where she looks forward to life with Tony, to comic commentary by three friends. Has any of the gods' victims been so merrily unknowing before the lightning struck?

She's already dead. Yet I think *Gypsy* is even harder to take. A hit, yes, again and again, and long may it be so; but this one really stings. *West Side Story* is about real people: real life, real love, and something is possible, for all the despair. The next Tony and Maria will bring their people together, somewhere. *Gypsy* treats show people: everything is about performance, so nothing is possible, for all the vitality. Nothing will come of nothing.

Or see it this way: *West Side Story* is about how bigotry destroys you. *Gypsy* is about how your mother destroys you. This show is The One That Got Away With It, shattering a cultural given, that all mothers are nurturing, loving, and self-sacrificing. *Gypsy* is about a mother who is a selfish, stupid, destructive piece of junk.

Stephen Sondheim has said that of all his shows—this is, of course, counting the bitterly middle-aged *Follies* with its blighted culture and wrecked marriages, the sylistically complex *Pacific Overtures*, the merry cannibals of *Sweeney Todd*, and the president-killers of *Assassins*—the most "difficult" was *West Side Story*. And, true, we've seen how impossible The Street thought the project until it actually came into the Winter Garden and made its history.

But surely *Gypsy*'s titanic protagonist makes the audience work very, very hard to like the show—even to like it despite the protagonist. She was Ethel Merman, so here was another star show, in the varied line of *The King and I, Top Banana, Wonderful Town, By the Beautiful Sea, Bells Are Ringing, Jamaica, Oh Captain!, Redhead,* and *The Sound of Music*. I intend this list to demonstrate how different each star show can be—*The King and I*'s powerful composition next to *By the Beautiful Sea*'s almost improvisational riffs on personality and locale; the impossibility of reviving *Redhead* while *Wonderful Town* and *The Sound of Music* make regular returns.

Some star shows can lose their stars, as the composition becomes more beloved than the central entertainer; *The Sound of Music* and *The Music Man* have been done with nobodies. And *The King and I* has "switched" its star's role with its supporting role, for Yul Brynner. But *Gypsy* not only holds out for stars but stands as a kind of Mother Courage, Isolde, Phèdre—not just prima-donna domain but the ultimate challenge. It's the musical's outstanding diva role. No wonder the whole thing got underway only after someone looked Merman in the eye and asked, more or less, Are you willing to act this time?

Merman was. She had played a fake Merman all her life; now she would play someone real, Gypsy Rose Lee's mother, called Rose. Billed as "a musical fable,"* Gypsy was based on Lee's memoirs, telling how she and her sister, June Havoc, were pushed into show biz. This brings us to another Arthur Laurents book, to a Jule Styne–Stephen Sondheim score; and to another Jerome Robbins staging.

However, unlike West Side Story, Gypsy was not dance theatre. The production as a whole had a strong sense of motion, partly urged on by vaudeville billing cards at stage right and left. Scene five is announced as BABY JUNE AND HER NEWSBOYS—LOS ANGELES, scene six as "HAPPY BIRTHDAY"—AKRON, scene ten as "DREAMS OF GLORY"—BUFFALO. Nevertheless, except for the onstage performance spots, an in one crossover called "Travelling" in which Rose kidnaps kids to fill out her daughters' act, the impromptu "rehearsal" of "All I Need Is the Girl," and a bit of walkabout for the trio "Together," Gypsy was strictly a play with songs. There was no equivalent to West Side Story's opening gang skirmishes, dance at the gym, "Cool," "Rumble," and dream ballet. But, again, West Side Story is romantic; it's what the 1950s did with operetta. Gypsy is realistic; it's what the 1950s did to musical comedy.

Here's life, truly, starting with a dysfunctional family of stage mother, favorite daughter, and unloved daughter. Merman's entrance, through the stage-left aisle of the Broadway Theatre, was that of a steamroller, coursing in to flatten everything in its path, starting with the niece-favoring talent scout Uncle Jocko, the father whose gold retirement plaque she pawns, restaurateurs, landlords, her daughters, and her boy friend. There is literally no one this woman won't do it to.

Yet she has charm. Her victims want to like her, want to be liked by her. We get to meet them in a book that isn't scaling the

---

* Here's a nice symmetry—the last great fifties musical echoes the first, Guys and Dolls, billed as "a musical fable of Broadway."

entertainment peaks from song to song but is, rather, telling the story and letting the songs bubble up where the plot needs to feel. Broadway has known plenty of backstagers—we've had a sample in *Me and Juliet, By the Beautiful Sea*, maybe *My Fair Lady* (it's rehearsal and performance, no?), and certainly *Mr. Wonderful*. But none of those showed us career movement, an up or down. *Me and Juliet* was life backstage in a hit show. *By the Beautiful Sea* was life on vacation between tours, days off from hell, if the cut comic song "Thirty Weeks of Heaven" is to be believed—it's another of those wonderful numbers that somehow creates fun out of terror ("The midnight train to Wichita that doesn't stop at Wichita . . ."). *Mr. Wonderful* did show an up—but a quick and sudden one. Please, Sammy, try the bigtime. No. *Please*. Okay. So he opens at a Big Miami Beach Motel and Wows 'Em All.

No, *Gypsy* was the one to show us what ups and downs await in the show biz, as they used to put it in *Gypsy*'s 1920s and 1930s. The show biz. It was a living, like any other. The plumbing biz. The construction biz. But Rose doesn't see it so. This biz is her ticket to ride, her mirror, portrait, ad, caption, headline. We see her push past amateur nights on to third-line vaudeville down to burlesque and back up, as her second daughter succeeds, onto a kind of back-street stardust. And all the way she is eating her young.

Seldom does a celebrity present her life to the public so unapologetically and honestly. Apparently, Gypsy Rose Lee told the musical's authors that they could do what they want as long as they called the show *Gypsy*. Sister Havoc held out for a long while, then thought, What the hell, it's me, isn't it? There were a few other bloops—Sondheim wanted to write the whole score, but Merman wouldn't trust an unproved composer and Jule Styne stepped in; one of the pair of the younger June and Louise was terrified of heights and destroyed the staging (and caused the dropping) of "Mama's Talkin' Soft," during which the girls were perched above the "Small World" scene, singing against it in cynical counterpoint; Jule Styne had to threaten to withdraw his music, note for note, to force Jerome Robbins to reinstate the cut "Little Lamb"; producer David Merrick decided to emasculate the overture, possibly the greatest a musical has ever had. Why? Because it was great and Merrick was a vindictive idiot? Why do supposedly great theatre men pull stunts like this? Maybe they're not great, after all?

Anyway, *Gypsy* surmounted its out-of-town problems and came in a super-hit, not with the longest original run but with the longest-lasting acclaim. Is this the best book of a fifties musical? No—*The King and I*. And second best, admittedly on a borrowing, is *My Fair Lady*. *Gypsy* is third best, but it is also the most dangerous book, and *that* leads us into the next era. Laurents presents an evil woman and does not redeem her. *Gypsy*'s mother is what she is, like it or not—this is the new part of the musical, because suddenly a popular art is an honest art—*Stop!* Pop is respectful, right? Gentle, conventional, pleasing.

Not this time. Even *West Side Story*, for all its comedy, is made of sweet, determined, or brutal characters who have sworn to Do It. Warriors, essentially. *Gypsy*, for all its comedy, is made of Rose, thrusting her daughters on stage in her stead:

> ROSE: I guess I did do it for me.
> LOUISE: Why, Mother?
> ROSE: Just wanted to be noticed.

That Rose sends Louise out into the sleazy darkness of burlesque to strip, losing her lover but creating a star, tells us what Rose is: an American. Nothing matters but making it, stardom. So the great, the telling moment in *Gypsy* is not the end but the first-act finale, when the song-and-dance boys and even starry Baby June have abandoned Rose, Herbie, and Louise. Designer Jo Mielziner placed them at a crossroads—more literally, a railroad station. This is when the stage placards spelled out 'TERMINAL': OMAHA. But what Mielziner presented was not terminal but inaugural. The backdrop's bottom half read as railroad track, lines running from stage left and right up toward the horizon. The top half read as overhead cable, lines running from stage left and right down toward the horizon, the two series of lines meeting at the center and moving on beyond the eye's sight. In other words: infinity. Unlimited choice. The future, more story, and anything is possible. A *crossroads*, I say. It was at this juncture that Rose turned on Louise—not turned *to*—and, in her spooky, obsessed way, preluded with the "I had a dream" motif and then ripped into "Everything's Coming Up Roses," as Louise and Herbie stared at her in utter dismay.

There are so many narratively or characterologically telling moments in this show that one doesn't know where to pin the medal. Let's at least cite received opinion that *Gypsy*'s score is one to inscribe in the book of classics, one whose every number is beloved—not just standouts such as the driving "Some People," with its relentlessly diatonic trio (on "I had a dream") or the svelte "You'll Never Get Away From Me," which two, as a pair, limn the paradoxical maniac and charmer sides of Rose's character.

But then, are there *standouts* in Gypsy's score? Isn't this one of those drop-one-number-and-the-entire-structure-collapses scores, even if Jerome Robbins did try to drop "Little Lamb" (but then how would we know Louise?) and co-producer David Merrick tried to destroy the overture? Work of this intensely creative caliber is no surprise from Stephen Sondheim. But it raises questions about composer Jule Styne's spotty career. Considering Jerome Kern's work as a whole, one finds a very few dud scores in something like forty titles. Richard Rodgers upheld an even higher level, though his very last works saw a true loss of power. The more variable Cole Porter often bounced from brilliant to merely okay; but okay Porter is still the goods.

Styne has varied far more widely: top in *High Button Shoes* (1947) and *Gentlemen Prefer Blondes* (1949), dull in *Two on the Aisle* (1951), sordid in *Hazel Flagg* (1953), top again in *Bells Are Ringing* (1956), suddenly amazing in *Gypsy*, top in the unappreciated *Do Re Mi* (1960), errant in *Subways Are for Sleeping* (1961), all-popular in *Funny Girl* (1964), slipping in *Hallelujah, Baby!* (1967) and *Darling of the Day* (1968), abysmal in *Look to the Lilies* (1970), and so on. Why, one asks, did Styne become so musically sophisticated, so suddenly, in *Gypsy*?—the "I had a dream" motif, which runs through the score, as does "May We [or Let Me] Entertain You?," from kiddy anthem to stripper's theme; that idea of playing the cynical "Mama's Talkin' Soft," against the idealistic "Small World," only "Mama's Talkin' Soft" is honest and "Small World" is a lie; then the fusion of the score's musical and verbal themes in Merman's eleven o'clocker, "Rose's Turn."

This last number alone is a classical site of symbolic importance in the musical's development, along with *On Your Toes*'s "Slaughter on Tenth Avenue," *Carousel*'s Bench Scene, the first five minutes of *Cabaret*, and the first five seconds of *Follies* (and prob-ably all the rest of *Follies* as well). In "Rose's Turn," many themes collide—the star stuff, the story stuff, the director–choreographer stuff, the musical-behaving-with-opera's-power stuff. It's literally, the climax of the 1950s, a hard-on, artistically speaking. Where exactly did Styne get this new, improved Styne from?*

I'd like to hear someone ask Stephen Sondheim about the extent of his *musical* influence on Jule Styne. Another question: why does everyone intelligent hate the movie? Granted, Natalie Wood as Louise is, as ever, a pretty girl who cannot act. But Rosalind Russell? Karl Malden? This is extremely correct casting, especially given Russell's clobbering power as the meanest of Roses, the truest, the mother of all mothers. Then, too, the movie is generally faithful to the show; it even runs the indispensable overture during the credits. Stage revivals with Angela Lansbury (from London) and Tyne Daly (after a national tour) have reaffirmed *Gypsy*'s place in American cultural history, each new Rose

---

* Styne's output cannot be analyzed without mention of *Say, Darling* (1958), often mistaken for a musical. The poster billed it as "a comedy about a musical": Richard Bissell wrote the novel *The Pajama Game*, worked on its Broadway adaptation, and got a novel out of that, called *Say, Darling*. Bissell then worked on *its* adaptation . . . into a play with a bit of singing. Styne and Comden and Green wrote the "score," actually a shred of a number here and there, the impromptu chanting of an old hymn, an audition in which everyone wants to sing "I Could Have Danced All Night." It was Styne-Comden-Green at their absolute worst, but Victor went ahead and recorded the show anyway, building snatches into full-out numbers and losing the theatre's two-piano accompaniment for a orchestration by Sid Ramin as if this were *Bells Are Ringing*. This has confused listeners about the nature of the show. Some readers may recall the Jean Arthur *Peter Pan*, mentioned earlier—but that was a fully realized musical staging (though still not a musical), with an orchestra accompanying the action and a handful of numbers. *Say, Darling* more properly may be typed with Eartha Kitt's first show after *New Faces of 1952*, a play called *Mrs. Patterson* (1954) with, again, a pit band and six songs by James Shelton.

to be compared with Merman in search of the true Rose of the world, for Merman's portrayal remains one of the greatest performances in the musical's history, I daresay possibly even the greatest.*

Opera has many such Great Roles—Otello, Tosca, Isolde, Boris Godunof, Norma, Manon, Violetta, Peter Grimes, Carmen, Iago, the Marschallin—each a significant addition to a singer's repertory. When in a career's course should one assume the role (Manon needs youth; Norma wants authority), whom to study it with, does one defy or genuflect to tradition?—all this is part of opera's lore, part of why its culture is so rich and also so demanding. One cannot know a little about opera any more than one can know a little about rock or a little about jazz or a little about Shakespeare and call oneself knowing. There is a canon of classics, ever-changing, an endless gallery of great singers of the past that grows larger with each generation, a thousand performances to attend, languages to master, texts to penetrate, variants to recognize.

By the end of the 1950s, the American musical had finally established its culture. It was still to an extent an ephemeral art, its performing materials sometimes tossed away or vaulted after a given title had played out its New York run and national tour, its standing among the intelligentsia shaky, its underlying energies seldom perceived by chroniclers, and its very existence unknown to the academy.

But the discovery of the original cast album in the 1940s, and its succeeding acculturation with the introduction of the LP, gave the music a foundation for stability, permanence. Productions no longer vanished when they closed, as, for instance *Show Boat*, *Strike Up the Band*, *Of Thee I Sing*, *The Cat and the Fiddle*, *Music in the Air*, and *Pal Joey* did when they were new. Major musicals owned more than memories now; the main reason why Lansbury's

---

* Merman assumed that she was the once and future Rose, and bitterly denounced Rosalind Russell's seizing (as Merman saw it) of the lead in the movie. Now It Can Be Told: after Merman's death, her knickknacks closet gave up discs of the *Gypsy* movie's prerecorded vocal tapes—not the improved Lisa Kirk tracks, dubbing for an overparted Russell, but Russell's inadequate originals. Party records at Merman's *je m'en fiche* soirées?

and Daly's Roses could be set next to Merman's for historical comparison was that anyone could revisit *Gypsy, 1959* by playing Columbia's cast album.

Even stagings were now to outlast the final performance. As we speak, somehow, some day, somewhere (Germany, probably: they love American musicals there), someone is putting on a *West Side Story* as staged when he played a Jet some years earlier in a mounting directed by someone who had played an earlier revival directed by one of Jerome Robbins's "people," who was in the first national tour. It's like a ballet traveling through the decades, maybe changing emphases here and there but planning to hew as closely as possible to what was seen at the premiere.

As for Great Roles, what else are Nathan, Adelaide, Sky, and Sarah, Anna and the King, "Hajj," Peter Pan, Henry Higgins and Eliza, Frank Loesser's Tony, maybe Candide's Cunegonde but certainly the Old Lady, Harold Hill, perhaps Rodgers and Hammerstein's Maria (she's not a substantial character in the manner of *Gypsy*'s Rose, but the booking attracts stars)? The 1950s did not produce a larger number of all-time important shows than the 1940s, but the higher evolutionary level can be detected in the much greater number of excellent but not enduring shows, the "second level," so to say—*A Tree Grows in Brooklyn, Fanny, Plain and Fancy*. One long forgot characteristic of the forties musical was the constant production of dreadful shows, the kind that even the experts know nothing about—*Crazy With the Heat, Viva O'Brien, The Lady Comes Across*.

The fifties equivalents are few; at that, they stand out because, in an era in which cast albums proliferated, the very few untaped titles look cheesy by default. Still, if one thinks of the musical as being divided into three parts—classic scores, good listens, and empty-the-place dirges—the 1920s count respectively a goodly amount; a lot; and a lot. The 1930s count a handful; some; and a lot. The 1940s count a lot; a few; and a ton. But the 1950s count a lot; a load; and a very few.

The musical in 1960, then, was in the spring of its golden age, forty years on. Of the founding punters, Jerome Kern, Cole Porter, the Gershwins, Vincent Youmans, Lorenz Hart, and De Sylva,

Brown, and Henderson were dead or withdrawn. Oscar Hammerstein climbed his last mountain that very year. Irving Berlin would produce one final score in 1962, a dull one.

But this spring was by its very nature endlessly expansive, because the musical's cultural prominence and economic power kept attracting new talents to replace their predecessors and pursue their innovations.

There were glitches: *A Tree Grows in Brooklyn* never quite worked. The *Candide* that Americans know today is a trivializing revision. *Juno* never got a fair hearing. No successor appeared to reposition the gay lorgnette that Cole Porter had aimed at the social contract. The star comic died out. But *West Side Story* and *Gypsy* triumphed—such brutal, realistic pieces in a medium of sweet fantasy. There had been a time, remember, when a "musical" meant Fred and Adele Astaire and a Gershwin score; or Ziegfeld and les girls: inconsequential fun.

Of course, Rodgers and Hammerstein changed that. But it is my notion that *West Side Story* and *Gypsy* changed that *again*. I don't see these shows as climaxes of the Rodgers and Hammerstein era as much as the first strikes in the next era, one in which the musical finally gives up its membership in the popular arts to confront its audience. Pop affirms you; art questions you. Pop is fraud; art is truth. Pop promotes authority, convention; art defies, escapes. Pop worships mother; art asks what she wants.

Not that the years after *West Side Story* and *Gypsy* immediately brought in the Fourth Age: there was more transition and discovery to come first, a capstone of musical comedy in *Hello, Dolly!*, the first concept musical in a generation, *Cabaret*, the beginning of Sondheim the composer.

No. As we pause, the Rodgers and Hammerstein effect has been edited but not transformed. What happened in *Show Boat* and *Oklahoma!* continued to happen. It just started to happen differently, with subjects, characters, and worldviews that perhaps more directly challenged the public than even *Show Boat*'s exposure of racism or *Oklahoma!*'s smokehouse squid of a Jud Fry could.

But let me point out one overwhelming musical development that will have grave impact on the fortunes of the musical: In

1956, every radio station in America was playing the *My Fair Lady* album.

Some ten years later, every radio station in America was playing the Beatles' *Sgt. Pepper's Lonely Hearts Club Band*.

The music was changing, to a form that Broadway could not use. Could not sing, could not dance to.

Index

CPSIA information can be obtained
at www.ICGtesting.com
Printed in the USA
FFOW04n1711020115
10013FF